Race, Gender and Sport

The experiences of ethnic 'Other' females have – until recently – been widely overlooked in the study of sport. There continues to be a need to produce critical scholarship about ethnic 'Other' girls and women in sport and physical culture, in order to represent their complex, multifarious and dynamic lived realities. This international collection of critical essays provides compelling insight into the lived realities of ethnic 'Other' females in sport.

Throughout the book, contributors either draw on the political consciousnesses of 'Other' feminisms, or privilege the voices of ethnic 'Other' girls and women so as to broaden, diversify and advance critical thinking pertaining to ethnic 'Other' females in sport and physical culture. The purpose of the collection is both to produce knowledge and privilege otherwise subjugated knowledges, which individually and collectively present counter-narratives that better speak to the lived realities of racially oppressed groups of women and girls.

Race, Gender and Sport: The Politics of Ethnic 'Other' Girls and Women is important reading for all students and scholars with an interest in the sociology of sport, gender studies, or race and ethnicity studies.

Aarti Ratna is a senior lecturer in the sociology of sport and leisure at Leeds Beckett University. Dr Ratna's scholarship is shaped by the contributions of Black feminist intellectuals, and she uses this theoretical lens to inform her research about race, gender, sport, leisure, and popular culture. Many of her publications have specifically focused upon the multifaceted subjectivities of British Asian female footballers. Her more recent projects aim to examine gender, belonging, diaspora communities and the changing leisure lifestyles of older South Asian men and women.

Samaya Farooq Samie is a critical educator whose interdisciplinary research interests include the fields of sociology, race and ethnic studies, south Asian studies, women and gender studies, post-colonial feminist epistemologies, sport and popular culture. Her published work focuses not only on the complex identity work of young British Pakistani Muslim men and their constructions of religious masculinities through sport and physical education, but also explores the intersections of gender, 'race', culture and religion in the lives of sporting (south Asian) Muslim women living in diaspora communities in the 'West'.

Routledge Critical Studies in Sport

Series Editors: Jennifer Hargreaves and Ian McDonald
University of Brighton

The Routledge Critical Studies in Sport series aims to lead the way in developing the multi-disciplinary field of Sport Studies by producing books that are interrogative, interventionist and innovative. By providing theoretically sophisticated and empirically grounded texts, the series will make sense of the changes and challenges facing sport globally. The series aspires to maintain the commitment and promise of the critical paradigm by contributing to a more inclusive and less exploitative culture of sport.

Also available in this series:

Soccer, Culture and Society in Spain
An Ethnography of Basque Fandom
Mariann Vaczi

Olympic Exclusions
Youth, Poverty and Social Legacies
Jacqueline Kennelly

Critical Geographies of Sport
Space, Power and Sport in Global Perspective
Edited by Natalie Koch

The Sexual and Gender Politics of Sport Mega-Events
Roving Colonialism
Heather Sykes

Race, Gender and Sport
The Politics of Ethnic 'Other' Girls and Women
Edited by Aarti Ratna and Samaya Farooq Samie

www.routledge.com/sport/series/RCSIS

Race, Gender and Sport

The Politics of Ethnic ‘Other’ Girls and Women

Edited by Aarti Ratna and
Samaya Farooq Samie

Routledge
Taylor & Francis Group
LONDON AND NEW YORK

First published 2018
by Routledge
2 Park Square, Milton Park, Abingdon, Oxon OX14 4RN

and by Routledge
711 Third Avenue, New York, NY 10017

Routledge is an imprint of the Taylor & Francis Group, an informa business

British Library Cataloguing in Publication Data
A catalogue record for this book is available from the British Library

Library of Congress Cataloging in Publication Data
A catalog record for this book has been requested

ISBN: 978-1-138-63966-9 (hbk)
ISBN: 978-1-315-63705-1 (ebk)

Typeset in Sabon
by Wearset Ltd, Boldon, Tyne and Wear

MIX
Paper from responsible sources
FSC® C013056

Printed and bound in Great Britain by
TJ International Ltd, Padstow, Cornwall

Contents

Notes on contributors vii
Acknowledgements xi

Introduction: sport, race and gender – the politics of ethnic 'Other' girls and women 1
AARTI RATNA AND SAMAYA FAROOQ SAMIE

1 Mapping the field: research about ethnic 'Other' females, sport and physical culture 10
AARTI RATNA AND SAMAYA FAROOQ SAMIE

PART I
Theoretical interventions and knowledge production **33**

2 De/colonising 'sporting Muslim women': post-colonial feminist reflections on the dominant portrayal of sporting Muslim women in academic research, public forums and mediated representations 35
SAMAYA FAROOQ SAMIE

3 Theoretical considerations in the examination of African American girls and women in sport 63
AKILAH R. CARTER-FRANCIQUE

4 Re-confronting whiteness: ongoing challenges in sport and leisure research 85
BECCY WATSON AND SHEILA SCRATON

PART II
Experiences at the intersections of identity **107**

5 'Using the pen as a weapon': the resistance of an outsider within 109
AARTI RATNA

6 Confronting the 'whiteness' of women's cricket: excavating hidden truths and knowledge to make sense of non-white women's experiences in cricket 126
RAFAELLE NICHOLSON

7 Ladies-only! Empowerment and comfort in gender-segregated kickboxing in the Netherlands 148
JASMIJN RANA

PART III
Everyday struggles and transformative practice **169**

8 Lorena 'La Reina' Ochoa: disidentifying toward brown solidarity 171
KATHERINE M. JAMIESON AND YEOMI CHOI

9 Do women get the offside rule? Female fans, labelling and stereotypes in Turkey 189
ITIR ERHART

10 Sport coaching and the inclusion of Black women in the United Kingdom 204
ALEXANDRA J. RANKIN-WRIGHT AND LEANNE NORMAN

Index 225

Contributors

Akilah R. Carter-Francique (PhD, University of Georgia) is an assistant professor in the Department of Health and Kinesiology at Prairie View A&M University. To date, her research interests seek to explicate the intersections of race/ethnicity and women in the contexts of sport and physical activity, education, and health. Having a specific emphasis on Black girls and women, Carter-Francique employs a critical interpretivist standpoint (e.g. Black feminist thought, Critical Race Theory) to illuminate experiential marginalizations and promote social justice strategies to redress inequalities. Dr Carter-Francique is the co-founder (with Dr Deniece Dortch) and director of *Sista to Sista*, a co-curricular leadership development programme designed to foster a sense of connectedness amongst Black female college athletes. She is the co-editor of *Critical Race Theory: Black Athletic Experiences in the United States.*

Yeomi Choi, PhD, completed her doctoral degree in the Department of Kinesiology at University of North Carolina at Greensboro (UNCG), with a focus in Sociohistorical Studies. Before studying at UNCG, Dr Choi received an MS in Sport History Studies and a BS in Sport and Leisure Studies from Korea National Sport University. Pursuing an interdisciplinary approach crossing sport studies, cultural studies, sociology, history, and feminist studies, her dissertation examined discursively produced transnational masculinities through mediated Korean-born sport celebrities playing in Major League Baseball. Dr Choi's current research interests centre around mediated (American) Asian sporting subjectivities considering the intersections of gender, class, race, sexuality, and nationality. Dr Choi has taught courses in both the US and South Korea including Sociocultural Analyses of Sport and Exercise; History and Philosophy of Sport, Physical Activity, and Physical Education; Introduction to Kinesiology; Introduction to Sociology; Korean Society and Multiculturalism.

Itır Erhart studied philosophy and Western Languages and Literatures at Boğaziçi University. She completed her MPhil in Philosophy at the University of Cambridge. In 2001 she started teaching at Istanbul Bilgi

University, Department of Media and Communication Systems. In 2006 she earned her PhD from Boğaziçi University in philosophy. In 2015 she became an associate professor. She is the author of the book *What Am I?* and several articles on gender, sports and media including 'United in Protest: From "Living and Dying with Our Colours" to "Let All the Colours of the World Unite"' and 'Ladies of Beşiktaş: A Dismantling of Male Hegemony at Inönü Stadium'.

Katherine M. Jamieson serves as Professor and Chair in the Department of Kinesiology and Health Science at California State University at Sacramento. Dr Jamieson's scholarly endeavours focus on physical activity and human movement(s), equity issues, and feminist-informed, interpretive forms of knowledge production. Her research has been published in *Sociology of Sport Journal*; *Journal of Sport and Social Issues*; *Avante*; *Reading Sport: Critical Essays on Power and Representation*; and *Contemporary Issues in Sociology of Sport*. Dr Jamieson is co-author (with Dr Maureen Smith) of *Fundamentals of Sociology of Sport and Physical Activity* (Human Kinetics, 2016).

Rafaelle Nicholson has recently completed a PhD thesis at Queen Mary University of London entitled '"Like a Man Trying to Knit?" Women's Cricket in Britain, 1945–2000'. Prior to this she gained a BA in Modern History and Politics at Merton College, Oxford, and an MSt in Women's Studies at Mansfield College, Oxford. She has published her research in *History of Education* and *Women's History Review*, and has also written freelance on women's cricket for, amongst others, ESPNcricinfo and *Wisden*.

Leanne Norman is a senior research fellow in the School of Sport, Leeds Beckett University. Her research utilises a sociological lens to examine the culture of coaching to address gender equality within the profession. She also leads work around understanding the relationship between gender and occupational well-being for coaches, examining the influence of gender on the coach-athlete relationship, and analysing the impact of components of coach education on coaching practices and relations. Dr Norman has written for a number of academic textbooks and has published widely in academic journals. She also works as a consultant with a variety of sporting organisations to improve diversity within their coaching and athletic workforce.

Jasmijn Rana is a PhD candidate at the Berlin Graduate School Muslim Cultures and Societies, Freie Universität Berlin, Germany, and a lecturer in cultural anthropology at Leiden University, the Netherlands. Her research focuses on daily life of young Muslim women in kickboxing and examines gender, race, the body and belonging in and through sports in Europe.

Alexandra (A.J.) Rankin-Wright is a researcher in the School of Sport at Leeds Beckett University, UK. Her PhD thesis examined racial and gender equality, diversity and coaching development pathways in sport organisations and national governing bodies in the UK. Using a Critical Race Theory approach and Black feminist lens, the research explored organisational perspectives towards racial and gender equality, and the experiences of under-represented Black coaches. Dr Alexandra Rankin-Wright works with a number of sporting organisations to improve racial and gender equality policy and practice.

Aarti Ratna is a senior lecturer in sociology of sport and leisure at Leeds Beckett University. Dr Ratna's scholarship is shaped by the contributions of Black feminist intellectuals, and she uses this theoretical lens to inform her research about race, gender, sport, leisure and popular culture. Many of her publications have specifically focused upon the multifaceted subjectivities of British Asian female footballers. Her more recent projects aim to examine gender, belonging, diaspora communities and the changing leisure lifestyles of older South Asian men and women.

Samaya Farooq Samie is a critical educator whose research interests are interdisciplinary, making contributions to the fields of sociology, race and ethnic studies, south Asian studies, women and gender studies, post-colonial feminist epistemologies and sociology of sport and popular culture. Dr Samie's published work focuses not only on the complex identity work of young British Pakistani Muslim men and their constructions of religious masculinities through sport and physical education, but also explores the intersections of gender, 'race', culture and religion in the lives of sporting (south Asian) Muslim women living in diaspora communities in the 'West'.

Sheila Scraton was Pro-Vice-Chancellor and Director of University Research at Leeds Beckett (formerly Metropolitan) University from 2004 to 2008, and retired in 2010 , where she holds an Emeritus chair. As Professor of Leisure and Feminist Studies she has led and contributed to research including cross-national qualitative work on women and sport, ethnicity and gender, women and football, older women and leisure, gender and physical education, leisure and feminist theory and intersectionality. She was a panel member for RAE2001 Unit 69 (Sport-related Subjects) and was the Deputy Chair of RAE2008 Unit 46 (Sport-related Studies). She has published extensively across leisure and sport studies, was the Managing Editor of *Leisure Studies* from 2000 to 2003 and is a current member of the advisory boards of *Leisure Studies*, *Journal of Sport and Social Issues* and *Sport, Education and Society*.

Beccy Watson is a Reader in the Institute for Sport, Physical Activity and Leisure at Leeds Beckett University, where her research focuses on interrelationships between gender, 'race' and class. Her work reflects critical, social analysis of leisure and sport and is informed by debates on intersectionality and the continuing significance of feminist epistemologies. Recent studies have focused on masculinity, gender and dance and the challenge of interdisciplinary research across leisure, sport and physical activity. Dr Watson has been a Visiting Research Fellow and a Visiting Scholar at Newcastle University (NSW, Australia) and the University of Texas at Austin (US), respectively. She has been closely involved with the Leisure Studies Association and until recently was one of the managing editors of the Routledge international journal, *Leisure Studies*.

Acknowledgements

The book reflects the intellectual endeavours of nine other scholars who contributed chapters to our edited collection. We praise them, we cherish their respective insights, and believe that together, we have renewed a much-needed critical dialogue in the sociology of sport for other scholars to join. We thank the contributing authors for their individual efforts, and for their patience with the editorial process.

We thank Dan Burdsey, who, at very short notice, read and provided comments in regards to both the Introduction and Chapter 1. Dan Burdsey, Ben Carrington and Jon Dart also offered timely advice during the editorial process, and we are grateful for their support. We also acknowledge and thank Kevin Hylton here for his critical guidance and feedback in terms of securing a book publication, and his ongoing support of the project.

We are both indebted to Stan Thangaraj, for his academic generosity, collegiate approach, and friendship. We also thank the anonymous reviewers for their kind and constructive comments, which we used to shape the production of the final manuscript. We would also like to acknowledge the research administration support of both Sabina Khan and Izram Chaudhry.

Aarti would personally like to express her gratitude to Dean Allen, Dan Burdsey and Philippa Velija for their respective friendships and long-standing academic solidarities. To Jennifer Hargreaves, my former PhD supervisor, who over the last 15 years or so has become/is like a mother-figure to me. If she did not open up the doors of academia to me, I am not sure I would be here now. I would also like to recognise my colleagues at Leeds Beckett University (too many to name in person) who as teachers and researchers inspire me, and show me how 'it's done' on a daily basis. I would, though, like to personally acknowledge Jason Arday, Viji Kuppan, Anne Flintoff, Sarah Squires, Lee Tucker, and last but not least, Beccy Watson, who have all in different ways listened when I most needed a friendly ear. Finally, my parents and family who support me through it all, and who make it all possible, thank you. To my husband Dan Massey and our children, Lennie and Saffron, thank you for your love, smiles and patience. And to Samie, finally, my dear friend, this book is for us, and all the things that we individually, and collectively, stand for.

Samie would like to personally extend her heartfelt gratitude to Professor Christina Hughes and Professor Andrew Parker. You were both early readers of my work, and have guided and supported me, and for this I will always be profoundly indebted to you. For the many Muslim women whose critical voices and actions inspire me, and drive my empirical work: Thank you! I know that this emotional journey is as empowering for you as it can be painful. Know that you are important, and that your perspectives and feminisms matter. Thank you to my academic colleagues: Gerald Griggs for the many wonderful personal tutorials during my undergraduate years; Malcolm MacLean for those coffee and cake breaks in which we satisfied our gluttonous urges, and indulged in delightful debate about all manner of insanity related to sport; and Dan Burdsey, Aarti Ratna and Mahfoud Amara for believing in my work and giving me the confidence to write what I write. Last but not least, I would like to thank my family, especially my parents whose lifetime of support, love and affection continue to nurture and sustain me. To my beloved Dad and my devoted brother, Mubs, thank you for supporting this cause, and for your earlier reviews of my work. Thank you also to my husband, Farid, and to my son, Aydin Samie, for your energy and spirit.

Introduction

Sport, race and gender – the politics of ethnic 'Other' girls and women

Aarti Ratna and Samaya Farooq Samie

The scholarship about ethnic 'Other' girls and women and their relationships to sport and physical culture has undoubtedly grown over the past three decades. Work that is progressive in this field demonstrates the importance of sport and physical culture as a popular and public arena to examine the reproduction (and resistance to) omnipresent structures of inequality and control (see e.g. Ahmad, 2011; Burdsey *et al.*, 2013; Hargreaves, 2000; Jamieson, 1998; Scraton *et al.*, 2005; Thangaraj *et al.*, 2016). There is a growing body of knowledge that aims to critically read the experiences and perspectives of ethnic 'Other' women and girls (see e.g. Birrell, 1989; Douglas, 2002; Douglas and Jamieson, 2006; Jamieson, 2003; McDonald and Birrell, 1999; Scraton, 2001; Smith, 1992). Many mainstream 'White' academic traditions and disciplines, such as sociology, psychology, cultural studies and so on, have moved beyond uncritical representations of racialised (female) 'Others' (Brah and Phoenix, 2004; Davis and Lutz, 2000). The belief that there are other ways of knowing the relationship between ethnic 'Other' girls and women, and their diverse, dynamic and polymorphous relationships to sport and physical culture, is beginning to gain some traction (see Ratna *et al.*, 2017; Toffoletti and Palmer, 2015). And different feminist perspectives, like Black feminist politics, have been used within sporting literatures (see e.g. Armstrong, 2007; Carter-Francique and Flowers, 2013; Pelak, 2005; Ratna, 2017; Scraton, 2001). The critical use of intersectional thinking, as advanced by scholars of colour more broadly, has helped to uncover and critically analyse the multiple realities of ethnic 'Other' women. For instance, Jamieson's (2003) appropriation of *mestiza* consciousness in/through studies of sport specifically questions the dualistic, linear and Western norms of thinking which polarise identities, desires and power structures. Using the work of Anzaldúa (1987), she persuades readers to think about identities, desires and power as not just existing between the 'borderlands' (between the southwestern US/Mexican border) but also in and between the artificial boundaries of subject positionings, which can result in ambiguous, contradictory, shifting and multifarious 'standpoints'. Nevertheless, epistemological and methodological concerns about the validity and quality of much of this literature remain. As we explicate in Chapter 1, when much of the so called 'critical' literature can itself still be implicated in the problematic reproduction of stereotypes about ethnic 'Other' family life, cultures and physical dispositions, it is a sign that progress has not only been limited, but in fact is quite narrow. Furthermore, even as research has begun to yield contradictory, shifting and multifarious 'standpoints' pertaining to ethnic 'Other' women, many studies continue to purport the positive influence of Western sport in liberating such groups of women, overlooking in turn the complex and unexpected ways in which power operates and circumscribes the life chances of different groups of people, at any given moment in time, in and across different societies (see e.g. Birrell, 1990).

This collection aims to respond to the lacuna in *critical* knowledge about ethnic 'Other' females in sport, so as to better represent their complex, multifarious and dynamic lived realities. Like a number of other critical feminist scholars (see e.g. Lewis, 1996) we too found ourselves embroiled in a pressing debate about who could and should research ethnic 'Other' women and girls. We both knew all too well that such discussions have (falsely) polarised relational identities (see e.g. Burdsey, 2007; Fletcher, 2014; Watson and Scraton, 2001) and distracted otherwise reflexive and engaged scholars from producing much needed critical research, both within and outside of the field. The challenges of reading and representing ethnic 'Other' women's bodies is not straightforward, regardless of 'who' the author is (Ratna, 2017). Much of the burden of representation has traditionally fallen on, and in many cases continues to fall on, Black and ethnic 'Other' scholars themselves; it is left to them to unhinge uncritical knowledge and/or redress the epistemic erasure of alternate ways of knowing and thinking with and through difference. Women of colour, according to Smith (1992: 244), because of their "shared historical traditions and personal experiences" can become "subjects of (their) own research rather than objects" by "developing critical thinking and a critical consciousness" so as to challenge "patterns of oppression and domination". Yet this kind of 'retreat response' from scholars, who do not share the identities of ethnic 'Other' girls and women, is not necessarily *the answer*. It reproduces the narrow viewpoint that consciousness of oppression is inextricably connected to bearing an identity of oppression, which, in turn, ignores how particular identities, at particular times and in certain contexts, may be marginalised, privileged, and linked to the complex interplay of both freedom and control. It also removes White men and women's responsibilities for addressing the lives of people different from themselves (Ratna, 2017; this volume), but it "ultimately paralyses meaningful discussion or advocacy" (Vertinsky and Captain, 1998: 536). As Vertinsky and Captain (1998: 536) eloquently state:

> [...] the most delicate secrets must be studied to bring about the healing process made possible by knowledge, and [...] outsiders have a role to play in explaining the travails of people whose experience they have not shared.

The final collection brings together voices and subjugated viewpoints from scholars, of various racial and ethnic backgrounds (English, and non-English speaking), geographies and personal and political sensibilities, who are working across various disciplinary boundaries and writing about the relationship between sport, physical culture, and the participation of ethnic 'Other' girls and women. As a part of this process, we connected with a range of scholars both male and female. But we do acknowledge that the final collection does reflect 'female' voices, and this was by no means deliberate or intentional. We recognise the possibility for many male scholars to struggle for and against the material and cultural structures that have traditionally limited females. Nevertheless, those who proactively responded to our call for contributions happened to be female, and in similar and different ways, they privilege theoretical frameworks that 'speak to them', and which inform their methodological choices and methods, to provide new and original approaches to analysing sport, physical culture and the lives of ethnic 'Other' girls and women.

What's in a name?

Through this very personal and political project, we pondered long and hard about the use and misuse of labels. A pertinent place to begin this discussion is to state, overtly, that the girls and women at the centre of this edited collection constitute a minority or majority ethnic population within the national boundaries of their 'home'. But regardless, and simultaneously, they are predominantly read and positioned as ethnic 'Other', meaning in this sense, 'different to the White, female body'. Of course, the language which can be used to represent the heterogeneity of ethnic 'Others' is not tension-free. For instance, the terms 'Black' and 'women of colour' hold different cultural and political meanings for people in America and in England (Brah, 1996; Mirza, 1997). Yet, to find another term to capture the politics of diverse groups of ethnic 'Other' girls and women is not straightforward either. For example, terms such as ethnic minority and ethnic majority; first world and third world; global north and global south; and one third world and two third worlds. For different reasons they can all be confusing and/or problematic. That is, differences between 'them' still become unintentionally masked and often universalised, and moreover, 'they' may represent a majority within a nation but still be publically and politically read and treated as minority: that is, 'Other' (Mohanty, 2003). Indeed, some groups of ethnic 'Other' girls and women may represent a minority within the nation, but their citizenship status means that they may view themselves as part of the social, cultural and political 'majority' (Brah, 1996). In this volume, the incorporation of diasporic groups within particular national boundaries is meant to trouble assertions about specific ethnic groups from 'there' (e.g. South and/or East Asia, South America and Africa) over 'here' (Australia/New Zealand, Europe and North America). We believe this elucidates the (re)construction of identities as not fixed to particular spaces (of origin) but dynamic and in tension across a number of transnational contexts, disrupting notions of core/periphery from both research and analysis (see e.g. Burdsey *et al.*, 2013; Carrington, 2010, 2015; Joseph *et al.*, 2012). Nevertheless, vernacular such as 'West' and 'non-West' are still common even though the processes of globalisation mean that those terms, in the late modern epoch, are becoming erroneous. The point is not to fragment the experience of different groups of ethnic 'Other' girls and women, so that they are read as quintessentially different from one another. But to assert that despite the differences within and between groups, they nevertheless possess agency and resistive power which unites their struggles for visibility, representation and acceptability in/through sport and physical cultures. As editors, we adopt the term ethnic 'Other' to centre the *politics* of how different groups of girls and women make sense of their lived materialities. In this volume, we have given flexibility to contributing authors to make their own decisions about labels and naming practices, rather than to overly police selected nomenclature. Thus, the varied labels evident throughout this collection may reflect popular terminology across different moments in time, dominant discourses in the academic literature, common parlances used across different geo-political sites, and as self-selected by the participants included in and across the different chapters.

Book structure

The chapters included in this edited collection are bound together in similar and different ways; they shift our analytical gazes from the supposed 'problems' of female ethnic 'Others' to debates about broader discourses, language, practices and social systems which operate in/through the domains of sport and physical culture. That is, the mechanisms of sport and physical culture which work to position 'them' as marginal, and 'Other'. This collection begins with a mapping the field chapter written by the editors, establishing what has been assumed to constitute the relationship between ethnic 'Other' females, sport and physical culture. We provide a theoretical critique of such work, reviewing persisting challenges and alternative ways of researching the lives and sporting preferences of different groups of ethnic 'Other' girls and women. By mapping the developments across this field of study, we offer theoretical ingredients for developing a counter-narrative to the prominent and problematic ways ethnic 'Other' girls and women are represented in/through sport and physical culture. The edited collection is then split into three key sections; that is, chapters that exemplify feminisms of the ethnic 'Other', stimulating debates about various disciplinary and methodological traditions as well as using connected theories and methods to critically read the lived, sporting, physical needs and desires of ethnic 'Other' girls and women. The chapters are specifically structured as follows:

Theoretical interventions and knowledge production: research in this section draws on important theoretical interventions to studies of sport that are significant to international scholars of sociology, cultural studies, feminism, race, diaspora and ethnicity. For example, Black feminist thinking (Carter-Francique's chapter) and Postcolonial feminist theories (Samie's chapter) are used to elucidate the complex manifestations of structural relations of power and agency. The theories adopted are not just drawn from discourses predominant in the West, but also engage subjugated ideologies and perspectives that expose structures and cultures of control, exclusion and oppression, and centralise the advocacy of the subaltern. Both Carter-Francique and Samie invite us to cross boundaries of knowledge/discipline, to find other ways of critically engaging with the different, changing and complex lived realities of ethnic 'Other' girls and women in sport. Meanwhile, Watson and Scraton draw on a critical feminist lens, to further (re)consider researching the sport and leisure experiences of ethnic 'Others' as White researchers. Their chapter not only lays bare the researchers' desire to confront the implications of Whiteness, in and through scholarship about race, gender and sport/leisure, but demonstrates how racialised scripts pertaining to 'Others' and the privileged 'White' self can be questioned, and unhinged throughout the research process, so as to better facilitate knowledge deconstruction and reconstruction.

Experiences at the intersections of identity: the collection of knowledge in this section of the book aims to use relevant theories and concepts to unearth and unpack the multiply constituted nature of identities, giving voice to a range of ethnic 'Other' girls and women (from different parts of the world) exploring the problems and possibilities of their sporting (and physical) engagements. Ratna, in her chapter, deconstructs and reconstructs, through an analysis of her own career, the intersections of race, gender and class. She argues that her outsider within status – as a British Asian woman in the elite, White and male spaces of academia – provides the creative energy to write back to systems and structures of domination, and representations of ethnic 'Others' more broadly in the field of sport studies. Nicholson explores the history of gendered and racialised myths of 'difference', that have arguably shaped the experiences of non-White female athletes right up to the present day. By consulting written diaries produced by White female cricketers, who participated in numerous international cricket tours during the postwar period, Nicholson examines the constructedness of White superiority. She further explores the effect this construction of 'Whiteness' had when non-White cricketers were encountered. Rana, through the kickboxing engagements of Dutch-Moroccan women, focuses upon the geographical, social and pious context of their bodily choices and experiences, presenting a narrative that speaks back to the Dutch government's neoliberal, integrationist rhetoric.

Everyday struggles and transformative practice: chapters in this section of the book employ theoretical lenses and different methodologies in order to centre the perspectives of ethnic 'Other' females, and their roles in the shaping and making of their sporting engagements as either coaches, fans, players, etc. Instead of viewing ethnic 'Other' girls and women as docile, and sport as a fixed and repressive body of power, the chapters in this section address the transformative agencies of ethnic 'Other' females. Thus they explore the structural continuities and changes that have impacted different ethnic 'Other' women's engagements with physical culture and sport. Jamieson and Choi – using a Chicana feminist lens – powerfully do this by re-addressing the neoliberal and consumptive goals of 'a global girl project', in order to contextualise the career of Mexican golfer Reina Ochoa and her disidentifying manoeuvres in/ through the professional game. Erhart, drawing upon the intersection of discourses about gender and ethnicity, reveals the pleasures and resistant practices of Turkish, Muslim women fans of men's football. Both of these chapters rely on and access knowledge contained in articles not written in English. Finally, Rankin-Wright and Norman critically debate the problems and possibilities of being a Black and/or South woman in/across the predominantly White and male spaces of the coaching workforce, in the UK. The authors, using Critical Race Theory and a Black feminist theoretical approach, make visible their research participants' struggles for recognition and respect.

Authors of this edited collection overall push the boundaries of knowledge production, to go deeper into their interrogations of hidden, complex and contested ways of understanding ethnic 'Other' girls and women's relationships to sport and physical culture. From this basis, we invite other scholars to join this dialogue, to work from our different social, geographic and political positionings as well as disciplinary boundaries in order to continue to advance a *critical* reading of the sporting, physical and social worlds of ethnic 'Other' girls and women. We recognise this process may engender epistemological tensions. But nevertheless, we urge scholars within and beyond the sociocultural studies of sport and physical culture, to take up this challenge, creating spaces in our scholarship to 'speak to' and 'hear our each other' into transformative knowledge production and practice (Vertinsky and Captain, 1998: 536; see also Ratna and Samie, Chapter 1 of this volume; Ratna *et al.*, 2017). In this vein, we call for our engagements in research to be politically motivated, using our research for humanitarian ends, and to make sport and physical culture truly inclusive and empowering for *all* those who may wish to be involved, in whichever way, and for whatever purpose.

Of course, as is quite often the nature of edited collections, we were unable to include or represent the experiences of many ethnic 'Other' girls and women, who remain overlooked in the academies of sport and knowledge production. Here we consider the political quests of intersex Indian athletes (Mitra, 2014), the feminine and national sensibilities of elite Japanese women footballers (Ho, 2014), the physical cultural practices of girls and women living across different parts of South America (Filho and Rubio, 2012), the imperial, indigenous, and new migration context of sport and physical culture for ethnic 'Other' females in Australia and New Zealand (Palmer and Masters, 2010; Nemani and Thorpe, 2016), and female participation in sport and physical cultures in the changing post-apartheid context of South Africa (Hargreaves, 2000; Pelak, 2005). Further still, we are cognisant of the under-representation of the lives and identities of minoritised White groups, who experience similar forms of racial and ethnic Othering, as well as the absence of testimonies pertaining to the experiences of dual heritage or multi-heritage groups of women within and across different national and diasporic boundaries. As Washington (1990: 32) states, these kinds of "heroic voices, and heroic images of ... [minoritised women and girls] (have been) suppressed", from institutions of research and knowledge production, as well as institutions of sport, and yet their "heroism" is what many within those culture depend on "for its survival" (see also Hargreaves, 2000). Nevertheless, we hope that the theoretical and empirical insights developed in this volume will stimulate further research about female ethnic 'Others' and their relationships with sport and physical culture.

References

Ahmad, A. (2011) 'British Muslim Female Experiences in Football: Islam, Identity and the Hijab', in D. Burdsey (ed.) *Race, Ethnicity and Football*. Oxford: Routledge.

Anzaldúa, G.E. (1987) *Borderland, La Frontera: The New Mestiza*; U.S.A.: Aunt Lute Books.

Armstrong, K. (2007) 'The Nature of Black Women's Leadership in Community Recreation Sport: An Illustration of Black Feminist Thought', *Women in Sport and Physical Activity Journal*, 16(1): pp. 3–15.

Birrell, S. (1990) 'Women of Color, Critical Autobiographies, and Sport', in Messner, M.A. and D.F. Sabo (eds) *Sport, Men and the Gender Order*. Champaign, Illinois: Human Kinetics: pp. 185–199.

Birrell, S. (1989) 'Racial Relations Theories and Sport: Suggestions for a More Critical Analysis', *Sociology of Sport Journal*, 6: pp. 212–227.

Brah, A. (1996) *Cartographies of Diaspora: Contesting Identities*. London and New York: Routledge.
Brah, A. and Phoenix, A. (2004) 'Ain't I a Woman? Revisiting Intersectionality', *Journal of International Women's Studies*, 5(3): pp. 75–86.
Burdsey, D. (2007) *British Asians and Football: Culture, Identity and Exclusion*. London: Routledge.
Burdsey, D., Thangaraj, S. and Dudrah, R. (2013) 'Playing through Time and Space: Sport and South Asian Diasporas', *South Asian Popular Culture*, 11(3): pp. 211–218.
Carrington, B. (2015) 'Assessing the Sociology of Sport: On Race and Diaspora', *International Review for the Sociology of Sport*, 50(4–5): pp. 391–396.
Carrington, B. (2010) *Race, Sport and Politics: The Sporting Black Diaspora*, Los Angeles. London, New Delhi, Singapore, Washington D.C.: Sage.
Carter-Francique, A.R. and Flowers, C.L. (2013) 'Intersections of Race, Ethnicity and Gender in Sport', in E.A. Roper (ed.) *Gender Relations in Sport*. Rotterdam, Boston, Taipei: Sense Publishers: pp. 73–93.
Davis, K. and Lutz, H. (2000) 'Open Forum: Life in Theory – Three Feminist Thinkers on Transition(s)', *European Journal of Women's Studies*, 7(3): pp. 367–378.
Douglas, D. (2002) 'To be Young, Gifted, Black and Female: A Meditation on the Cultural Politics at Play in Representations of Venus and Serena Williams', *Sociology of Sport Online – SOSOL*, 5(2): pp. 1–16.
Douglas, D. and Jamieson, K. (2006) 'A Farewell to Remember: Interrogating the Nancy Lopez Farewell Tour', *Sociology of Sport Journal*, 23: pp. 117–141.
Filho, M.A.T. and Rubio, K. (2012) 'Between the Confrontation and the Concession: The Identities of Brazilian Olympic Female Athletes', *International Journal of Humanities and Social Science*, 2(20): pp. 44–51.
Fletcher, T. (2014) '"Does He Look Like a Paki?" and Exploration of "Whiteness", Positionality and Reflexivity in Inter-racial Sports Research', *Qualitative Research in Sport, Exercise and Health*, 6(2): pp. 244–260.
Hargreaves, J.A. (2000) *Heroines of Sport: The Politics of Difference and Identity*, Oxon, New York: Routledge.
Ho, M.S. (2014) 'Is Nadeshiko Japan "Feminine"? Manufacturing Sport Celebrity and National Identity on Japanese Morning Television', *Journal of Sport and Social Issues*, 38(2): pp. 164–183.
Jamieson, K.M. (2003) 'Occupying a Middle Space: Toward a Mestiza Sport Studies', *Sociology of Sport Journal*, 20: pp. 1–16.
Jamieson, K.M. (1998) 'Reading Nancy Lopez: Decoding Representations of Race, Class and Sexuality', *Sociology of Sport Journal*, 15: pp. 343–358.
Joseph, J., Darnell, S., and Nakamura, Y. (2012) *Race and Sport in Canada: Intersecting Inequalities*. Toronto: Canadian Scholar Press.
Lewis, G. (1996) 'Situated Voices: "Black Women's Experience" and Social Work', *Feminist Review*, 53: pp. 24–56.
McDonald, M.G. and Birrell, S. (1999) 'Reading Sport Critically: A Methodology for Interrogating Power', *Sociology of Sport Journal*, 16(4): pp. 283–300.
Mitra, P. (2014) 'Male/Female or Other: The Untold Stories of Female Athletes with Intersex Variations in India', in J. Hargreaves and E. Andersen (eds) *The Handbook of Sport, Gender and Sexuality*. London and New York: Routledge: pp. 384–394.

Mohanty, C.T. (2003) *Feminism without Borders: Decolonizing Theory, Practicing Solidarity*, Durham and London: Duke University Press.
Nemani, M. and Thorpe, H. (2016) 'The Experiences of Brown "Female" Bodyboarders: Negotiating Multiple Axes of Marginality', in Thorpe, H. and Olive, R. (eds) *Women in Action Sport Cultures: Identity, Politics and Experience*, London: Palgrave Macmillan: pp. 213–234.
Palmer, F.R. and Masters, T.M. (2010) 'Māori Feminism and Sport Leadership: Exploring Māori Women's Experiences', *Sport Management Review*, 13: pp. 331–344.
Pelak, C.F. (2005) 'Negotiating Gender/Race/Class Constraints in the New South Africa', *International Review for the Sociology of Sport*, 40(1): pp. 53–70.
Ratna, A. (2017) 'Black Women, Black Voices: The Contribution of a Spivakian and Black Feminist Analysis to Studies of Sport and Leisure', in J. Long, T. Fletcher and R. Watson (eds) *Sport Leisure and Social Justice*. London: Routledge: pp. 153–167.
Ratna, A., Samie, F.S., Jamieson, K. and Thangaraj, S. (2017) 'Learning Lessons from the Feminisms of Ethnic "Others"', in L. Mansfield, J. Caudwell, B. Watson and B. Wheaton (eds) *The Handbook for Feminisms in Sport, Leisure and Physical Education*. Basingstoke: Palgrave (in press).
Scraton, S.J. (2001) 'Reconceptualising Race, Gender and Sport: The Contribution of Black Feminism', in B. Carrington and I. McDonald (eds) *Race, Sport and British Society*. London: Routledge: pp. 170–187.
Scraton, S., Caudwell, J. and Holland, S. (2005) '"Bend it Like Patel" Centring "Race", Ethnicity and Gender in Feminist Analysis of Women's Football in England', *International Review for the Sociology of Sport*, 40(1): pp. 71–88.
Smith, Y.R. (1992) 'Women of Color in Society and Sport', *Quest*, 44: pp. 228–250.
Thangaraj, S., Arnoldo, C. and Chin, C. (eds) (2016) *Asian American Sporting Cultures*: New York: New York University Press.
Toffoletti, K. and Palmer, C. (2015) 'New Approaches for Studies of Muslim Women and Sport', *International Review for the Sociology of Sport*, DOI: 10.1177/1012690215589326.
Vertinsky, P. and Captain, G. (1998) 'More Myth than History: American Culture and the Representations of the Black Female's Athletic Ability', *Journal of Sport History*, 25(3): pp. 532–561.
Washington, M.H. (1990) 'The Darkened Eye Restored: Notes Toward a Literary History of Black Women', in H.L. Gates (ed.) *Reading Black, Reading Feminist: A Critical Anthology*, New York: Penguin Books: pp. 30–45.
Watson, B. and Scraton, S. (2001) 'Confronting Whiteness: Researching the Leisure Lives of South Asian Mothers', *Journal of Gender Studies*, 10(3): pp. 265–277.

Chapter 1

Mapping the field

Research about ethnic 'Other' females, sport and physical culture

Aarti Ratna and Samaya Farooq Samie

Introduction

This chapter critically charts research about race, gender and sport, particularly as it pertains to the representation of ethnic 'Other' girls and women's voices, identities and experiences in sport and physical culture.[1] In mapping developments in the field, our objectives are twofold. First, to interrogate the theoretical interjections and critical turns in knowledge production, that shape the predominant representations of different groups of ethnic 'Other' girls and women, across time and space. And second to critically assess the theoretical contours that have broadened knowledge, and expose moments when researchers have (perhaps inadvertently) limited the possibility for further 'critical' insights to be produced. We begin with a broad debate about sport, race relations and gender, and emphasise the omission of knowledge about ethnic 'Other' girls and women during the 1970s and 1980s, as well as the largely positivistic, androcentric, assimilationist, ethnocentric and Eurocentric thinking which has colonised much of the scholarship in the sociology of sport. Moving on from this, we problematise both the reproduction of dominant discourses about (some) ethnic 'Other' girls and women *and* the cultural institution of sport. Reflecting on subjugated knowledges and the agencies of ethnic 'Other' females, we critically debate the turn in knowledge production which sensitises the politics of difference and intersectionality. The final section of this chapter provides a critique of the growing body of scholarship about ethnic 'Other' girls and women, sport and physical culture, since the turn of the millennium produced in, by and predominantly for Western countries. Although the narrative developed is generally ordered from past to present, we do not suggest that shifts in knowledge production are by any means linear, becoming more progressive with the march of time (see Caudwell, 2011). Instead, we note that the process has been rather patchy and is characterised by peaks and troughs in critical understanding as well as progressions and regressions in theoretical engagement, in and across particular moments of time. Whilst we attempt to provide a critical review of pertinent scholarly work written about particular gendered ethnic 'Other' groups, we remain mindful of one important fact: that this reflection cannot be deemed 'complete' by any means. Oppressive forces of power and control will be experienced differentially in and between ethnic 'Other' girls and women, and we do want to conflate and/or universalise group experiences (see below for further debate). Yet we cannot review the particular histories, voices, dynamic and manifold experiences of every group – who may fall within the ethnic 'Other' female label – in one chapter either. Instead, our intention for this chapter is to examine the interplay between structural determinants and systems of power, and the complexities and vagaries of particular ethnic 'Other' female experiences, and their agentic beings and becomings, purely as a means to illustrate critical issues and turns in knowledge production. This is our critical reading, but one which we sincerely hope provides an avenue and platform for other scholars who may also wish to further interrogate such issues in their own studies as well as to interrogate what this may mean for the sporting, physical needs, pleasures, experiences and endeavours of different groups, within and across broader ethnic 'Other' female groupings.

Sport, race relations and gender: the problems and perils of categorical research

In 1989 Birrell published what many sports scholars deem to be a canonical text in sport studies. *Race Relations Theories in Sport* heightened awareness about the extent to which the complex issues of race, ethnicity, cultural difference and so on were either being obscured or explored superficially. When we first encountered this text in the early 2000s, being amongst a handful of non-White feminist (and female) scholars trying to get ahead in what remains a predominantly White, masculinist institution, we embraced it for many reasons. We were concerned about the ways in which issues of race, ethnicity and gender had traditionally been documented (by White, Western researchers, in and through *selected* epistemological, ontological and methodological traditions) written in and predominantly produced for English speaking countries (or 'the West'). That earlier discussions of racial and gendered tropes were replete with a plethora of omissions, inaccuracies and misrepresentations about non-White women and girls, and their multifarious relationships to sport and physical culture. Yet at the time of Birrell's publication, little attention had been placed on such issues. Only a handful of critical sport scholarship about non-White women and girls even existed within the sub-discipline of sport sociology, or sport and leisure studies (see e.g. Douglas, 1988a, 1988b; Raval, 1989; Trivedi, 1984), and most of what was produced was unpublished (and therefore not widely available to the general public, or for citation in scholarly or other intellectual contexts) (e.g. Abney, 1988;

Alexander, 1978; Barclay, 1979; Murphy, 1980). Some critical literature about minoritised females did exist, but it was published in cultural studies or mainstream sociology, and did not deal with sport per se. Throughout the 1970s and 1980s, for instance, Black feminist theorists were critiquing the essentialism and the referentiality in theorising 'woman' in (secular, liberal) feminist theory and political activity (Davis, 1981; *Feminist Review*, 1984) and Black feminist politics were taking aim at the concept of "global sisterhood" for its failure "to fully take on board the power relations that divided" women (Brah and Phoenix, 2004: 76). (South) Asian feminists, too, were vigorously challenging the essentialist connotations of racism, rejecting in particular universalist theories of 'Other' women's identity as unjust and oppressive (Amos and Parmar, 1984; Grewal *et al.*, 1988; Trivedi, 1984). However, sports scholars rarely engaged with this broader spectrum of feminist thinking and/or critical studies of race, controlling and limiting, in turn, the ways that ethnic 'Other' women and girls' engagement with sport was known and understood (both within and beyond the sporting literature).[2]

Instead, sport was romanticised as an arena for social and civic progress, and positioned as an essential 'social service' and an integral feature of 'social planning in Britain' (Coghlan and Webb, 1990; DoE, 1975). That is, sport was portrayed as an arena for racial progress, a force for good (Carrington, 2010). Issues of racial inequalities were explored idiosyncratically and represented as a 'thing' that Black men were believed to live with as the otherwise meritocratic system of sport adapted and adjusted (see Birrell, 1989). During the 1960s and 1970s, researchers sought to develop "a generalized sociological framework for the analysis of race, racism and race relations" (Jarvie and Reid, 1997: 213; see also Cashmore, 1996), but gender was rarely considered as a relevant or necessary area of social inquiry. The persistence of racial myths and fallacies about 'natural' physical strengths, and 'intellectual' inadequacies of certain (male) cultural groups (e.g. African Americans) dominated the literature (e.g. Kane, 1971). As Wiggins (1989: 158) noted, "people from all walks of life – coaches, athletes, trainers, cultural anthropologists, psychologists, sociologists, physical educators, biologists, medical doctors, and sportscasters" were putting forward "their own theories regarding racial differences and their possible effects on sport performance", especially as it related to Black (male) athletes. Likewise, quantitative studies that privileged androcentric and positivistic epistemologies erased females from this documented knowledge, and rarely critiqued the character of racial oppressions either. For example, researchers seldom questioned the production of "stereotypes, prejudices and myths about ethnic minority groups" and the various contributions this type of thinking had on strengthening discrimination against, and legitimising the under-representation of ethnic minority peoples within certain sports (Jarvie and Reid, 1997: 211; see also Coakley,

1986; Eitzen and Sage, 1978; Spracklen, 2008). In fact, despite a wealth of literature tracing the role of sport in distributing, establishing and maintaining "dominant patterns of social organisation and [...] power" within and beyond the colonies (Houlihan, 1991: 10; see also Dunae, 1988; Mangan, 1986; Stoddart, 1988), much of this earlier research ignored the impact of colonial legacies in manufacturing racial mythologies between White and non-White peoples in the metropolis. For instance, scholarship of the time frequently overlooked the impact of historical connections between certain sports, and the assumed racial and ethnic differences that categorised and juxtaposed Whites as superior saviours and leaders (read: colonisers) and represented non-Whites as inferior, backward and the uncivilised 'Others' (read: colonised) (see Birrell, 1989; Carrington, 2010; Wiggins, 1989). Likewise, the position and actions of sporting White women during this imperial age was, and still is, relatively overlooked (Nicholson, this volume). The sports literature was, instead, polarised, with discussions about gender centralising the experiences of White (typically middle-class, able-bodied, heterosexual) women, and talk of race privileging African Caribbean or African American men (Birrell, 1989, 1990; Bruening, 2005; Hargreaves, 2000; Scraton, 2001). When attention was paid to diverse ethnic cultural groups, predominantly White, fe/male researchers perpetuated ethnocentric perceptions about the agentic capacity of non-White females (see e.g. Carrington *et al.*, 1987; Leaman, 1984; Leaman and Carrington, 1985; Lewis, 1979), overlooking how factors such as 'White patriarchy' and/or 'racism' itself (the institution, ideologies, practices and product) negatively impacted women of colour in sport (see Raval's 1989 response to Carrington *et al.*'s. 1987 work). Birrell (1989, 1990) suggested that to move beyond bias models of understanding, race needed to be viewed as more than just a descriptive variable. More research was required in order to examine how ideologies about race produced racial categorisations, that over time and across different context developed and crystallised into dominant racial relations of power and control. She argued that materialist theories, for instance, offered the potential to critically understand racial relations as shaped by both capitalist and colonial projects (Birrell, 1989). At this time, she proposed a cultural studies solution to further exploring the social constructions of race:

> [...] the field [the socio-cultural analysis of sport] might benefit from a blending of materialist and cultural analyses of the sort that cultural studies offers [...]. The analysis would be critical and reflexive; it would take into account the contours of the particular relations of dominance and subordination that exist among groups located at the intersections of class and racial conflicts; it would be grounded in a historical analysis or the origins of such relations; it would carefully attend to the production of ideologies of dominance and subordination; and it would

> utilize analytical strategies that respect the dialectical relationship between material conditions and cultural reproduction.
>
> (Birrell, 1989: 220)

Of course, not all research produced on Black and ethnic 'Others' during the 1980s was complicit in perpetuating racial mythologies or Eurocentric ideologies. Researchers did recognise that White, African Caribbean and South Asian women all faced different opportunities and restrictions in relation to all aspects of their life within (British) society. Many called for "research on (racial) minorities" to entail a focus on ethnicity and the notion of "groups within groups within groups" (Fleming, 1994: 169; see also Raval, 1989). The reliance on quantitative methodologies greatly impeded progress towards more radical and critical interventions. Ethnic 'Other' female groups were represented as 'hard to reach', yet very few concrete efforts were made to consider, much less to engage, these diverse communities of women.

Dominant discourses, subjugated knowledges and (political) agency

At the turn of the millennium – almost a decade after Birrell's poignant call for more 'critical scholarship' to be produced on the sporting experiences of women of colour – we were disturbed by the fact that scholarly (and political) enquiries about the structures, cultures and discourses omnipresent in sport and society remained scarce, and narratives about the agentic potential of ethnic 'Other' girls and women 'inside' of these spaces were still subjugated. Exceptions, did, of course, exist (see Douglas, 2002; Hargreaves, 2000; Jamieson, 1998, 2003; Scraton, 2001; Smith, 1992). The critical contribution by Hargreaves' *Heroines of Sport*, published in 2000 as a collection of essays about "different groups of women whose stories had been excluded from previous accounts of women's sports and female heroism", was crucial in complicating otherwise uncritical and essentialist debates about issues of race, ethnicity and gender (2000: 8). This seminal work situated Black women in South Africa; Muslim women from the Middle East; Aboriginal women from Australia and Canada; and lesbian and disabled women from different countries worldwide, as active agents in the making and shaping of their own lives and sporting endeavours. It drew attention to the everyday agencies and acts of resistance that collectively marked the experiences of women who existed on the margins of sport, in terms of race, ethnicity, disability, sexuality, class and culture, and who were otherwise forgotten or excluded from intellectual debates about sport (ibid.: 5). Despite this promising turn, the wider body of research in this area was heavily skewed, focusing either on African American (Black) women or South Asian women (in Britain). The sporting preferences of other ethnic 'Other' females, at this time, often elided between popular representations of both Black and South Asian girls and women (and mostly in relation to a US or UK context respectively). What is more, the quality of a lot of the so-called 'critical' scholarly work on race, ethnicity and minoritised women and girls, produced since the turn of the millennium and published in and for English-speaking countries, was mixed (see also Ratna, 2015, 2016).

On the one hand, problems of past research persisted, despite claims that scholarship and thinking had evolved to now include an increasingly global, neoliberal and neocolonial epoch. In reality, intellectual inquiries throughout the 1990s and mid-2000s continued to drive and value particular types of narratives, that ultimately left intact functionalist notions about the value of Western sports and societies. For instance, the metanarrative of 'inadequacies' in non-White peoples (and not in European systems, structures and ideologies) was still dominant (as it had been throughout the 1980s and early 1990s), but was being used to brush aside prejudicial practices that contributed to the underrepresentation of diverse minority ethnic 'Others' (see e.g. St. Louis, 2003, 2004). This phenomenon was originally evident in claims that attributed the low involvement of South Asian (men) in Rugby League, with the beliefs that they had 'small statures', lower thresholds for pain and were culturally non-violent, and non-competitive (Long *et al.*, 1995, 1997). It was also highlighted in crudely racist and fallacious allegations that South Asian men avoided football because they were 'too frail for contact sports' (Burdsey, 2007; Fleming, 2001). We were disgruntled by this phenomenon of manufacturing uncritical and singular claims, and circulating them as legitimate 'truths' and 'facts' from the field. As South Asian females – one a British Hindu Gujarati and the other a British Pakistani Muslim – we recall how this kind of thinking also compounded the Western obsession to make sense of the low sport participation trends amongst 'our kind' in the West. Researchers privileged, for instance, the notion that South Asian women and girls were caught in between conflicting cultures, and restrained by the prevalence of ethnically and culturally acceptable gender-specific roles that privileged family commitment, honour and academic achievements ahead of sports and their own needs and interests (see Figueroa, 1993; Hall, 1995; Johnson, 2000; Maguire and Collins, 1998; Porter, 2001; Rai and Finch, 1997; Taylor and Toohey, 1999; Tirone and Pedlar, 2000; Verma and Darby, 1994). Other work stipulated that girls were restricted from pursuing physical activity due to the negative attitudes and disapproval of parents and other respected elders (Ismond, 2003; Porter, 2001). The (mis-)representation of South Asian cultures, and the dominant framing of South Asian women as subjects and objects of their family, culture and religion, subsequently meant that White fe/male, Western, secular liberal feminist researchers looked first to 'evidence' of restrictive parents preventing their daughters from engaging in physical activity, than to any other causal explanations (e.g. fears of revealing bodies in public, and concerns about 'acceptable' body size and shape; see Scraton, 2001). Suffice it to say, research about body image, eating disorders etc. amongst South Asian females remains scarce even today, whilst there is an abundance of research that compares participation trends between and across White and non-White cultures (Fischbacher *et al.*, 2004; Gill *et al.*, 2002; HEA, 2000; Rowe and Champion, 2000; Snape, 2005). There is no problem comparing trends, however, when the trend analysis is used to reinforce and strengthen pre-determined assumptions about the largely negative impacts of ethnicity, and often religion on such females' opportunities for sport, it is entirely problematic. "Subjugated knowledges" become replaced with metanarratives that further enable researchers to retain control over the histories, lived biographies, realities and "truths of various subordinate groups" (Jarvie and Reid, 1997: 216; see also Collins, 1991).

The rhetoric of ethnic 'Other' female absenteeism and/or underrepresentation from certain Western sports took on a new agenda, especially in the European literature, as political concern about the unwillingness of foreigners to integrate and/or assimilate to White/Western structures heightened. Functionalist claims about sports potential to reign in self-alienating 'Others' began dominating discussions, especially when it came to making sense of Muslim communities (see e.g. Klein and Kothy, 2001; Walseth, 2007; Walseth and Fasting, 2004). Whilst the bulk of this research raised awareness of the exclusive nature of sport, it also did in ways that relied on, and further perpetuated, a 'cultural conflict' framework that collectively depicted these racialised and religionised groups as a 'problem' (see e.g. De Knop *et al.*, 1996; Elling *et al.*, 2001; Klein and Kothy, 2001). What remained absent was a critical unhinging of the extent to which sport institutions were themselves traditionally structured to appropriate and reinforce European (often, nationalist and assimilatory) agendas and perspectives whilst also giving lip service to the rhetoric of inclusion (see Burdsey, 2007). In fact, even when attention turned to the agentic capacity of women from these communities, researchers were preoccupied with defining their resistance, not necessarily to overturn racist, Eurocentric structures within sport, but on fighting discriminatory 'backward' traditions within their own culture and against their own men (see e.g. Pfister, 2000). As Samie (2013) states, the latter point has, of course, been used to further support claims about such women as oppressed by their own cultures and men.

In reality though, agency and empowerment can operate in multiple ways and at different levels, ranging from collective organisation and mass demonstrations, to silence as an individual act of resistance in and of itself (Mirza, 1997; Ratna *et al.*, 2017). It is also likely to include acts of individual negotiation and compliance, and we would be remiss in our analysis if we failed to mention that alternate readings of ethnic 'Other' women's agentic tactics did exist, of course. Here we reflect on Ratna's 2008 study of sporting British Asian girls in which deprioritisation of race was utilised, not as a way to escape one's cultural or ethnic identity, but as a way to cope in the White spaces of women's football. We also consider the critical work of Black feminists who suggested that silence itself is a powerful agentic technique that allows women, otherwise bound by racist and derogatory stereotypes, to resist telling their stories so as to prevent their lives and existence from being misconstrued under a Western ethnocentric gaze (see e.g. Collins, 2000; Douglas, 2002). In other words, reluctance to share lived experiences of truth has allowed certain groups of ethnic 'Other' women to retain power over their own histories (Ali *et al.*, 2010). However, as our own experiences of studying sport sociology in the UK and attending international conferences across Europe, America and Australia have shown, these 'alternative' bodies of knowledge have remained subjugated (e.g. see Ratna, this volume). They are either excluded from most graduate and postgraduate courses, or overshadowed at conferences dominated by the sheer volume of essentialist critiques, that further bolster and corroborate stereotypic assumptions (see Samie's personal narrative as outlined in Ratna *et al.*, 2017). Hence, when ethnocentric representations of gender relations of power and control within ethnic 'Other' communities are re-presented, for instance, as the 'primary' issues that affect the lives of certain groups of women, the entire process of knowledge construction becomes complicit in both cultivating, and legitimising narrowed ways of knowing race relations, gender and difference. It is itself a way to police and control what is known and what remains unknown about ethnic 'Others' (see Samie, 2013). It strengthens essentialist Eurocentric (master) metanarratives, bolstering documented 'truths' and purported facts that reinforce the dominant (masters') viewpoint (Samie, 2013, this volume; Samie and Sehlikoglu, 2014; Ratna *et al.,* 2017). Furthermore, it thwarts progressive debates and undermines efforts to rupture Eurocentric thinking. Toffoletti and Palmer (2015) allude to this, stating that the narrowed emphasis of research on ethnic 'Other' females and sport has overlooked alternative realities, such as their experiences of sport fandom (e.g. Erhart, 2011; this volume; Ratna, 2014), sports consumption (e.g. Armstrong, 2001; Shankar, 2013), sports leadership (e.g. Armstrong, 2007; Koca and Öztürk, 2015; Palmer and Masters, 2010), and as sports coaches (Borland and Bruening, 2010; Rankin-Wright and Norman, this volume).

In the context of the US, predominant racial tropes positioned African American females as 'natural' athletes (Carrington, 2010) and the sporting visibility of elite athletes justified this narrative (Scott and Pitsiladis, 2007; Withycombe, 2011). Yet at the same time, as Carby (1982) rightly attests, White fe/male researchers have not always represented the realities of Black women as part of their feminist agendas (see also Birrell, 1990), and even when they have (added Black women to White feminist research agendas) this has often been in "tokenistic" ways (Alexander-Floyd, 2012: 9). This has helped to advance evidence of hierarchical demarcations between Black and White women. It is evident in literary texts where Black (read: African American) women have traditionally been positioned in one of two ways: either as 'self-doubting, retentive and mute' or 'aggressive, powerful matriarchs' (see Collins, 2000; Washington, 1990). The insidious effects of this kind of racist intellectualising are also evident in sport. Consider, for example, the fact that Black women's athletic abilities have not only been framed in relation to White women's understandings of femininity and patriarchy (see Douglas, 1988a, 1988b), but that they have often been juxtaposed in derogatory ways to traditional representations of White femininity. Black women are hypervisible in the sporting literature, and are frequently re-presented as too muscular and thus not 'real' women (see Cahn, 1994; Mowatt *et al.*, 2013; Vertinsky and Captain, 1998) compared to White women, who are frequently characterised in terms of their (alleged) piety, purity, submissiveness and domesticity (Ross, 2009).[3] Black women have also been portrayed as hypersexual, often animalistic, spectacles for leisure consumption (see Carrington, 2010; Hall, 1997; and Mowatt *et al.*'s 2013 discussions about the eroticisation of Saartjie Baartman's naked Black [South African] body dubbed the 'Hottentot Venus' and displayed at exhibitions in London and Paris for public amusement and critique). At other times, the 'tokenistic' addition of Black women to White feminist research allowed researchers to make salient White women's sufferings (see Alexander-Floyd, 2012). Crenshaw (2006) uses the term "representational intersectionality", to further debate the ways Black women's experiences only become worthy of consideration when they are re-presented in relation to the ontological security of White women. She refers to this as the 'bait-and-switch' strategy (see also Hargreaves, 2000). It is explicit in the re-presentation of Black female tennis players, sisters Venus and Serena Williams, as Black female Amazonians, which not only implies the presence of racial threat (read: overtly masculine Black women) but is popularly thought to unfairly impact White (read: dainty, feminine) female players (Spencer, 2004; see also Douglas, 2002; Ifekwunigwe; 2009; Withycombe, 2011). That this type of representation is compounded by, and continues to perpetuate racial fallacies, rooted in colonialist thinking, should not be ignored. It is, of course, yet another example of how 'truths', facts and evidence about ethnic 'Other' females continue to privilege the (heterosexual) able-bodies of White women. Indeed, when representations of real African American women and/or their bodies rarely move beyond this level of analysis and racial stereotyping, it is a problematic reminder of how the Black sportswoman (read: historical caricatures fetishised by researchers and historians alike) is "unknown and, of course, unheralded" within mainstream and sporting literature (Oglesby, 1981: 1).

In this way, even when claims to move beyond assimilatory, androcentric, Eurocentric and ethnocentric visions of the world were made, they also continued to facilitate (White, secular, liberal) fe/male researchers' interpretations of ethnic 'Other' female cultures as essentially inferior, failing or falling short in some way. The material affect of this kind of non-representation or misrepresentation has had damaging consequences for the public good of ethnic 'Other' women (see e.g. Bruening, 2005; Ratna, 2017; Vertinsky and Captain, 1998). It has muted the voices of real women, limiting, in turn, the possibilities of knowing the investments and power of the ethnic 'Other' woman as separate to, and something other than, the formation and representation of the White, Western, fe/male 'Subject' (see Ratna, 2017; Spivak, 1988). For varied groups of ethnic 'Other' girls and women, it has allowed researchers to present certain types of evidence as the only form of valid 'truth'. Such narratives subvert attention from the structures and cultural orthodoxies of sport which reproduce relations of power between women and men, and within and across different racial and ethnic groups. They also espouse an 'oppression olympics' to see 'who' is most likely to suffer from the greatest form of inequality, and which factors are at the 'root' of all oppressions (Hancock, 2011; Yuval-Davis, 2012; see also Birrell, 1990; Hall, 1996; Messner, 1992). For instance, some Marxist influenced readings of feminism still purport to show the class system of oppression as fundamentally significant to the liberation of different (racial and ethnic) groups of women (King and McDonald, 2007). Such a hierarchy of oppression discourse forecloses a critical understanding of the complex and unexpected ways power operates, circumscribing the life chances of different groups of people in any given society, at any given moment in time (Birrell, 1990). As Scraton asserts (2001), sports scholars failed to unpack the complexities of multiple axes of oppression, and so did not fully understand the racialised, gendered and classed histories and cultures of sport as well as how that fosters the creation of particular sporting identities, resistances and personal pleasures (see also Jamieson, 1998, 2003; Thangaraj *et al.*, 2016).

The politics of difference, intersectionality and voice

Engaging with the concept of difference, both Hargreaves (2000) and Scraton (2001) have indeed interrogated the social identities of women as multiple, hybrid and evolving across time and space. Brah (1996), in particular, connects the level of structural and institutional to the everyday manifestation of difference, and the impact of this upon the lived circumstances, personal realities and choices of people living at the intersections of particular social categorisations. Thus, she argues that biographies are relational and connected to wider social structures and histories in multiple and complex ways. The scholarship of ethnic 'Other' feminist intellectuals has been particularly significant in drawing attention to this multidimensional aspect of identities, and has been debated by scholars in relation to sport (e.g. Birrell, 1989, 1990; Jamieson, 1998, 2003; King and McDonald, 2007; McDonald and Birrell, 1999; Scraton, 2001; Smith, 1992). Crenshaw's (1989) critical application of Black feminist ideas to an unpacking of intersectionality has particularly gained much traction in and across the academic community, including within the sociocultural analysis of sport and leisure (e.g. Adjepong, 2015; Carter-Francique and Flowers, 2013; Ratna, 2013; Watson and Scraton, 2013). Crenshaw specifically argued through her critical analysis of violence against women of colour in the US, that thinking structurally and politically about intersections of identity elucidates how feminist and anti-racist practices have both functioned in tandem, to obliterate remedial actions that may specifically benefit the materialities of women of colour. This is because women of colour are often 'split' across divergent agendas that do not coalesce. More critical efforts to represent the lives of ethnic 'Other' women were clearly needed to move beyond simplistic notions of how they may be 'different', and inferior to the subject positions of White, sporting females. An engagement with research that addressed the complex needs of female ethnic 'Others', their lived ontology and agentic possibilities, was also needed to reposition otherwise marginalised, and often muted, women as 'subjects' of research, as opposed to mere objects of inquiry and knowledge production. The latter approach was necessary, since even researchers who had claimed to centralise real women's voices, ultimately overlooked the "flesh-and-blood realities of racial [and gendered] oppression" (Birrell, 1990: 197). The resulting scholarship failed to critically read sport as a manifestation of complex and fluid relations of power (Birrell and McDonald, 2000).

Today, there is a growing corpus of research that explores the critical issues of race and ethnicity, as it pertains to women and girls' experiences of sport, leisure and physical culture. Some researchers have sought to remedy many of the earlier pitfalls by honouring or privileging the voices, authenticities, experiences and perspectives of ethnic 'Other' women and girls (see e.g. Jamieson, 1998, 2003; McDonald and Birrell, 1999; Scraton, 2001; Smith, 1992). Within America, an emerging body of research is evident in regards to Asian Americans, Latinas, Mexicanas, First Nation people, and their multiple and complex engagements in sport, using new and interesting blends of Black feminism, queer of colour feminism, chicana feminism, chicana cultural studies, cultural geographies and area studies (Douglas and Jamieson, 2006; Hanson, 2005; Jamieson, 1998, 2003, 2005; Jamieson and Choi, this volume; King, 2015; Ratna *et al.*, 2017; Thangaraj *et al.*, 2016; Van Ingen *et al.*, 2016). There is growing evidence of mainstream 'White' academic traditions and disciplines (e.g. sociology, psychology, cultural studies and so on) moving beyond non-inclusive, uncritical and irrational representations of the racialised 'Other', to centralise the notion of 'intersectionality', and the multiple oppressions experienced at varying levels by all women (Anzaldúa, 1987; Brah and Phoenix, 2004; Collins, 2000; Crenshaw, 1989; Davis and Lutz, 2000). There is also evidence of research critically pushing the boundaries of knowledge production, signalling other ways of knowing the relationship between ethnic 'Other' girls and women, and their diverse, dynamic and polymorphous relationships to sport and physical culture (Ratna *et al.*, 2017).

However, even as alternative and 'Other' feminist voices have become more salient in highlighting how (and the extent to which) the epistemic worldview of 'White/Western middle class feminists' as privileged and 'everyone else' as being inferior has overlooked how 'Other' women have also struggled and resisted (a universal form of) patriarchy "in their own rights, in their own unique ways both inside/outside of the feminist movement" (Amos and Parmar, 1984: 7), epistemological concerns about the relationship between discourse, power, and agency remain. In this regard, knowledge about ethnic 'Other' girls and women's lives is still relatively subjugated (Alexander-Floyd, 2012; Collins, 2000). Indeed, intersectionality has been critiqued, with some arguing that it has become about everyone else apart from Black women, and they are either viewed as no longer facing inequality and/or that their subjectivities have been decentred from intersectional thinking (Alexander-Floyd, 2012). Alexander-Floyd (2012: 9) summarises that:

> [...] the current focus on intersectionality within the social sciences is, in fact, a post-Black feminist approach, one that disappears or re-marginalises Black women.

In fact, despite the abundance of sport literature on African American women, relatively little is known about the lives, experiences and identities of women of the African diaspora, in the places that they are known to reside in significant numbers, as majority or minority populations, outside of America, and across other parts of the world e.g. from within Europe or indeed from within Africa itself (Ratna, 2015, 2016). Accounts of other ethnic groups, e.g. South American, Aboriginal, and women from the Far East in sport also remains sparse (Carter-Francique and Flowers, 2013; Hargreaves, 2000; Ho, 2014; Jamieson, 2003; Kietlinski, 2011; King, 2015; Tseng, 2015). Yet, the increased visibility of diverse groups of ethnic 'Other' women on (Western) sports fields or courts, continues to be naively heralded as a sign of 'equity' in sports (Kivel *et al.*, 2009).

Despite the increasingly positive influence of postmodern feminist politics, to make visible the particular standpoints and experiences of different groups of women, and extend knowledge of previously neglected aspects of racialised identities, such as age, generation, sexuality and disability, the pitfalls of earlier 'add-and-stir' approaches, evident in early bias and assimilation models, are still apparent in some research on race and ethnicity. On the one hand, the desire to be inclusive of difference has become an end in and of itself, at times reducing identities, social positions and re-positionings to a hybrid mélange of endless heterogeneity. Additionally, Alexander-Floyd (2012) argues that whilst intersectionality has been increasingly mobilised in more contemporary research, one of the main problems is that it remains, on the whole, disconnected from context, power relations and structures of inequality (see also Bilge, 2014; Hylton, 2005). That is, researchers have become more preoccupied with just "multiplying identity categories rather than constituting a structural analysis or political critique" (Crenshaw, 1989 cited in Alexander-Floyd, 2012: 4). At times, this has obscured structural and ideological functions of modern sport, instead of exposing, for instance, the complex and un/expected ways unequitable relations of power are fostered and maintained (see Ali *et al.*, 2010). At other times, researchers have simply looked to issues of difference to further reinforce a clear sense of distance between Western and non-Western issues. Worse still, research about certain minority groups continues to be implicated in perpetuating untruths, and/or strengthening the durability of cultural and racial stereotypes that are themselves informed and compounded by narrow, and often Anglo and European, interrogations of the cultures of ethnic 'Others' (see e.g. Samie's 2013, Samie and Sehlikoglu's 2014, and Toffoletti and Palmer's 2015 work on Muslim women and sport for an elaboration of this debate).

Bar a few select critical publications that explore the valuable contribution of Black feminisms, transnational feminisms and postcolonial feminisms (see e.g. Burdsey *et al.*, 2013; Douglas, 2002; Hayhurst, 2011; Jamieson, 2003; Mowatt *et al.*, 2013; Ratna *et al.*, 2017; Samie, 2013; Samie and Sehlikoglu, 2014; Scraton, 2001; Thangaraj *et al.*, 2016; Toffoletti and Palmer, 2015), the voices and writings of alternative feminist movements remain under-appreciated, and counter-narratives that better speak to the lived realities of racially diverse groups men and women are virtually absent. This phenomenon prevails despite the fact that a number of ethnic female 'Others' (predominantly of non-Western heritage) have been at the forefront of subverting Anglo/Eurocentric perspectives pertaining to the racialised female 'Other' (both within and beyond the sporting literature). Consider, for instance, the influential contributions of Black feminist, chicana feminists and postcolonial feminists who have boldly chosen to 'write back' to White/ned feminism and neo-colonialism, as way to better exert and re-position their political agency, and remember and revive 'erased' cultural histories. Here, we also reflect (and celebrate) such contemporary sports research that seeks to rejuvenate ethnic 'Other' female cultural histories, political thoughts and actions (see e.g. Armstrong, 2007; Borland and Bruening, 2010; Carter-Francique, this volume; Douglas, 2002; Douglas and Jamieson, 2006; Jamieson and Choi; this volume; Ratna, this volume; Ratna *et al.*, 2017; Samie, this volume; Versey, 2014) as well as cast a wider focus on different and emerging physical cultures (see e.g. Kedhar, 2014; Kipnis and Caudwell, 2015; Leseth, 2014; Nemani and Thorpe, 2016; Pollard and Guell, 2012; Ratna, this volume; Wheaton, 2014). Despite the generally progressive move away from functionalist perspectives of sport, many international sport-for-development initiatives continue to hark on about sport as a vehicle for good. It is most evident in claims that sport can 'empower' (read 'free') girls and young women from the shackles of their religions, cultures, families and so on (see Darnell and Hayhurst, 2011; Jeanes *et al.*, 2014; Kay, 2009; Samie *et al.*, 2015 for a more comprehensive discussion of this issue).

Concluding thoughts

The scholarship about ethnic 'Other' girls and women and their relationships to sport and physical culture has undoubtedly grown since Birrell (1989), and then Scraton (2001), made their particular calls for more radical advances in the field. Knowledge has steadily risen within the field whilst it is still the case that feminist, critical race scholars and other sociologists from outside of the field, very rarely critique sport as a significant area of analysis. The body of work that is progressive demonstrates the importance of sport and physical culture as a popular and public arena to examine the reproduction (and resistance to) omnipresent structures of inequality and control. Nevertheless, within the field, persisting issues related to the positivistic, assimilation, androcentric, ethnocentric and Eurocentric approaches to research, impinge on the quality of the scholarship produced; many of the studies reproduced problematic stereotypes about ethnic 'Other' family life, cultures and physical dispositions as well as provided a surface-level analysis that mostly failed to critically interrogate the political implications of being an 'outsider' within the unequitable, able-bodied, gendered, sexualised and White fields of sport and physical culture.

We argue that there continues to be a need to produce *critical* scholarship about ethnic 'Other' girls and women in/through sport and physical culture, in order to represent their complex, multifarious and dynamic lived realities, as they see them, and as significant to their own senses of self. Moreover, employing theoretical lenses and methodologies to centre the perspectives of ethnic 'Other' females, shifting them from objects to subjects of analysis, and to expose structures and cultures of control, exclusion and oppression. This task may involve de-colonising the research process and crossing boundaries of knowledge/discipline to find other ways of critically engaging with the different, changing and complex lived realities of ethnic 'Other' girls and women (Birrell, 1989, 1990; Jamieson in Adams *et al.*, 2016; Ratna *et al.*, 2017). This edited collection seeks to do just this, and the authors of the chapters included in this volume – in similar and different ways – respond to such a call, providing new and original approaches to analysing the lives of ethnic 'Other' girls and women.

As outlined in the introduction, conceptually, this book draws on a range of literatures rooted in the political consciousness of what can be called 'Other' feminisms to (a) privilege the voices of ethnic 'Other' girls and women and (b) broaden, diversify and advance critical thinking pertaining to their engagements with sport and physical culture. Our intention is both to produce knowledge and privilege otherwise subjugated knowledges, that individually and collectively present counter-narratives that better speak to the lived realities of racially oppressed groups of women and girls. The contributors of this book have, in different and compelling ways, tried to grapple with and better consider how to be more sensitive, tactful, reflective and reflexive in "[...] *whose* truth they were telling" when they constructed the final textual narrative for wider reading (read: knowledge consumption) (Van Ingen, 2013: 100). And throughout our journey as writers and editors, we have continuously asked ourselves pressing questions that encourage us to think more deeply and critically about 'what (has) framed (our own) seeing' as minoritised ethnic women (from the UK and US respectively) and as academic scholars whose voices remain marginalised, at large. Making visible the cultural assumptions, context, and meanings that are captured and privileged in this book, has genuinely been a very personal and political process of knowledge construction for us. We are proud of all the contributors and truly believe that with this contribution, significant steps can be taken to challenge hegemonic discourses in which an array of ethnic 'Other' women's stories have been previously misread, from the perspectives of (White and often male) elites. In this regard, we passionately invite our readers "to step outside" cultural boundaries and backgrounds, "to set aside (any) social inherited ethnocentrism" so as to "apprehend the world from the viewpoint of other human beings who live by different meaning systems" (Spradley, 1980: vii–viii). In regard to this, we invite scholars in and beyond the field of sport and sociocultural studies to respond to our contribution and also to (re-)discover and (re-)envision the experiences of multiple ethnic 'Other' women from a set of marginalised perspectives, joining us in dialogue, in order to advance the development of *critical* and politically-informed scholarship.

Notes

1 In this chapter, in an attempt not to flatten differences between ethnic 'Other' girls and women, we acknowledge distinctions in and between 'them' and where relevant, use the categorisations offered by the author of the literature being cited.
2 It is worth mentioning that a number of sport scholars have indicated that researchers from feminist studies and/or critical race studies rarely critiqued sport as a significant facet of social life either (see e.g. Ansari, 2004; Birrell, 1990; Carrington, 2010, 2012; Hylton, 2005; Jamieson, 1998, 2003).
3 It should be added that these traits are rarely idealized in discussions juxtaposing White and South Asian, and/or Muslim females, presumably because they challenge the durability of Eurocentric claims that Western White women are in a more progressive position.

References

Abney, R. (1988) The effects of role models and mentors on the careers of Black women athletic administrators and coaches in higher education. Unpublished doctoral thesis, University of Iowa.

Adams, M.L., Helstein, M.T., Kim, K-Y., McDonald, M., Davidson, J., Jamieson, K.M., King, S. and Rail, G. (2016) 'Feminist Cultural Studies: Uncertainties and Possibilities', *Sociology of Sport Journal*, 33: pp. 75–91.

Adjepong, A. (2015) '"We're, Like, a Cute Rugby Team": How Whiteness and Heterosexuality Shape Women's Sense of Belonging in Rugby', *International Review for the Sociology of Sport*, DOI: 10.1177/1012690215584092.

Alexander, A. (1978) Status of minority women in the AIAW. Unpublished Masters thesis, Temple University.

Alexander-Floyd, N.G. (2012) 'Disappearing Acts: Reclaiming Intersectionality in the Social Sciences in a Post-Black Feminist Era', *Feminist Formations*, 24(1): pp. 1–25.

Ali, S., Mirza, H., Phoenix, A. and Ringrose, J. (2010) 'Intersectionality. Black British Feminism and Resistance in Education: A Roundtable Discussion', *Gender and Education*, 22(6): pp. 647–661.

Amos, V. and Parmar, P. (1984) 'Challenging Imperial Feminism', *Feminist Review*, 17: pp. 3–19.

Ansari, H. (2004) 'Introduction: Racialization and Sport', *Patterns of Prejudice*, 38(3): pp. 2009–2012.

Anzaldúa, G.E. (1987) *Borderland, La Frontera: The New Mestiza*, U.S.A.: Aunt Lute Books.

Armstrong, K. (2007) 'The Nature of Black Women's Leadership in Community Recreation Sport: An Illustration of Black Feminist Thought', *Women in Sport and Physical Activity Journal*, 16(1): pp. 3–15.

Armstrong, K. (2001) 'Black Women's Participation in Sport and Fitness: Implications for Sport Marketing', *Sports Marketing Quarterly*, 10(1): 9–18.

Barclay, V.M. (1979) Status of Black women in sports among selected institutions of higher education. Unpublished Masters thesis, University of Iowa.

Bilge, S. (2014) 'Whitening Intersectionality: Evanescence of Race in Intersectionality Scholarship', in W.D. Hund and A. Lentin (eds) *Racism and Sociology*, Zurich, Munster: Lit Verlag: pp. 175–206.

Birrell, S. (1990) 'Women of Color, Critical Autobiographies, and Sport', in M.A. Messner and D.F. Sabo (eds) *Sport, Men and the Gender Order*, Champaign, Illinois: Human Kinetics: pp. 185–199.
Birrell, S. (1989) 'Racial Relations Theories and Sport: Suggestions for a More Critical Analysis', *Sociology of Sport Journal*, 6: pp. 212–227.
Birrell, S. and McDonald, M.G. (2000) *Reading Sport: Critical Essays on Power and Representation*, Boston: North University Press.
Borland, J.F. and Bruening, J.E. (2010) 'Navigating Barriers: A Qualitative Examination of the Under-representation of Black Females as Head Coaches in Collegiate Basketball', *Sport Management Review*, 13: pp. 407–420.
Brah, A. (1996) *Cartographies of Diaspora: Contesting Identities*, London and New York: Routledge.
Brah, A. and Phoenix, A. (2004) 'Ain't I a Woman? Revisiting Intersectionality', *Journal of International Women's Studies*, 5(3): pp. 75–86.
Bruening, J.E. (2005) 'Gender and Racial Analysis in Sport: Are All the Women White and All the Blacks Men?' *Quest*, 57: pp. 330–349.
Burdsey, D. (2007) *British Asians and Football: Culture, Identity and Exclusion*. London: Routledge.
Burdsey, D., Thangaraj, S. and Dudrah, R. (2013) 'Playing through Time and Space: Sport and South Asian Diasporas', *South Asian Popular Culture*, 11(3): pp. 211–218.
Cahn, S.K. (1994) *Coming on Strong: Gender and Sexuality in Twentieth Century Women's Sport*, New York: Free Press.
Carby, H. (1982) 'White Woman Listen! Black Feminism and the Boundaries of Sisterhood', in the Centre for Contemporary Culture Studies' (eds) *The Empire Strikes Back: Race and Racism in 70s Britain*, London: Routledge: pp. 212–235.
Carrington, B. (2012) 'Introduction: Sport Matters', *Ethnic and Racial Studies*, 35(6): pp. 961–970.
Carrington, B. (2010) *Race, Sport and Politics: The Sporting Black Diaspora*, Los Angeles, London, New Delhi, Singapore, Washington D.C.: Sage.
Carrington, B., Chivers, T. and Williams, T. (1987) 'Gender, Leisure and Sport: A Case-study of Young People of South Asian Descent', *Leisure Studies*, 6: pp. 265–279.
Carter-Francique, A.R. and Flowers, C.L. (2013) 'Intersections of Race, Ethnicity and Gender in Sport', in E.A. Roper (ed.) *Gender Relations in Sport*, Rotterdam, Boston, Taipei: Sense Publishers: pp. 73–93.
Cashmore, E. (1996) *Making Sense of Sport*, Routledge, London.
Caudwell, J. (2011) 'Sport Feminism(s): Narratives of Linearity?', *Journal of Sport and Social Issues*, 35(2): pp. 111–125.
Coakley, J. (1986) *Sport in Society: Issues and Controversies* (Third Edition), St. Louis: Times/Mosby.
Coghlan, J.F. and Webb, I.M. (1990) 'Development of High Performance and Mass Participation in Sport and Recreation', in J.F. Coghlan and I.M. Webb (eds) *Sport and British Politics Since 1960*, London, New York, Philadelphia: The Falmer Press: pp. 100–125
Collins, P.H. (2000) *Black Feminist Thought: Knowledge, Consciousness and the Politics of Empowerment* (Second Edition), New York and London: Routledge.
Collins, P. H. (1991) 'Toward an Afro-Centric Feminist Epistemology', in S. Kemp, and J. Squires (eds) *Feminisms*, Oxford: Oxford University Press.

Crenshaw, K. (2006) '"Mapping the Margins": Intersectionality, Identity Politics and Mapping the Margins', *Kvinder, Køn & Forskning,* 2–3: pp. 7–20.
Crenshaw, K. (1989) 'Demarginalizing the Intersections of Race and Sex: A Black Feminist Critique of Antidiscrimination Doctrine, Feminist Theory and Antiracist Politics', *University of Chicago Legal Forum,* 1(8): pp. 139–167.
Darnell, S.C. and Hayhurst, L.M.C. (2011) 'Sport for Decolonisation: Exploring a New Praxis of Sport for Development', *Progress in Development Studies,* 11(3): pp. 183–196.
Davis, A. (1981) *Women, Race and Class,* London: Women's Press.
Davis, K. and Lutz, H. (2000) 'Open Forum: Life in Theory – Three Feminist Thinkers on Transition(s)', *European Journal of Women's Studies* 7(3): pp. 367–378.
De Knop, P., Theeboom, M., Wittock, H. and DeMartelaer, K. (1996) 'Implication of Islam on Muslim Girl's Sport Participation in Western Europe', *Sport, Education and Society,* 1 (2): pp. 147–164.
Department of Education (DoE) (1975) 'Sport and Recreation', in B. Houlihan (ed.) (1991) *The Government and Politics of Sport,* London: Routledge.
Douglas, D. (2002) 'To Be Young, Gifted, Black and Female: A Meditation on the Cultural Politics at Play in Representations of Venus and Serena Williams', *Sociology of Sport Online – SOSOL,* 5(2): pp. 1–16.
Douglas, D. (1988a) 'Discourses on Black women – a history of silence: A review of relational analysis in education and sports literatures'. Paper presented at The North American Society for the Sociology of Sport Conference, Cincinnati.
Douglas, D. (1988b) 'Race, class and sex: Toward a relational level of analysis of Black women's responses to oppression in sport'. Paper presented at the R. Tait McKenzie Symposium on Sport, Knoxville, TN.
Douglas, D. and Jamieson, K. (2006) 'A Farewell to Remember: Interrogating the Nancy Lopez Farewell Tour', *Sociology of Sport Journal,* 23: pp. 117–141.
Dunae, P. (1988) 'Education, Emigration and Empire: The Colonial College, 1887–1905', in J.A. Mangan. (ed.) *Benefit Bestowed? Education and British Imperialism,* Manchester: Manchester University Press: pp. 193–210.
Eitzen, D.S. and Sage, G. (1978) *Sociology of Sport* (Second Edition), Dubuque, Iowa: Wm. C. Brown.
Elling, A., De Knop, P. and Knoppers, A. (2001) 'The Integrating and Differentiating Significance of Sport', in J. Steenbergen, P. De Knop and A. Elling (eds) *Values and Norms in Sport,* Oxford: Meyer and Meyer Sport: pp. 73–94.
Erhart, I. (2011) 'Ladies of Besiktas: A Dismantling of Male Hegemony at Inönö Stadium', *International Journal for the Sociology of Sport,* 48(1): pp. 83–98.
Feminist Review (1984) 'Many Voices, One Chant: Black Feminist Perspectives', *Feminist Review* 17(1): pp. 3–19.
Figueroa, P. (1993) 'Equality, Equity and Physical Education', in J. Evans. (ed.) *Equality, Equity, and Physical Education,* London: Falmer Press.
Fischbacher, C.M., Hunt, S. and Alexander, L. (2004) 'How Physically Active are South Asians in The United Kingdom? A Literature Review', *Journal of Public Health,* 26(3): pp. 250–258.
Fleming, S. (2001) 'Racial Myths and South Asian and Black Physicality', in B. Carrington and I. McDonald (eds) *Race, Sport and British Society,* London and New York: Routledge: pp. 105–120.

Fleming, S. (1994) 'Sport and South Asian Youth: The Perils of "False Universalism" and Stereotyping', *Leisure Studies*, 13(3): pp. 159–177.
Gill, P.S., Kai, J., Bhopal, R.S. and Wild, S. (2002) *Health Care Needs Assessment: Black Minority Ethnic Groups*, Abingdon: Radcliffe Medical Press Ltd.
Grewal, S., Kay, J., Landor, L., Lewis, G. and Parmar, P. (eds) (1988) *Charting the Journey*, London: Sheba.
Hall, A.M. (1996) *Feminism and Sporting Bodies: Essays on Theories and Practise*, Ann Arbor, Michigan: University of Michigan Press.
Hall, K. (1995) '"There's a Time to Act English and a Time to Act Indian": The Politics of Identity Amongst British-Sikh Teenagers', in S. Stephens (ed.) *Children and the Politics of Culture*. Princeton, New Jersey: Princeton University Press.
Hall, S. (ed.) (1997) *Representations: Cultural Representations and Signifying Practices*, London, California, New Delhi: Sage.
Hancock, A.-M. (2011) *Solidarity Politics for Millennials*, New York: Palgrave Macmillan.
Hanson, S.L. (2005) 'Hidden Dragons: Asian American Women and Sport', *Journal of Sport and Social Issues*, 29(3): pp. 279–312.
Hargreaves, J.A. (2000) *Heroines of Sport: The Politics of Difference and Identity*, Oxon, New York: Routledge.
Hayhurst, L.M.C. (2011) 'Corporatizing Sport, Gender and Development: Postcolonial IR Feminisms, Transnational Private Governance and Global Corporate Social Engagement', *Third World Quarterly* 32(3): pp. 531–549.
Health Education Authority (HEA) (2000) *Black and Ethnic Minority Groups in England: The Second Health and Lifestyle Survey*, London: Health Education Authority.
Ho, M.S. (2014) 'Is Nadeshiko Japan "Feminine"? Manufacturing Sport Celebrity and National Identity on Japanese Morning Television', *Journal of Sport and Social Issues*, 38(2): pp. 164–183.
Houlihan, B. (1991) *The Government and Politics of Sport*, London, New York: Routledge.
Hylton, K. (2005) 'Race, Sport and Leisure: Lessons from Critical Race Theory', *Leisure Studies*, 24(1): pp. 81–98.
Ifekwunigwe, J.O. (2009) 'Venus and Serena Are "Doing it" for Themselves: Theorizing Sporting Celebrity, Class and Black Feminism for the Hip-Hop Generation', in B. Carrington and I. McDonald (eds) *Marxism, Cultural Studies and Sport*, London and New York: Routledge: pp. 130–153.
Ismond, P. (2003) *Black and Asian Athletes in British Sport and Society*, Basingstoke and New York: Palgrave Macmillan.
Jamieson, K. (2005) '"All My Hopes and Dreams": Families, Schools, and Subjectivities in Collegiate Softball', *Journal of Sport and Social Issues*, 29(2): pp. 133–147.
Jamieson, K.M. (2003) 'Occupying a Middle Space: Toward a Mestiza Sport Studies', *Sociology of Sport Journal*, 20: pp. 1–16.
Jamieson, K.M. (1998) 'Reading Nancy Lopez: Decoding Representations of Race, Class and Sexuality', *Sociology of Sport Journal*, 15: pp. 343–358.
Jarvie, G., and Reid, I. (1997) 'Race Relations, Sociology of Sport and the New Politics of Race and Racism', *Leisure Studies*, 16(2): pp. 211–219.

Jeanes, R., Magee, J., Kay. T. and Banda, D. (2014) 'Sport for Development in Zambia: The New or Not So New Colonisation?' in *Native Games: Indigenous Peoples and Sport Post-Colonial World*, accessed at http://dx.doi.org/10.1108/s1476-2854(2013)0000007011 on 23 November 2016.

Johnson, M.R.D. (2000) 'Perceptions of Barriers to Healthy Physical Activity among Asian Communities', *Sport, Education and Society*, 5(1): pp. 51–70.

Kane, M. (1971) 'An Assessment of Black is Best', *Sports Illustrated*, 18 January, pp. 72–83.

Kay, T. (2009) 'Developing through Sport: Evidencing Sport Impacts on Young People', *Sport in Society*, 12(9):1: pp. 177–1191.

Kedhar, A. (2014) 'Flexibility and Its Bodily Limits: Transnational South Asian Dancers in an Age of Neoliberalism', *Congress of Research in Dance*, 46(1): pp. 23–41.

Kietlinski, R. (2011) *Japanese Women and Sport: Beyond Baseball and Sumo*, London: Bloomsbury Academic.

King, R. (2015) *Asian American Athletes in Sport and Society*, New York and Oxon: Routledge.

King, S.J. and McDonald, M.G. (2007) '(Post)identity and Sporting Cultures: An Introduction and Overview', *Sociology of Sport Journal*, 24: pp. 1–19.

Kipnis, H., and Caudwell, J. (2015) 'Boxers of Kabul: Women, Boxing and Islam', in C.R. Matthews and A. Channon (eds) *Global Perspectives on Women in Combat Sports: Women Warriors around the World*, London and New York: Palgrave Macmillan: pp. 41–56.

Kivel, B.D, Johnson, C.W. and Scraton, S.J. (2009) '(Re)Theorizing Leisure, Experience and Race', *Journal of Leisure Research*, 41(4): pp. 473–493.

Klein, M.L. and Kothy, J. (2001) 'Social Conflicts in Interethnic Sport Contacts: A Comparative Study in Local Football Leagues'. Paper presented at the 6th annual congress of the European College of Sport Science.

Koca, C., and Öztürk, P. (2015) 'Gendered Perceptions about Female Managers in Turkish Sports Organisations', *European Sport Management Quarterly*, 15(3): pp. 381–406.

Leaman, O. (1984) *Sit on the Sidelines and Watch the Boys Play: Sex Differentiation in Physical Education*, York: Longman for Schools Council.

Leaman, O. and Carrington, B. (1985) 'Athleticism and the Reproduction of Gender and Ethnic Marginality', *Leisure Studies* 4: pp. 205–218.

Leseth, A.B. (2014) 'Experiences of Moving: A History of Women and Sport in Tanzania', *Sport in Society: Cultures, Commerce, Media and Politics*, 17(4): pp. 479–491.

Lewis, T. (1979) 'Ethnic Influences on Girls' P.E.', *British Journal of Physical Education* 10, p. 132.

Long, J., Carrington, B. and Spracklen, K. (1997) '"Asians Can't Wear Turbans in the Scrum": Explorations of Racist Discourse Within the Professional Rugby League', *Leisure Studies* 16(4): pp. 249–260

Long, J., Tongue, N., Spracklen, K. and Carrington, B. (1995) *What's the difference?* Leeds: Leeds Metropolitan University, The Rugby Football League, Leeds City Council.

Maguire, B. and Collins, D. (1998) 'Sport, Ethnicity, and Racism: The Experience of Asian Heritage Boys', *Sport Education and Society* 3(1): pp. 79–81.

Mangan, J.A. (1986) *Games Ethic and Imperialism*, Middlesex: Viking.

McDonald, M.G. and Birrell, S. (1999) 'Reading Sport Critically: A Methodology for Interrogating Power', *Sociology of Sport Journal*, 16(4): pp. 283–300.

Messner, M. (1992) 'White Men Misbehaving: Feminism, Afrocentricism, and the Promise of a Critical Standpoint', *Journal of Sport and Social Issues*, 16(2): pp. 136–144.

Mirza, H.S. (1997) *Black British Feminism: A Reader*. London: Routledge.

Mowatt, R.A., French, B.H. and Malebranche, D.A. (2013) 'Black/Female/Body Hypervisibility and Invisibility', *Journal of Leisure Research*, 45(5): pp. 644–660.

Murphy, M.D. (1980) The Involvement of Black in Women's Athletics in Member Institutions of the AIAW. Unpublished Doctoral thesis, University of Florida.

Nemani, M. and Thorpe, H. (2016) 'The Experiences of Brown "Female" Bodyboarders: Negotiating Multiple Axes of Marginality', in H. Thorpe and R. Olive (eds) *Women in Action Sport Cultures: Identity, Politics and Experience*, London: Palgrave MacMillan: pp. 213–234.

Oglesby, C. (1981) 'Myths and Realities of Black Women in Sport', in T.S. Green, C.A. Oglesby, A. Alexander and N. Franke (eds) *Black Women in Sport*, Reston, Virginia: American Alliance for Health, Physical Education, Recreation and Dance: pp. 1–13.

Palmer, F.R. and Masters, T.M. (2010) 'Māori Feminism and Sport Leadership: Exploring Māori Women's Experiences', *Sport Management Review*, 13: pp. 331–344.

Pfister, G. (2000) 'Doing Sport in A Headscarf? German Sport and Turkish Females', *The Journal of Sport History*, 27(30): pp. 497–523.

Pollard, T.M. and Guell, C. (2012) 'Assessing Physical Activity in Muslim Women of South Asian Origin', *Journal of Physical Activity and Health*, 9: pp. 970–976.

Porter. S. (2001) *Sport and Ethnic Minorities Communities: Aiming at Social Inclusion*. Research Report 28. Sport Scotland. pp. 1–57

Rai, D.K. and Finch, H. (1997). *Physical Activity from Our Point of View. Qualitative Research amongst South Asian and Black Communities,* London: Health Education Authority.

Ratna, A. (2017) 'Black Women, Black Voices: A Spivakian and Black Feminist Approach to Researching the Lives of Black Women', in J. Long, T. Fletcher and B. Watson (eds) *Sport, Leisure and Social Justice*, London: Routledge: pp. 153–167.

Ratna, A. (2016) 'Why do we (still) know so little about Black women and sport?' Extended paper presented at Diversity, Equity and Inclusion seminar series, Leeds Beckett University, Leeds.

Ratna, A. (2015) 'Why do we (still) know so little about Black women and sport?' Paper presented at the North American Sociology of Sport Society, Santa Fe.

Ratna, A. (2014) ' "Who are ya?" The National Identities and Belongings of British Asian Football Fans', *Patterns of Prejudice*, 48(3): pp. 286–308.

Ratna, A. (2013) 'Intersectional Plays of Identity: The Experiences of British Asian Female Footballers', *Sociological Research Online*, accessed at www.socresonline.org.uk/18/13.html on 9 December 2016.

Ratna, A. (2007) 'A "Fair Game?": British Asian Females' Experiences of Racism in Women's Football', in J. Magee, J. Caudwell, K. Liston and S. Scraton (eds) *Women, Football and Europe: Histories, Equity and Experiences*, Oxford, UK: Meyer and Meyer Sport: pp. 77–96.

Ratna, A., Samie, F.S., Jamieson, K. and Thangaraj, S. (2017) 'Learning Lessons from the Feminisms of Ethnic "Others"', in L. Mansfield, J. Caudwell, B. Watson and B. Wheaton (eds) *The Handbook for Feminisms in Sport, Leisure and Physical Education*, Palgrave (in press).
Raval, S. (1989) 'Gender, Leisure and Sport: A Case Study of Young People of South Asian Descent', *Leisure Studies*, 8: pp. 237–240.
Ross, J.R. (2009) 'Black Female Athletes as the Ultimate Other: Breaking Free from the Controlling Images', *The Moving Towards Justice Series: A Project of NAGWS' Inclusion and Social Justice Committee*, 1(1): pp. 1–22.
Rowe, N. and Champion, R. (2000) *Sport Participation and Ethnicity in England*, London: Sport England.
Samie, S.F. and Sehlikoglu, S. (2014) 'Strange, Incompetent and Out-of-Place. Media, Muslim Women and the London 2012 Olympics', *Feminist Media Studies* 15(3): 363–381.
Samie, S.F., Johnson, A.J., Huffman, A.M. and Hillyer, S.J. (2015) 'Voices of Empowerment: Women from the Global South Re/negotiating Empowerment and the Global Sports Mentoring Programme', *Sports in Society*, 18(8): pp. 923–937.
Scott, R.A. and Pitsiladis, P. (2007) 'Genotypes and Long Distance Running: Clues from Africa', *Sports Medicine*, 37(4): pp. 424–427.
Scraton, S.J. (2001) 'Reconceptualising Race, Gender and Sport: The Contribution of Black Feminism', in B. Carrington and I. McDonald (eds) *Race, Sport and British Society*, London: Routledge: pp. 170–187.
Shankar, S. (2013) 'Affect and Sport in South Asian American Advertising', *South Asian Popular Culture*, 11(3): pp. 231–242.
Smith, Y.R. (1992) 'Women of Color in Society and Sport', *Quest*, 44: pp. 228–250.
Snape, R. (2005) 'Steps to Health: An Evaluation of a Project to Promote Exercise and Physical Activity amongst Asian Women in a Post-industrial Town in England', *Managing Leisure*, 10(1): pp. 145–155.
Spencer, N.E. (2004) 'Sister Act VI: Venus and Serena at Indian Wells: "Sincere Fictions" and White Racism', *Journal of Sport and Social Issues*, 28(2): pp. 115–135.
Spivak, G.C. (1988) 'Can the Subaltern Speak?', in C. Nelson and L. Grossberg (eds) *Marxism and the Interpretation of Culture*, London: Macmillan: pp. 271–313.
Spracklen, K. (2008) 'The Holy Blood and the Holy Grail: Myths of Scientific Racism and the Pursuit of Excellence in Sport', *Leisure Studies*, 27(2): pp. 221–227.
Spradley, J.P. (1980) *Participant Observation*, New York: Holt, Rinehart and Winston.
St. Louis, B. (2004) 'Sport and Common-sense Racial Science', *Leisure Studies*, 23(1): pp. 31–46.
St. Louis, B. (2003) 'Sport, Genetics and the 'Natural Athletes': The Resurgence of Racial Science', *Body and Society*, 9(2): pp. 75–95.
Stoddart, B. (1988) 'Sport, Cultural Imperialism, and Colonial Response in the British Empire', *Comparative Studies in Society and History*, 30(4): pp. 649–673.
Taylor, T. and Toohey, K. (1999) 'Sport, Gender and Cultural Diversity: Exploring the Nexus', *Journal of Sport Management*, 13(1), pp. 1–17.

Thangaraj, S., Arnaldo, C. and Chin, C.B. (eds) (2016) *Asian American Sporting Cultures*, New York and London: New York University.
Tirone, S., and Pedlar, A. (2000) 'Understanding the Leisure Experiences of a Minority Ethnic Group: South Asian Trends and Young Adults in Canada', *Society and Leisure*, 23 (1): pp. 145–169.
Toffoletti, K. and Palmer, C. (2015) 'New approaches for Studies of Muslim Women and Sport', *International Review for the Sociology of Sport*, DOI: 10.1177/1012690215589326
Trivedi, P. (1984) 'To Deny Our Fullness: Asian Women in the Making of History', *Feminist Review*, 17(1): pp. 37–50.
Tseng, Y.-H. (2015) 'Reproduction of the Female Image and Nationalism in Taiwanese Sport Documentaries', *International Review for the Sociology of Sport*, DOI: 10.1177/1012690214568732.
Van Ingen, C. (2013) ' "Seeing What Frames Our Seeing": Seeking Histories on Early Black Female Boxers', *Journal of Sports History*, 40(1): pp. 93–110.
Van Ingen, C., Sharpe, E., and Lashua, B. (2016) 'Neighbourhood Stigma and the Sporting Lives of Young People in Public Housing', *International Review for the Sociology of Sport*, DOI: 10.1177/1012690216641146.
Verma, G.K. and Darby, D.K. (1994) *Winners and Losers: Ethnic Minorities in Sport and Recreation*, London and Washington D.C: The Farmer Press.
Versey, H.S. (2014) 'Centering Perspectives on Black Women, Hair Politics, and Physical Activity', *American Journal of Public Health*, 104(5): pp. 810–815.
Vertinsky, P., and Captain, G. (1998) 'More Myth than History: American Culture and the Representations of the Black Female's Athletic Ability', *Journal of Sport History*, 25(3): pp. 532–561.
Walseth, K. (2007) 'Bridging and Bonding Social Capital in Sport – Experiences of Young Women with an Immigrant Background', *Sport, Education and Society*, 13(1): pp. 1–17.
Walseth, K. and Fasting, K. (2004) 'Sport as a Means of Integrating Minority Women', *Sport in Society*, 7(1): pp. 109–129
Washington, M.H. (1990) 'The Darkened Eye Restored: Notes Toward a Literary History of Black Women', in H.L. Gates (ed.) *Reading Black, Reading Feminist: A Critical Anthology*, New York: Penguin Books: pp. 30–45.
Watson, B. and Scraton, S.J. (2013) 'Leisure Studies and Intersectionality', *Leisure Studies*, 32(1): pp. 35–47.
Wiggins, D.K. (1989) 'Great Speed but Little Stamina. The Historical Debate over Black Superiority', *Journal of Sport History*, 16(2): pp. 158–185.
Wheaton, B. (2014) 'Lifestyle Sport for all women: understanding belonging and exclusion for minority ethnic and older participants'. Paper presented at *Sporting Females: Past, Present and Future*, Leeds Beckett University, Leeds.
Withycombe, J.L. (2011) 'Intersecting Selves: African American Female Athletes' Experiences of Sport', *Sociology of Sport Journal*, 28: pp. 478–493.
Yuval-Davis, N. (2012) 'Dialogical Epistemology – An Intersectional Resistance to the "Oppression Olympics" ', *Gender and Society*, 26(1): pp. 46–54.

Part I

Theoretical interventions and knowledge production

Chapter 2

De/colonising 'sporting Muslim women'

Post-colonial feminist reflections on the dominant portrayal of sporting Muslim women in academic research, public forums and mediated representations

Samaya Farooq Samie

The plethora of academic research and mediated coverage about Muslim women and sport tries to make sense of a range of factors that influence Muslim women's access to and experiences of participating in sport (Johnson, 2000; Martin and Mason, 2003; Pfister, 2010a). Toffoletti and Palmer (2015: 7) summarise these factors as *familial influences* (Kay, 2005, 2006), *sociocultural expectations of Muslim femininities* (Nakamura, 2002), *patriarchy* (Hargreaves, 2007), *ethnic identity* (Abdul Razak *et al.*, 2010; Johnson, 2000) and *religion* (Benn *et al.*, 2011; De Knop *et al.*, 1996; Pfister, 2003; Walseth and Fasting, 2003). More recently, researchers have turned their attention to recognising and making visible previously subjugated knowledge pertaining to Islam's view of sports. Walseth and Fasting's (2003) work primarily drew attention to scriptures such as Qur'anic verses, and written accounts of the Prophet Muhammad's teachings (commonly known as Hadith). It also captured the stories, experiences and voices of Egyptian Muslim women negotiating their access and entry participation in certain sports on their own culturally-specific and religious terms. Meanwhile, Benn *et al.* (2011) have included the work of Islamic feminists, and documented the experiences of Muslim female sports practitioners, coaches, and professors and teachers from diverse Islamic countries to highlight how Muslim women are challenging authoritarian Islamic political and patriarchal regimes to reclaim their right to access sport. Despite these advancements, the pervasiveness of essentialist and monolithic discourses in constructing 'sporting Muslim women' as different, strange, incompetent and out-of-place is still very evident at multiple levels, from sporting institutions and the mainstream media (Samie, 2013, 2014; Samie and Sehlikoglu, 2014) to western academic institutions and scholarship (Ratna *et al.*, 2017). Hence, the need to think more critically about the "production of knowledge" (Toffoletti and Palmer, 2015: 2–3) is crucial if we are to move beyond and disrupt the universalising and polarising metanarratives that are borne out of racist and imperialist epistemologies (Ratna *et al.* 2017). In fact, in an era of rising right-wing populism – where politicians and those within the public sphere vehemently and openly make generalised claims about Islam (being the identifiable, single biggest threat to democracy), and casually represent 'Muslim women' as *subordinate* and *oppressed*, to imply that a profound, impenetrable polarity between Muslim/Islamic identities and non-Muslims people is an uncontestable truth and fact that liberals should no longer ignore nor tolerate – this need to be cognizant of how the activity of research can itself be implicated in the "worst excesses of colonialism" is more important than ever (Smith, 1999: 33).

Rooted in and informed by a post-colonial feminist perspective, this chapter exposes the colonising agendas manifest in much of the intellectual discursive knowledge, in/formal discussions and mediated representations produced about the 'sporting Muslim woman'. It is an expansion of the set of concerns that I shared in a co-authored chapter titled 'Learning Lessons from Other Feminisms' (see Ratna *et al.*, 2017). It is also a theoretical contribution, since much of my work to date has been empirically grounded in unhinging and decentring metanarratives about Islam, sport and Muslim people (see e.g. Farooq, 2011; Farooq and Parker, 2009; Samie, 2013, 2014, 2015; Samie and Sehlikoglu, 2014). By adopting a 'decolonising' approach, emphasis is placed on unhinging dominant assumptions about sporting Muslim women, their lives and experiences of sport: assumptions that rely on neo/colonial suppositions to portray Muslim women as controlled or regulated subjects of patriarchal, paternal, and authoritarian theocratic structures. In so doing, I also recover subjugated perspectives (i.e. unreported truths) and replace untruths that circulate various segments of academic sporting infrastructures and institutions that I, myself, have encountered, or had to overcome in the decade that I have been researching this field. My decolonising efforts in this chapter are shaped by my own journey, as a sporting Muslim female and an academic, who has connected with hundreds of sporting Muslim women (from different ethnic, racial, class and geographical backgrounds and political sensibilities) who feel disillusioned at being 'written out' (read: hidden, ignored, overlooked and trivialised) of dominant narratives of sporting Muslim women. The overarching purpose of this discussion is to outline how and why what is so frequently known, or talked about in relation to the 'sporting Muslim woman' comes to be intellectualised as *relevant*, *truthful* and *factual*, and why certain aspects concomitantly remain unknown, and absent from dominant portrayals, discussions and representations about sporting Muslim women.

The chapter begins with a broader discussion of colonisation and the historical construction of certain discursive knowledge about Islam, Muslim culture and Muslim women that sets 'Them' apart from western civilisation as ultimately different and 'Other'. This section also focuses on how this discursive knowledge has and continues to infiltrate and shape intellectual/academic, popular and political representations of Muslim women both within and beyond the sporting context. Having outlined the fundamental premise around which colonisation operates to control the ways in which Muslim women are, and can be known, the chapter then discusses the core principles of decolonising research agendas, especially as it relates to making sense and unhinging discursive representations about 'sporting Muslim women'. The final subsections of this chapter draw attention to recurring metanarratives through which negative assumptions about sporting Muslim women are continuously made.

Colonisation: outlining the historical premise and goal

Colonisation has come to denote a variety of phenomena, from "the most evident economic and political hierarchies to the production of a particular cultural discourse" that infiltrate and influence western scientific, public and political categorisations, as well as (mediated) imagery (Mohanty, 2002: 18). For this chapter, I engage the latter concept to consider how 'colonising agendas' have infiltrated various formal scholarly pursuits of 'knowledge production' and informal imaginative, anecdotal constructions and representations of Islam and Muslim people, privileging Anglo, American and Eurocentric philosophies, ideologies and analytical categories that (a) juxtapose differences as 'bad', 'backward' and 'degenerative' and (b) produce certain kinds of knowledge, scholarship and 'truth' that ultimately depict Islam, Muslim culture and Muslim women as always *less than*, and *inferior* to western cultures and western women (Mohanty, 1988: 61; Said, 1978, 1997). There is already a well-established body of scholarship that outlines the extent to which, for instance, the practice of veiling and gender segregation in Muslim cultures was homogeneously depicted by European colonisers as symbolising everything *backward* and *wrong* with Muslim people, reinforcing the views of Christian polemics, that Islam was a *menace* (Rodinson, 1991), a "primitive" and doctrinarian school of thought that controlled its believers (Patai, 1973: 143–144) and sanctioned sexual indulgence amongst men while pledging women to "maternity and masculine pleasure" (Berque, 1964: 172–173; Grace, 2004).

In fact, despite the wider (feminist and political) objectives to subvert exclusionary and discriminatory epistemologies and inspire a deconstruction of the privileged and legitimate 'word' in the social sciences, there is also evidence that some leftist and (second-wave) feminist researchers have relied on these colonialist representations to continue to make sense of Muslim women. It is reflected in representations, produced by intellectuals and journalists, that perpetuate one-dimensional insights into the position of Muslim women by relying on 'problem' issues such as polygamy, forced marriages, confinement of women in the home, veiling, sex-segregation, honour killings, arbitrary divorce and genital cuttings to (a) depict Muslim women as passive victims and docile recipients of feudal, patriarchal and degenerative systems in which men dominated, and women served on men's terms, and (b) synonymously position European White women as educated, independent, modern and in control of their bodies and sexualities (see e.g. Brooks, 1995; Chesler, 2005; Goodwin, 1995). Universalising *all* Muslim women as somehow *always* being adversely affected by these practices has provided a way to not only set the conditions, but control and police the parameters of how Islam, Muslim culture and Muslim women are known, identified, classified and portrayed to European/American/western audiences, legitimising in turn the modes of thinking that are accepted as the most *plausible* and *factual*, and subjugating (read: writing-out) the possibility of knowing alternative and competing perspectives, subjectivities and truths that also exist.

Decolonising research principles

The term 'decolonisation' has frequently been used by indigenous researchers, or researchers working in and for indigenous contexts, to inspire research protocols, and methodologies that deconstruct (or 'take apart') known stories, otherwise consumed and accepted as 'fact' or as 'truth' to reveal "underlying texts" and privilege subjugated knowledge, perspectives and voices (Smith, 1999: 3). Decolonising agendas call upon researchers working with vulnerable, marginalised and/or threatened communities to weave together contextual histories, politics, and cultural considerations of indigenous peoples in "respectful, ethical, sympathetic and useful" ways (ibid.). That is, researchers are encouraged to think critically about the process of research (methods used, hypotheses, assumptions, judgements and analyses made) when working with vulnerable communities of people that are frequently positioned in and through misrepresentations and stereotypes that pathologise their existence as somehow always being *less than*, and/or *inferior* to the western ways of living or being. This style of research is not unique to indigenous researchers, although the term decolonising is used primarily by indigenous researchers. Anti-racist (critical) researchers, Chicano scholars, and Black and Asian feminists have all drawn attention to and critiqued colonising agendas that are evoked when certain kinds of research methods/strategies, and analytical/theoretical frameworks are used, and have called for researchers to rethink and work against, rather than through, colonising and colonised discursive depictions (see e.g. Amos and Parmar, 1984; Bhavnani, 1993). To some degree, the desire of 'Third Wave' feminism in the west to move beyond non-inclusive, uncritical and irrational representations of the 'Other' has also been influenced by decolonising philosophies, although the term 'deconstruction' is more commonly used. Post-structural feminists, for instance, have sought to honour the authenticities and individual experiences of non-dominant people, including women and children in developing countries, as well as young western women. They have also widely theorised the relationship between discourse, power, and agency, especially in relation to disenfranchised, or 'minority' groups (see Butler, 1990, 1993; Foucault, 1980; Hekman, 1990). These contributions have certainly thwarted the mainstream homogenising of peoples that desensitise notions of 'difference' by introducing the notion of 'intersectionality' and multiple oppressions experienced at varying levels by all women (Brah and Phoenix, 2004; Davis and Lutz, 2000).

Although the word 'decolonising' has not necessarily been utilised in discussions about sporting Muslim, there is a small collection of critical sports research that seeks to recover subjugated voices, perspectives, and ignored histories to move beyond essentialist metanarratives (Samie, 2013, 2014, 2015). Amara (2008) for instance alludes to a steady and productive presence of Muslim women from a range of different Islamic countries at the African, Pan-Arab, and Asian Mediterranean games, as well as the Islamic Solidarity Games. Ahmed (2009a, 2009b), herself a participant of the British Muslim women's futsal team that competed in the 2005 Islamic Women's Games, provides a lucid account, both of the largely negative experiences that veiled Muslim women have competing in British sporting contexts because of the overwhelming Islamophobia and racism, and the history and context of the Islamic Women's Games that first originated in Iran. There is also a burgeoning collection of work that has evolved out of multicultural discourses to highlight sporting Muslim women's multifarious and dynamic perspectives on sport, physical activity and leisure as well as their agentic struggle against conservative paternalistic structures (Walseth, 2006a, 2006b) and their challenge and attack on establishment Islamic structures erected by men (Benn *et al.*, 2011; Hargreaves, 2000). Benn *et al.*'s collection of work stands out particularly because it engages the work of Muslim scholars, Muslim sports advocates and Islamic feminists to showcase Muslim women's struggle on their own terms (out there on the peripheries) and helps to facilitate a reconceptualisation of Muslim women as being 'active agents', not merely passive objects. The inclusion of this largely subjugated knowledge produced by "Muslim scholars, practitioners, and leaders" within the scientific community of sport, for wider consumption by sports scholars in and around the 'world' has been celebrated as a productive (post-structural, post-modern) step towards listening to other perspectives and capturing how those different to us (in the west) exist (ibid.: 4; Toffoletti and Palmer, 2015). This diversity in research on sporting Muslim women is certainly a progressive step; however, as I will evidence later in this chapter, essentialist assumptions that juxtapose a modern, rational and progressive west against an unmodern, irrational and backward Islam still abound in in/formal academic forums, published literature and mediated reportings on sporting Muslim women.

My decolonising approach

In this chapter, the decolonising process starts with recognising that "people everywhere have a way of life [...] a culture of their own", that if we are to "truly understand", we must first "take (it) seriously" (Brunt, 1999: 506). This is not a culturally relativist plea to ignore or negate the real problems that do often exist within Islamic communities, especially towards women and girls. It is also not a call to adopt anti-western research agendas, nor does it ignore the inherent challenges of constructing problematic assumptions about a homogenous 'west'. Instead it is a call to us all to take the difficult, but necessary, steps to genuinely move beyond modernity and its assumption of an all-embracing objective truth so that we can (a) recognise how certain discursive truths about 'sporting Muslim women' have been constructed, and (b) rise to the challenge of rectifying the ontological and epistemological distortion that either ignores, trivialises or contains real sporting Muslim women under essentialist metanarratives that claim to give voice to their experiences, but, in fact, reinforce and sustain the 'west is best' philosophy. For me, the politics and ethics of post-colonial feminists allows me to (a) unhinge the organising premises of Anglo/Eurocentric perspectives pertaining to the racialised 'Other' so as to (a) move beyond universalist theories of 'Other' women's cultural practices as unjust and oppressive and (b) dismantle the essentialist connotations of (secular, liberal, feminist) epistemologies that have typically neglected the agentic capacity of 'Other' women to historically struggle and resist oppressive regimes and practices in their own own unique ways both inside and outside of the feminist movement (Ahmed, 2000; Amos and Parmar, 1984).[1]

A critical starting point in this decolonising process is inscribing and accepting that a distinction between 'Muslim women' as a "category of discourse" and Muslim women as "concrete historical subjects with diverse social and personal biographies and orientations" exists (Brah, 1993: 443; see also Afshar, 1994). For the purposes of this chapter, this means recognising the many ways in which *real* sporting Muslim women's lives and identities have been essentialised, homogenised and/or discursively represented, in and through neo/colonial metanarratives, as a "singular, homogenous group" (Samie, 2013, 2014; Toffoletti and Palmer, 2015: 11) bound by the "*sameness* of their oppression" (read: barriers and struggles to access sport) (Mohanty, 1988: 65). It also means coming to terms with, and unhinging the extent to which these crude processes of categorisation and representation not only "police what is (and should)" be known about these women, but also reaffirm "the 'word' (and perspectives) of those who have [unfairly claimed] the power [and the right] to define or authorize the criteria" for what constitutes a sporting Muslim woman (Ahmed, 1998: 80–90). Samie and Sehlikoglu (2014) allude to this point, highlighting the extent to which mediated representations have contributed to an understanding of sporting Muslim women as only ever being 'strange, incompetent and out-of-place' in modern western sorting arenas like the Olympics, by failing to report on unveiled Muslim women, or Gold medal winning Olympic heroines, as 'sporting Muslim women'.

Decolonising the 'sporting Muslim woman': epistemological and ontological questions

Having outlined the historical basis and goals of colonising discourses and decolonising methodologies, I now allude to a set of neo-colonial assumptions and metanarratives that (a) manufacture homogeneous representations in which certain Islamic requirements and other practices are depicted not only as the 'real problems' to/for sporting Muslim women's advancement in the competitive arena, but cast as the antithesis of progressive politics, modern and/or scientific reasoning, and (b) privilege secular, liberal feminist principles as somehow the *only* genuine/legitimate way for sporting Muslim women to cultivate and embody agentic power to liberate themselves from the oppression of Islamic regimes.

Islam and Muslim culture as erecting practical and ideological barriers

There is no denying that the collection of academic scholarship and mediated reporting (both produced and published in and for western audiences) that initially interrogated Muslim females' experience of sport, physical education and leisure perpetuated the notion that Islamic requirements *inhibited* or presented real challenges to Muslim females' full participation in sport (Bee, 2005, 2007; Benn, 1994, 1996, 2000, 2002; Carrington *et al.*, 1987; Carrington and Williams 1988; Carroll and Hollinshead 1993; Dagkas and Benn 2006; De Knop *et al.*, 1996). In fact, this notion dominated discussions about sporting Muslim women in the west despite the fact that alternative readings pertaining to Islam's 'favourable' view of sport by Islamic/Muslim (and feminist) scholars did exist in various intellectual domains (al-Qaradawi, 1992a, 1992b; Bernat, 1989; Ibrahim, 1982; Ismail, 1999; Naciri, 1993; Sfeir, 1985). In this earlier literature, unravelling Islam's position on sport meant determining to/for western audiences whether it was legal (acceptable, 'halal') for Muslim women to engage in sport, and also sensitising these audiences to what was deemed 'taboo' (Benn, 2005; Johnson, 2000; Walseth and Fasting, 2003). In many cases, the (often feminist, secular, liberal, democratic) desire to both make sense of regulated Muslim females, and to also free 'Them' from their cloistered spaces fuelled the need to raise awareness about the genuine plight and suffering of those 'rare' Muslim women who did venture into sport. Stories of real (read: 'flesh and blood') Muslim women who suffered the wrath of fundamentalist/Islamist groups were universally adopted to represent not only the *subject* of Muslim women and sport itself, but came to define the parameters of knowing and speaking for *all* Muslim women's experiences. A fitting example that has often been (over)reported in western media is the case of Hassiba Boulmerka, famous for both winning the gold medal for the 1500 metres at the 1992 Barcelona Olympics and for being fiercely criticised, and receiving death threats from some fundamentalist groups within Algeria for revealing too much flesh during the race.[2] Boulmerka's plight forced her into exile to Europe in order to continue competing (Morgan, 1998; Hargreaves, 2000). Although Boulmerka's story has also been starkly contrasted to Nawal el-Mountawakel's more 'positive' experience of winning the women's 400 metres hurdles event at the 1984 Summer Olympics (Hargreaves, 2000), my own experiences show that it has also been used by journalists, sports researchers and lecturers to (a) initiate discussions on the topic of Muslim women and sport, (b) homogeneously represent the pressures that other *Arab* and *North African* Muslim women face, and (c) warn of the inherent dangers of 'Islamic fundamentalist' thinking. In a *New York Times* article titled 'Muslim Women's Exclusion is Target of New Campaign', representatives of Atlanta Plus (a European women's group which comprises women from France, Belgium, Germany, Sweden, Canada and the United States) allude to the suffering of Muslim women from multiple countries (Algeria, Morocco and Tunisia, as well as Iran, Kuwait, Pakistan, Saudi Arabia, Qatar and the United Arab Emirates), warn about the "Koranic admonition that women may uncover only their hands and face" and blame foreign 'conservative' Islamic countries for not simply harbouring discriminatory attitudes towards women and sport, but for exporting "this problem" to immigrant groups in the west (Simmons, 1995). Instead, Muslim countries are depicted as lagging behind the progressive western nations, and against this backdrop, the group members emerge as important and brave heroines that take on the challenge of transforming oppressive and degenerative regimes abroad and in the west. In fact, their struggle for gender equality is described as 'tough', reinforcing the perception that European women are burdening themselves with the feminist duty to empower and rescue (both migrant and non-migrant) Muslim women who are represented as not being able to help themselves. Although there is evidence of researchers questioning the fallacious nature of such representations (Nakamura, 2002; Walseth and Fasting, 2003), it remains the case that stories of sporting Muslim women's plight continue to outweigh stories of success, progression and advancement. From the UK to France, Belgium, Germany, Netherlands, Australia, Canada and the United States, the concern around barriers and challenges has invariably dominated a plethora of public, political, media and academic discussions as an almost unchallengeable truth. In some instances, success stories are shared with disclaimers that warn the reader about the "reality" – that progress has been both "gradual" and minimal, and that women in Islamic countries are a small minority in the competitive sports arena" (Pfister, 2010b: 38). However, the 'competitive sport arena' in this example refers primarily to western international competitive sporting events, not other global sporting events where Muslim women competed. Samie and Sehlikoglu's (2014) work serves to remind us that 'success' when it comes to discussions of sporting Muslim women is defined primarily in terms that reaffirm Muslim women's struggle to overcome copious adversities, such as lack of sporting provisions in Islamic countries, and the generally unsupportive conditions under which Muslim females across the 'Islamic/Muslim world' struggle to even obtain minimal access, and not necessarily on winning medals. At other times, alternative histories, such as the historical, cultural and/or political dynamics of different sports and their integration in different majority Muslim nations, are overlooked (Amara, 2013, 2016; see also Al-Jazeera, 2013) so as to exacerbate and accentuate claims of Muslim cultures lagging behind the west.

In the majority of discussions pertaining to struggle and barriers, *how sport* and *participation* have been defined (as terms and concepts), and then investigated and reported, either through published academic scholarship, formal and informal sport, physical activity and/or physical education and leisure forums, and mediated coverage is rarely questioned. Toffoletti and Palmer (2015: 7) do note that "*participation*" has typically denoted *active* participation – that is, the "physical activity of playing sport or exercising", thereby overlooking "other forms of participation in sport, as consumers of sport experiences and sport media". This is a valid point, but neglects to mention that in many cases of researching religious or other impediments to Muslim women's engagement in sport, *sport* has actually also denoted western-styled, western-fashioned sport and leisure activities, even when researchers claim to have adopted the "widest sense" to consider "all aspects of physical activity" (Benn *et al.*, 2011: 1). Meanwhile, *participation* has denoted engagement in western activities, under conditions that prioritise and privilege secular (western) etiquettes. Researchers have, of course, alluded to *alternative* sporting arenas where Muslim women compete (Ahmed, 2009a, 2009b; Amara, 2008) and also called for more inclusive measures to be adopted in sport so as to move beyond simply 'one-model' systems of sport (Benn, 2000, 2002). Nevertheless, much of the initial process for producing knowledge and 'truth' about Muslim women's struggles to access or participate in sport did utilise and rely on evidence of Muslim women's absence from western sporting contexts and/or their 'special' requests for accommodating religious observance to manufacture and reinforce the concern about 'barriers and challenges' (Bee, 2005, 2007; Benn, 1994, 1996, 2000, 2002; Carrington *et al.*, 1987; Carrington and Williams 1988; Carroll and Hollinshead 1993; Dagkas and Benn 2006; De Knop *et al.*, 1996). In these instances, we cannot overlook the inherent arrogance that also implies (a) *only* western-fashioned sport constitutes proper, real or genuine 'sport'; and (b) *only* engaging under secular conditions demonstrates any kind of 'real success' or progress for Muslim women. In fact, it remains the case that much of the research on sports potential for promoting social inclusion of minorities – especially Muslim women – into majority cultures is borne out of, if not compounded by, the belief that engagement in western sport will bring the unsettled outsiders into the fold of normal society, and that participating without 'special' requests symbolises unfettered acceptance of western values and western practices.

On other occasions, when researchers have either talked about alternative forms of sports participation amongst Muslim females at academic sporting conferences or entered these spaces, the focus (or 'the story') that is inevitably told rests on (a) exposing the *different* conditions under which Muslim women engage so as to demystify the 'Other' and (b) measuring how 'good' or 'bad' this difference is for Muslim women (Hillyer, 2008, 2011). In both instances, the audience is overwhelmingly reminded about the extent to which Muslim women are (willingly and unwillingly) regulated. To really accentuate the notion of unmodern and unprogressive practices regulating Muslim female bodies, two elements of Islamic culture are emphasised: namely, veiling and sex-segregation.

Veiling as the 'problem'

Despite the fact that some sports organisations, like FIFA, have come to now allow certain types of head veils to be worn, *veiling* in general, and especially during sport, is still a contentious issue within and across diverse sporting institutions. Over the years, it has been intellectualised to and for western audiences of sports coaches and sports practitioners as a dangerous garment; indeed, this is why FIFA (allegedly) initially imposed a ban against hijab in 2007 (Ayub, 2011; Esfandiari, 2007). Samie and Sehlikoglu (2014) provide a comprehensive overview of the contentious representations pertaining to the inclusion of the veil ahead of and during the 2012 Olympics, outlining how some questioned whether it was a sign of progression or regression for women, while others coalesced it with western acceptance of Islamist Wahabi sympathies. Muslim women who have worn head veils or full-bodied garments during western sporting events have frequently reported being subjected to verbal insults and/or racial abuse (Abu-Arif, 2008; Ahmed, 2009a; Benn and Ahmad, 2006). Others have been dismissed from sport, banned from playing (Ayub, 2011; Matus, 2004) or been forced to choose between competing in sports or their religious commitments (Sports Plus, 2009). Of course, these kinds of 'flesh and blood' stories of struggle have been included in the sporting literature and in the liberal) media, prompting some to claim that the real voices of Muslim women are now being captured. However, my own experiences of talking to sports coaches, teachers, sport policy makers and practitioners from both the UK, many parts of Europe and the US, and of delving into blogs, op-eds and other mediated reportings about Muslim women and sport have shown that these stories are also often accompanied with public and political debate that seeks to rationalise whether the act of 'banning' or asking someone to 'leave the sports field' can in fact be deemed *racist* (read: irrationally prejudiced) or based on scientific concerns (read: rational, reasonable, logical). This is particularly evident in mediated coverage of Asmahan Mansour, the 11-year-old who was asked to remove her hijab during play, but was told to leave the field when she refused (Feminist Wire, 2012) and FIFA's disqualification of the Iranian women's soccer team for wearing the hijab (Moghtader, 2011). As one respondent to Moghtader's article noted, "What if (the hijab) gets in a knot around someone's neck and cuts off the air to one of the players? What can the ref do? Rip the hijab off? It would cause riots around the world" (Bobalu). In this exchange, the underlying public message is clear: it is in fact the 'west' that is struggling (equally) to deal with the illogical requests of 'Others', and not necessarily Muslim women who are the (only) legitimate targets or victims. In fact, when Cindy van den Bremen, the Dutch designer of sport headscarves, wrote about the process and challenge of designing an acceptable (Velcro) version of the sport headscarf, she described her design as a "modern interpretation of Islam" (Breman, 1999).[3] Interestingly enough, even as the notion and concept of 'sports hijabs' are becoming a trendy phenomenon, alternative forms of 'Islamic' attire are still viewed with hostility (e.g. the burkini ban on some of France's beaches). In 2009, I attended a guest lecture on Muslim women and sport at a British higher education institution. The lecturer so vividly juxtaposed the inclusion of the traditional (non-sporty) 'hijab' on 'our soil' (read: here in the UK, in some western school sports, physical education programmes and community level sports programmes) with the forced unveiling of Muslim girls and women in certain Islamic countries (e.g. Turkey where the secular political values have long dictated the removal of the veil in public settings). In this instance, the UK was depicted as embracing a generous and diplomatic position when compared to the oppressive regime of Turkey that was forcing its women to do something that perhaps they do not wish to do. "We're several steps ahead", the lecturer remarked, prompting many to question why we even needed to accept the hijab if Islamic countries were rejecting it. The same lecture also chastised Saudi Arabia and Iran for forcing women to veil. Of course, I understood that the fundamental essence of the lecture was to denounce any kind of 'forced' obligations (clothing-related or otherwise), however I could not ignore the very uncomfortable political undertones, especially when, even in discussions about rising Islamophobia in the UK, cases of discrimination (of women having their veils ripped off or women being spat at for wearing a veil in England) were so (conveniently) ignored.

An important additional point about veiling to mention here is that over the years, a number of non-Muslim female athletes have chosen to wear sports garments that cover the entire body, including the head in some cases, without being shunned as 'strange'. The late Florence Griffith and Allyson Felix of the USA, and Cathy Freeman of Australia are a few examples of female athletes who have worn tight full-bodied leotards, with both Griffith and Freeman actually covering the head too. Yet Muslim women who have worn (tight) full-bodied leotards (e.g. Ruqaya al-Gassra of Bahrain) have consistently been negatively represented in western media and asked to explain their decisions (see e.g. Amara, 2012; Pye, 2008; Samie and Sehlikoglu, 2014). My own experiences of discussing the politics of this issue at sports workshops have often resulted in a number of colleagues telling me that, as far as they saw it, the *real problem* was that Muslim women's decision to wear the full-bodied attire was based *solely* on religious doctrine to cover the body, and not scientific reasoning about, for instance, the leotard improving aerodynamics. Of course, I asked how my academic colleagues could so confidently claim to 'know' that 'aerodynamics' or anything else for that matter was not also a reason, or one of many reasons for selecting such attire. I appreciated and valued this kind of debate, because it has allowed me to ascertain untold 'truths', especially those that are often unreported in literature, but which we hold as a matter of fact, or which we only choose to whisper in changing rooms or exchange in hushed private conversations. In these instances, I was always struck by the fact that these sporting intellectuals could (a) so casually trivialise any woman's choice to 'cover up' – there are women who chose veiling, after all; (b) that they could so easily negate veiling (of the head and/or body) as empowering for some who chose to wear such attire; and (c) they could 'read' the use of the leotard by Muslim women as both the embodiment of *restriction* and unprogressive ideas, and yet attribute the same garment on a non-Muslim female body as evidence of scientific and technological advancements.[4] In these instances, the overarching metanarrative reminded sporting audiences that participating under western conditions or secular etiquettes is better and safer to *hijabed* alternatives.

Gender segregation as the 'problem'

The notion of segregated sporting arenas has fuelled hysteria about the extent to which women are regulated and/or completely excluded from entering 'men's spaces' (e.g. female ban from football stadiums in Iran; Braunshweiger, 2016; Corbett, 2008). In many cases, sports authorities have even raised concerns about accommodating such requests in western contexts (Elling *et al.*, 2001; Walseth and Fasting, 2004). Yet what is often overlooked is that gender segregated provision has also resulted in sporting developments specifically for women in these countries, and that it is Muslim men who are excluded from these 'female-only' spaces (Eqbali, 2007). Although increasing efforts are made to recognise the importance of female-only sporting spaces that give women an opportunity to compete (Pfister, 2003), much of this work also trivialises the life-long engagement of these women in such arenas as unrealistic (Pfister, 2000). It is poignantly illustrated in the following excerpt about Iranian women's engagement in rugby.

> [...] some Iranian women proudly see themselves as the most emancipated in the Middle East but still have to combine their careers and leisure activities with traditional expectations, childbearing, cooking and cleaning [...]
>
> (Corbett, 2008: 4–5)

Inherent in these neo-colonialist assumptions is the belief that religious observance of any kind cannot result in real empowerment of women because religion brings with it irrational and authoritarian/patriarchal rules that render women subordinate to men. The notion that Muslim women and western women may have shared struggles against capitalist patriarchy, for instance, is completely overlooked. Instead the evidence and claims that are made serve as yet another reminder of how Muslim women and western women are simply 'too different', and how their lives and needs are completely incompatible. The statement "Iranian women still have a long way to go before they are truly competitive in the international arena" is made to add a final punchy reminder, in case the reader forgets this point! The international competitive arena denotes, of course, western sporting events like the Olympics, not other global sporting arenas (or organic sporting spaces) where Iranian Muslim women and many other Muslim women from diverse Islamic and non-Islamic countries have made significant advancements on their own terms.

At times, neo-colonialist discourses have represented the different conditions under which some Muslim women compete as irrational. The ways in which the (alleged) banning of photographers at sporting events like the Islamic Women's Games or other segregated organic sporting spaces has been intellectualised to and for western audiences is a prime example of this. To the western world that relies so heavily on global media coverage from satellite and cable television, newspapers, and radio for sponsorship, commodification etc. it is an especially bizarre (and insular) way to market sports. On the other, it has been codified as being deeply rooted in paranoia about unrelated males and the wider issue of modesty. Although media coverage of these events is rare, female radio and print-media journalists, and female western sports advocates who have entered these spaces have often made excessive references to the restrictive garments that women continue to wear when they are competing in segregated spaces (BBC, 2005; Hillyer, 2011). This analysis operates to remind the western audience that (a) western and Muslim women's lives are as polarised as possible, and (b) that even in controlled spaces Muslim women are not 'free' from authoritarian rule. What is overlooked, however, is the need to understand the cultural context, instead of assume that all sports need to or should evolve or be commercialised in the same way that western sports are. Moreover, these assumptions ignore the fact that in many cases, some women may still wear body-covering garments because the 'outsider' (researcher, journalist) who has stepped into their world has done so (a) without fully understanding the cultural relevance/importance of veiling to these women and their cultures; and (b) disregarded the fact that photographs (and videos) capture the full aesthetics of the person that is being observed. In other words, still images are powerful artifacts, as well as socially and politically constructed representations of social life and the people within it (Rose, 2001). Once captured there is no way to control who sees these images and how they interpret or represent them. Hence, preventing photographers from entering female-only spaces can also be a powerful, and empowering, way to retain control over how one's body is displayed to millions of people around the world; and allowing 'outsiders' to bring cameras into these protected spaces can in fact be a gesture of goodwill and of trust, which is then later abused and violated to portray 'controlled' women.

The metanarrative of Islamic requirements or Muslim culture erecting ideological and practical barriers has thus not only evolved to mean 'impeding' engagement in western events, but taken various forms to further bolster claims of cultural incompatibilities, of an impenetrable clash between two civilisations long defined as being embroiled in ideological, philosophical and, more recently, political conflicts with each other. More worryingly, the corpus of knowledge that legitimates a cause for concern around certain Islamic ways of engaging in sport, remains centred on and informed by the firm belief that western traditions are better than, superior to and the only (reasonable) replacement for what has been depicted as regressive and unmodern Islamic thinking, even though, in reality, many fundamental tenets of western, secular sporting traditions are also problematic for many sports advocates and feminists alike. Here I consider the long standing struggle for many female athletes and sports feminists to challenge, overturn and take aim at sporting etiquettes, and practices that overtly sexualise, and trivialise, women's engagement (e.g. Nicole Cook's and Jess Varnish's experiences of sexism in cycling are but two very recent examples, Ingle, 2016). Yet the same concerns around revealing dress codes, sexual tensions and derogatory hypersexualised representations of sporting women's bodies, when presented by Muslim women, are represented in ways that attribute it a 'Muslim problem' that is deeply rooted in religious practices that have no place in a modern, progressive, democratic world. Moreover, because Muslim women's bodies are still frequently understood as the locus of religious interpretations that rest on acceptable, good and/or honourable femininity being dependent on the covering of women's nakedness (the basic premise of how Qur'anic concept of modesty is itself analysed), even when shared concerns are legitimately expressed, the metanarratives still reinforce the juxtapositions between Muslim women's controlled sexuality (e.g. covering up), and the sexual liberation that western women cherish, value and appreciate (e.g. not covering). Moreover, by representing modesty as a solely 'Muslim' problem, researchers have long ignored how revealing dress codes can be a concern for women from all backgrounds regardless of religious affiliation, cultural and/or ethnic make-up, class, and/or sexual orientation. Instead, the 'Other' experience is not only measured against white, middle-classed, western women's experience, but labelled as 'lacking' and tied to "so-called feminist notions of what constitutes 'good' or 'bad' practice" (Amos and Parmar, 1984: 11).

Muslim men as violators of gender equality and distorted representations of agency

In more recent years, increasing efforts have been made to celebrate and recognise Muslim women's agency. Researchers like Benn *et al.* (2011: 4), for instance, utilise subjugated knowledge produced by "Muslim scholars, practitioners, and leaders" within the scientific community of sport. This has been celebrated as a productive (post-structural, post-modern) step towards listening to other perspectives and capturing how those different to us (in the west) exist (Toffoletti and Palmer, 2015). Consulting Muslim scholars is seen as a 'good enough' attempt to both gain 'pure' or unbiased knowledge from insiders, and to redress or even overcome the challenges of essentialism in much of the published work on Muslim women and sport. However, it is a very naïve claim, one that is itself informed by reductive assumptions such as that only Muslims can know the experiences and perspectives of other Muslims. The question of *who* should speak is an entirely valid one, but *how* we seek to obtain these voices (methodologically) and the *ways* in which we analyse and represent these perspectives to our readers (epistemologically and ontologically) is even more important. In the spirit of thinking reflexively and always seeking ways to unravel what is known and how it has come to be known as such, I think it is pertinent to (a) reflect on the ways in which 'agency' has been defined and understood within this new body of research; and (b) outline some of the popular ways in which knowledge from a socially, culturally and politically diverse movement is being used to explain sporting Muslim women's 'unique' position. It is important to mention that it is not my intention to engage in a critical debate about whether Islamic feminism should be viewed as a strand of feminism or Islamism. Nor do I wish to dissect the legitimacy of different claims made by many Islamic feminists. Nevertheless, I do think it is important to contextualise the diverse and varied opinions and perspectives that have shaped this collective discourse and practice, before I outline how it is being utilised by sports researchers.

Islamic feminism, in many ways, is an umbrella term that encapsulates the very broad and diverse descriptions, perspectives and voices of Muslim scholars (mostly women, but also men) who offer various critiques of Islamic history, doctrine, practice and culture. The overarching aim is to give voice to Muslim women, and this is done through three specific avenues or *typologies*: modern or pragmatic Islamic feminist perspectives, secular Islamic perspectives, and traditionalist perspectives. While the first two perspectives can be broadly characterised as being concerned with identifying masculine authoritarianism and patriarchy as the cause of Muslim women's oppression, the latter, on the whole, embrace the notion that 'all is the will of the God' (a claim that has been vehemently rejected by the global feminist movement and by many secular Islamic feminists). These initial perspectives have enormous implications and consequences, both on what social justice for Muslim women means and entails, and how it needs to be fought for. Hence, modern, pragmatic and/or secular Islamic feminists often fight to reclaim their status as *equals* to (and the same as) men by historicising the contexts under which the Qur'an was first written, and recovering feminist perspectives on scriptures to challenge and/or overturn male-centric truths that are believed to be responsible for positioning Muslim women as inferior subordinates to men. They also work to empower Muslim women to seek political and legal reform in their countries to challenge the male-centred conditions that negatively impact their lives. Traditionalist Islamic feminists, however, do not necessarily view or support this kind of 'anti-male' or female-against-male approach as the only solution for women's empowerment. Notwithstanding differences within traditionalist Islamic feminist perspectives, suffice it to say that traditionalists revere the notion of a dual-sex society – one in which men and women are accepted as *equal* but *different* – as opposed to one in which women usurp men's position (see e.g. Faruqi, 1994).[5] Despite this enormous variety, when sports researchers have utilised so-called 'Muslim knowledge' to move beyond essentialist representations of Muslim women as 'oppressed', they have predominantly relied on the views and theoretical perspectives of secular Islamic feminists who insist that Islamic doctrine has been interpreted for them by men and thus reinterpret scripture and exegetical traditions to challenge various forms of injustice in both Muslim majority nations and Muslim communities (see e.g. Waljee, 2008; Benn *et al.*, 2011). Of course, some traditionalist viewpoints are also included, but as I will outline later, these are used to reinforce and emphasise the notion of difference, and complete 'Otherness' of Muslim females and Islamic thinking. Secular Islamic feminist interpretations of agency have been utilised to homogeneously characterise, represent and almost romanticise Muslim women's agency as nothing more than an attack on Muslim men's authoritarian decision-making, and a struggle against patriarchal structures to *only* be equal to men, or have the same access and rights as men. By privileging the 'word' and perspectives of predominantly secular Islamic feminists and/or those Muslim activists who celebrate the female-versus-male approach as the only path towards empowerment and agency, sports researchers not only further corroborate the secular western liberal feminist agenda, but they (inadvertently) polarise, often also demonise and silence, those segments of the Muslim population that have in many ways already been conceptualized as too radical and unmodern to rationalise under western feminist perspectives. Here I refer to those Muslim women (and men) who accept traditionalist Islamic perspectives, find empowerment on precisely these terms, do not believe they 'need saving' through western interventions and have the capacity to create their own culturally and religiously-specific ways to engage in a range of physical activities that sit outside of conventional understandings of what real 'sport' is and can be. Relying on secular perspectives to define agency thus carries with it many problematic and essentialist claims that inevitably represent Islamic thinking, and traditionalist values as antithetical to women's empowerment and the objectives of progressive politics (Mahmood, 2005).

As outlined earlier, there are times when conservative Islamic interpretations and perspectives have been used, and this is typically in relation to the sociocultural constructedness of Muslim women's bodies. For instance, sporting discourses have relied only on interpretations that situate Muslim women's bodies as either being "the embodiment of destruction (*fitna*), the symbol of disorder" and the "representative of the dangers of sexuality and its rampant disruptive potential" (Mernissi, 1975: 45), or as depicting something "shameful" and/or provocative that must be covered from public view (depicted in the word "*awra*" or "*aura*") (Arebi, 1994: 10; see also Hargreaves, 2000; Sfeir, 1985; Watson, 1994). These perspectives do indeed infiltrate certain Islamic cultures, but they are not the *only* perspectives. Alternative readings about Muslim women's position and bodies do indeed exist, and they celebrate the power, privilege, capability and importance that some Muslims believe God bestowed upon women.[6] When the only representations of Muslim women's bodies that are outlined and evidenced by and for sporting audiences (academics or practitioners) are negative, the underlying messages imply that Muslim women's bodies only carry negative meanings, hence 'sporting Muslim women' remain discursively represented as nothing more than regulated bodies: i.e. physically regulated bodies that need to be accompanied by males (chaperoned) in certain public spaces or excluded from these altogether (Pfister, 2003; Sfeir, 1985); and culturally regulated bodies that are under scrutiny from those within their own communities to ensure that women observe, embrace and reinforce customary notions of honour that are rooted in paternalistic ideals (Di-Capua, 2005; Hargreaves, 2007; Kay, 2005, 2006). Against this backdrop, Muslim women's agency comes to be understood as a reactionary backlash to being controlled by men in their communities (Samie in Ratna *et al.*, 2017); and surveillance becomes a problem that only exists within Muslim communities. The notion that Muslim identities are under increasing scrutiny from majority cultures is completely overlooked. This does of course reflect the social and political actions of some Muslim women living within and beyond Islamic jurisprudence, but it is certainly not the *only* form of agency. Mahmood's (2005) canonical text, *Politics of Piety*, provides a compelling insight into the ways that Muslim females who embrace "Islamic forms of sociability" (xxii) and traditionalist values of Islam, find "emancipatory possibilities" (2), and acquire influence and authority within these conditions. Overlooking alternative possibilities for how Muslim women might create agency means that the metanarrative of being controlled and always regulated remains not only intact, but engulfs the actions, stories and perspectives of some Muslim women – who often also write from and about conditions relating to conservative Islam and have looked to the second-wave of global feminist movement for 'remedies' – to situate *all* Muslim women under these representations.[7] Hence efforts to recover subjugated voices and knowledge from and about Muslim women silence and/or ignore diverse sporting Muslim women who do not share similar values and perspectives on agency and empowerment. The notion that Muslim women remain always trapped, always juxtaposed against "social, cultural and political powers" in both the so-called 'Islamic East' and the 'secular West' and squeezed in-between the "conflicting views by traditionalist and moderate jurists" prevails (Abusharuf, 2006: 715). My own journey with diverse Muslim women has shown me that multiple Muslim female identities do exist, and those who embody this diversity are not silent or absent from day-to-day life. My empirical work on heterosexy Muslim women (Samie, 2013, 2014) and tomboy Muslim girls (Samie, 2015) tries to recover some of the silenced voices that I have encountered in my research journey, but much more still needs to be done. Toffoletti and Palmer (2015) invite contemporary researchers to engage transnational feminist perspectives and to move beyond a focus on 'active participation' to include for instance sports consumption. This is indeed an important step, but it is not enough to simply look at how Muslim women consume sport if *how* we continue to understand *consumption* remains defined by an essentialist metanarrative that labels any kind of 'Other', alternative and non-traditional forms of sport consumption by and amongst Muslim women as 'less than' or inferior to western modes of sports consumption.

Conclusion

Throughout this chapter I picked apart the various essentialist representations about 'sporting Muslim women' so as to work against, and not with, colonizing discourses that further plunge us into hierarchical and binary juxtapositions that ultimately position Muslim women as regulated subjects that are 'less than' and 'inferior' to their western counterparts. Adopting a post-colonial decolonising perspective allowed me to grapple with how scholarship, in/formal discussions, and discursive projections rooted in, and compounded by neo/colonial ideas have been intertwined in the activity of knowledge/message production to construct, influence and control contemporary (western, secular liberal feminist) categorisations and representations of Islam, Muslim females and sport. It also allowed me to recover subjugated perspectives, knowledge, realities and truth(s). Drawing on Mohanty's (2003) work, Toffoletti and Palmer (2015: 12) invite us to be more cognizant of the process of recovering voice by raising epistemological questions about "how knowledge about Muslim women in sport is produced, by whom and why". Mohanty's earlier work asks us to think more critically about the "space/location" and the "politics of the production of particular knowledge" (1991: 3). In this chapter, the purpose of asking these questions was to (a) expose the durability of imperialist ideologies; (b) better understand the art of 'claims-making' itself; and (c) unhinge essentialist claims. When so much of the evidence on 'sporting Muslim women' overwhelmingly points to and corroborates the metanarratives, it is very challenging to resist reinforcing, privileging, and/or bolstering the "conventional European genealogy of thought", and refrain from juxtaposing non-western culture, society and its peoples as still "catching up with the West" or questioning the 'western-ness' of those deemed 'Others' (see Rodriguez *et al.*, 2010: 1). Even though this was not an empirical paper, I tried to recover subjugated perspectives so as to replace colonialist thinking with alternative knowledge. Some of this alternative knowledge comprises subjugated perspectives that are grounded by my own experiences, both of what it means to be a Muslim woman engaged in an array of different sports and cultural pastimes, and a researcher in the field. At all times I tried to remain sensitive towards the many Muslim women whom I have encountered and who have shared with me their stories, journeys, accomplishments and struggles to be something – someone that is more than, that exists beyond, and outside of colonising and colonised constructions and representations of 'sporting Muslim women' (these stories are captured in my empirical work, Samie, 2013,

2014, 2015). I have often been asked to 'explain' these participants' commitments to Islam and the western way of life by both Muslim and non-Muslim scholars who see 'Them' as somehow being incomplete: not fully western and not fully Muslim, simply 'too different' to make sense of. These assumptions infuriate me. They stem from myopic essentialist worldviews that seek to define the authentic identity of sporting Muslim women, as being simply '*this*' or '*that*'. In reality, the

> identity of (Muslim women) is not a straight jacket or dress or veil. It is an active, living, changing process, which demands a rereading of our history, and a reshaping of ourselves and our societies in the light of present challenges and future goals.
>
> (El Sadaawi, 1999 in Kassab, 2010: 95)

In an increasingly global and pluralist world, where ideas are always dynamic, shifting, evolving, and where people are more likely to (socially, culturally and politically) commute between different cultures (regardless of their geographical positioning), we need to better Muslim women's identities if we are to move beyond oscillating from one extreme homogenising depiction (*all* Muslim women as regulated) to another (*all* Muslim women fighting to be free from control are against men). In my own post-colonial research, I find it valuable to consider hyphenated identities. These are not identities that are 'trapped' on or straddling the margins as is often portrayed.

> [...] [I]dentity is about hierarchies which are constantly in flux and need to be seen in context. [And] any politics constituted around the primacy of one axis of differentiation (e.g., gender, race, religion or class) over all others [is] limited in its ability to do justice to the everyday experiences to those who "move in and out of different identities [...] and their mixed allegiances".
>
> (Davis and Lutz, 2000: 369–370)

Although this concept is typically used to make sense of people and identities that emerge in diaspora, it can also help contemporary researchers to think through and better understand how elements of identities and perspectives concomitantly evolve and emerge (both in a metaphorical and literal sense) out of the politics of marginalisation, of feeling both 'inside and outside', of non-belonging, rootlessness and being culturally homeless in their home (Bhabha, 1994; Hall, 2000a, 2000b). It is a more dialectical approach, one that affords a recognition of individuality and particularity of each woman and their everyday within specific contexts, and one that also recognises that feelings of being always challenged (by dominant elites from and within the west) apply to those living in Islamic and Muslim countries too, perhaps not in the same or on equal terms, but they do apply, especially as the neoliberal agenda seeks to expand and spread the 'west is best' rhetoric to the world. The need to think critically about the process of knowledge production requires us to be more cognizant of whose perspectives we are airing and privileging when we speak of broad concepts such as 'sport participation', 'agency', and of course 'empowerment'. Decolonising philosophies such as the ones outlined in this chapter can provide crucial points of discussion that can inspire critical points of departure in future discussions about sporting Muslim women, regardless of the politics of location or geography.

Notes

1 Collectively, decolonizing methodological approaches have been described differently, as "researching back" (see Burger, 1990), "writing back" (Ashcroft, *et al.*, 1989: 2) or "talking back" (Smith, 1999). What binds these approaches together is the fundamental commitment to recover colonised peoples, and their struggle(s) for self-determination, and its requirement for researchers to understand the effect, consequences and impact of the legacies of colonialism.

2 There are of course many other 'flesh and blood' stories that have been raised over the years to ensure that western audiences never forgot about Islam's derogatory treatment of women (see Samie and Sehlikoglu, 2014, and Amara, 2012). In many of these cases, stories about pushy, 'backward', controlling and unreasonable males forbidding sport or making scathing and hostile remarks about those Muslim women who 'dared to enter' sport are all used to eventually attribute reasonable blame to Islamic obligations and requirements for *pardah* (veiling) and the segregation of the sexes, a point that is discussed later.

3 It is important to mention that Muslim women have also been involved with inventing cunning solutions to help them access western sport on their terms. This includes the hijood (a combination of a hoodie and a hijab), the burkini (the full-bodied swimming attire) and the use of various head coverings, such as caps and bandanas that cover the hair and not the neck. These kinds of inventions have often been problematised instead of being celebrated as a sign of agency.

4 There is in fact limited research on the history and the use of the leotard in sport, but there is evidence that when it was first designed, it was marketed as a 'versatile' garment that would provide 'maximum comfort' (Strong, 1981) and "freedom to women" by "stretching with the body" (Adler, 1980: 137). Many forms of the leotard have existed over the years, including those stretchy, nylon and spandex leotards that became the basic fitness fashion of the 70s (see also Hauglad, 2012).

5 Under these perspectives, men are accepted as being responsible for women's physical, mental, and economic welfare regardless of whether they choose to work or not, because women bear the physiological (and often psychological) weight (or pressure) of physically having children, as well as dealing with financial and other negative consequences from taking leave from work to raise children. Secular, liberal feminists in the west and secular Islamic feminists (both within and beyond the west) have taken aim not only at how equality is conceptualised under these kinds of traditionalist agendas, but reject such claims for rendering women dependent on male wages (and thus vulnerable and subordinate to men).

6 The elevated status of women in Islam is also outlined when the Prophet is quoted as saying "paradise lies at the feet of the mother". Whilst this reinforces the maternal nature of women, it also attributes the fate of the greatest reward a believing Muslim can seek at the 'feet' of women. In another example, nursing women are depicted as impactful 'bread winners' who nurture not merely their children but the next generation of leaders (men and women), and their husbands are obligated to pay them a wage for taking on the burdensome responsibility of weaning the children as well as enduring the physical and psychological effects of childbirth (Qur'an 2:233).

7 I do not wish to undermine or overlook the possibility that the latter effort (of secular Islamic feminists looking to the west) may have been borne out of looking at commonalities between Muslim women and western women; however, it is important to be cognizant of the fact that even these forms of alternative feminisms (that are literally being led by Muslim women) bring with them the epistemological biases of modernity and the need to embrace universalist claims/agendas on women's issues (e.g. separating religion and state; empowerment being about being equal with and to men; see Moghissi, 1999).

References

Abdul Razak, M.T., Omar-Fauzee, M. and Abd-Latif, R. (2010) 'The Perspective of Arabic Muslim Women toward Sport Participation', *Journal of Asia Pacific Studies*, 1: pp. 364–377.

Abu-Arif, N. (2008) 'Denmark's Veiled Soccer Star'. Islam Online. Accessed online at: www.islamonline.net/servlet/Satellite?c=Article_C&cid=1212925458987&pagename=Zone-English-News

Abusharuf, A. (2006) 'Women in Islamic Communities: The Quest for Gender Justice Research', *Human Rights Quarterly*, 28(5): pp. 714–728.

Adler, France-Michèle. (1980) *Sportsfashion*, New York: Avon Books.

Afshar, H. (1994) 'Muslim Women in West Yorkshire Growing up with Real and Imaginary Values Amidst Conflicting Views of Self and Society', in H. Afshar and M. Maynard (eds) *The Dynamics of 'Race' and Gender: Some Feminist Interventions*, London: Taylor and Francis.

Ahmed, S. (1998) *Differences that Matter: Feminist Theory and Post-Modernism*, Cambridge: Cambridge University Press.

Ahmed, S. (2000) 'Boundaries and Connection: Introduction', in S. Ahmed, J. Kilby, C. Lury, M. McNeil and B. Skeggs (eds) *Transformations: Thinking Through Feminism*, Routledge: London and New York.

Ahmad, A. (2009a) 'Challenging Misconceptions: The British Muslim Women's Futsal Team'. Paper Presented at the Race, Ethnicity and Football conference. University of Brighton, 22 May 2009.

Ahmad, A. (2009b) 'The Women's Islamic Games: An Exploration of the British Muslim Women's Experiences of Competitive Sport'. Paper presented at the 16th International Association of Physical Education and Sport for Girls and Women *conference*. University of Stellenbosch, South Africa, 17 July 2009.

Al-Jazeera (2013) 'Football Rebels: Mekhloufi and the FLN Team'. Accessed online at: www.aljazeera.com/sport/football/2013/03/201331912371852641 3.html

al-Qaradawi, Y. (1992a) *The Lawful and the Prohibited in Islam*, Kuwait: International Islamic Federation of Student Organizations.

al-Qaradawi, Y. (1992b) *The Status of Women in Islam*, Cairo: Islamic Home Publishing and Distribution.
Amara, M. (2008) 'The Muslim World in the Global Sporting Arena', *The Brown Journal of World Affairs*, 14(2): pp. 67–76.
Amara, M. (2012) 'Veiled Women Athletes in the 2008 Beijing Olympics: Media Accounts', *International Journal of the History of Sport*, 29(4): pp. 638–651.
Amara, M. (2013) 'The Pillars of Qatar's International Sport Strategy', e-international, 29 November 2013. Accessed online at: www.e-ir.info/2013/11/29/the-pillars-of-qatars-international-sport-strategy/
Amara, M. (2016) 'Sport, a Serious Matter in the Arab World?' Accessed online at: http://i3saw.org/en/category/congresses/congress-stirling-2017
Amos, V. and Parmar, P. (1984) 'Challenging Imperial Feminism', *Feminist Review*, 17(1): pp. 3–19.
Arebi, S. (1994) *Women and Words in Saudi Arabia: The Politics of Literary Discourse*, New York: Columbia University Press.
Ashcroft, B., Griffiths, G., and Tiffin, H. (1989) *The Empire Writes Back: Theory and Practice in Post-Colonial Literatures*, London: Routledge.
Ayub, A. (2011) 'A Closer Look at FIFA's Hijab', *SAIS Review*, XXXI (1): 43–50.
BBC (2005) Taking on Tehran. BBC Radio Four. 11 January 2005.
Bee, P. (2005) 'The Veil is Slowly Lifting for Muslim Women Athletes', *Guardian* newspaper, sport supplement. 11 October 2005.
Bee, P. (2007) 'Running Under Cover', *Guardian* newspaper. 20 November 2007.
Benn, T.C. (1994) Physical Education: A Field Study Investigation into An Interface of Cultures. Unpublished Master of Arts Thesis, University of Leicester.
Benn, T.C. (1996) 'Muslim Women and Physical Education in Initial Teacher Training', *Sport, Education and Society*, 1(1): pp. 5–21.
Benn, T. (2000) 'Towards Inclusion in Education and Physical Education', in A. Williams (ed.) *Primary School Physical Education: Research into Practice*, London: Routledge: pp. 118–135.
Benn, T. (2002) 'Muslim Women in Teacher Training: Issues of Gender, "Race" and Religion' in D. Penney (ed.) *Gender and Physical Education*, London: Routledge: pp. 57–79.
Benn, T. (2005) '"Race" and Physical Education, Sport and Dance', in K. Green and K. Hardman (eds) *Physical Education: Essential Issues*, Thousand Oaks: Sage Publications.
Benn, T.C. and Ahmad, A. (2006) 'Alternative Visions: International Sporting Opportunities for Muslim Women and Implications for British Youth Sport', *Youth and Policy*, 92, Special Issue: pp. 119–132.
Benn, T., Pfister, G. and Jawad, H. (eds) (2011) *Muslim Women and Sport*, London: Routledge, pp. 1–10.
Bernat, M.A.E. (1989) *Islam and Games*, Tadkeshwar: Surat; Gujrat; India. Translated into English from Gujarati by Hussain, M.F.Q. Gujarat, India.
Berque, J. (1964) *The Muslim Arabs*, New York: Praeger.
Bhabha, H.K. (1994) 'Remembering Fanon: Self, Psyche and the Colonial Condition', in P. Williams and L. Charisman (eds) *Colonial Discourse and Postcolonial Theory*, New York: Harvester Wheatsheaf.

Bhavnani, K. (1993) 'Talking Racism and the Editing of Women's Studies', in D. Richardson and V. Robinson (eds) *Introducing Women's Studies: Feminist Theory and Practice*, London: Macmillan.

Brah, A. (1993) '"Race" and "Culture" in the Gendering of Labour Markets', *New Communities*, 19(3): pp. 441–458.

Brah, A. and Phoenix, A. (2004) 'Ain't I a Woman? Revisiting Intersectionality', *Journal of International Women's Studies*, 5(3): pp. 75–86.

Braunshweiger, A. (2016) 'Banned from Stadiums for Being a Woman in Iran', New York: Human Rights Watch.

Breman, CVD (1999) 'A Modern Interpretation of the Headscarf'. ISIM Newsletter. Vol. 4/99.

Brooks, G. (1995) *Nine Parts of Desire: The Hidden World of Islamic Women*, New York: Bantam Books.

Brunt, L. (1999) 'Thinking about Ethnography', *Journal of Contemporary Ethnography*, 28(4): pp. 500-509.

Burger, J. (1990) *The Gaia Atlas of First Peoples*, London: Gaia Books.

Butler, J. (1990) *Gender Trouble*, New York: Routledge.

Butler, J. (1993) *Bodies that Matter: On the Discursive Limits of 'Sex'*, New York: Routledge.

Carrington, B. and Williams, T. (1988) 'Patriarchy and Ethnicity: The Link Between School Physical Education and Community Leisure Activities', in J. Evans (ed.) *Teachers, Teaching and Control in Physical Education*, London: The Falmer Press: pp. 83–96.

Carrington, B., Chivers, T. and Williams, T. (1987) 'Gender, Leisure and Sport: A Case Study of Young People of South Asian Descent', *Leisure Studies* 6(2): pp. 265–279.

Carroll, B., and Hollinshead, G. (1993) 'Ethnicity and Conflict in Physical Education', *British Educational Research Journal*, 19(1): pp. 59–76.

Chesler, P. (2005) *The Death of Feminism: What's Next in the Struggle for Women's Freedom?* New York: Palgrave.

CNN News (2011) 'FIFA Defends Hijab Ban after Iranian Team Forfeits Olympic Qualifier'. Accessed online at: http://edition.cnn.com/2011/SPORT/football/06/07/football.iran.hijab.fifa/index.html

Corbett, D.R. (2008) 'Sport, Gender and Ethnicity: Inclusion and Exclusion'. Paper presented at the IOC IV World Conference on Women and Sport: 'Sport as a Vehicle for Social Change'. Dead Sea, Jordan, 8–10 March 2008.

Dagkas, S. and Benn, T. (2006) 'Young Muslim Women's Experiences of Islam and Physical Education in Greece and Britain: A Comparative Study', *Sport, Education and Society*, 11(1): pp. 21–38.

Davis, K. and Lutz, H. (2000) 'Open Forum: Life in Theory – Three Feminist Thinkers on Transition(s)', *European Journal of Women's Studies*, 7(3): pp. 367–378.

De Knop, P., Theeboom, M., Wittock, H. and DeMartelaer, K. (1996) 'Implication of Islam on Muslim Girl's Sport Participation in Western Europe', *Sport, Education and Society*, 1(2): pp. 147–164.

Di-Capua, Y. (2005) 'Women, Gender, Sports and the Female Body: Arab States', in S. Joseph and A. Najmabandi *et al.* (eds) *Encyclopaedia of Women and Islamic Cultures*, Leiden: Brill: pp. 440–441.

Elling, A., De Knop, P. and Knoppers, A. (2001) 'The Integrating and Differentiating Significance of Sport', in J. Steenbergen, P. De Knop and A. Elling (eds) *Values and Norms in Sport*. Oxford: Meyer and Meyer Sport.

Eqbali, A. (2007) 'Iranian Women Tackle Rugby in Islamic Republic'. Accessed online at: www.middle-east-online.com/ENGLISH/?id=22828 (27 December 2009).

Esfandiari, G. (2007) 'Football Board Fails to Sanction Muslim Hijab'. Accessed online at: www.payvand.com/news/07/mar/1374.html

Esfandiari, G. (2010) 'No Hijab on the Soccer Field'. Accessed online at: www.payvand.com/news/10/apr/1035.htmlwww.payvand.com/news/10/apr/1035.html

Farooq, S. (2011) '"Tough Talk", Muscular Islam and Football: Young British Pakistani Muslim Masculinities', in D. Burdsey (ed.) *'Race', Ethnicity and Football: Persisting Debates and Emergent Issues*, London: Routledge.

Farooq, S. and Parker, A. (2009) 'Sport, Physical Education and Islam: Muslim Independent Schooling and the Construction of Masculinities', *Sociology of Sport Journal*, 26(3): pp. 277–295.

Faruqi, L.A. (1994) *Women, Muslim Society and Islam*. (2nd edition). Indiana, USA: American Trust Publication.

Feminist Wire (2012) 'The Hijab on the Pitch'. Accessed online at: www.thefeministwire.com/2012/08/the-hijab-on-the-pitch/

Foucault, M. (1980) *Power/Knowledge: Selected Interviews and Other Writings (1972–1977)*, Suffolk, UK: The Harvester Press.

Goodwin, J. (1995) *Price of Honour: Muslim Women Lift the Veil of Silence on the Islamic World*, London: Warner Books.

Grace, D. (2004) *The Woman in the Muslin Mask: Veiling and Identity in Postcolonial Literature*, London, Sterling, Virginia: Pluto Press.

Hall, S. (2000a) 'Who Needs "Identity"?' in P.D. Gay, J. Evans and P. Redman (eds) *Identity: A Reader*, London: Sage.

Hall, S. (2000b) 'Old and New Identities, Old and New Ethnicities', in L. Back and J. Solomos (eds) *Theories of 'Race' and Racism*, London: Routledge.

Hargreaves, J. (2000) 'The Muslim Female Heroic: Shorts or Veils?' in J. Hargreaves (ed.) *Heroines of Sport: The Politics of Difference and Identity*, London: Routledge.

Hargreaves, J. (2007) 'Sport, Exercise and the Female Muslim Body', in J. Hargreaves and P. Vertinsky (eds) *Physical Culture, Power and the Body*, London: Routledge: pp. 74–100.

Hauglad, K. (2012) 'Leotard'. Accessed online at: http://fashion-history.lovetoknow.com/clothing-types-styles/leotard.

Hekman, S.J. (1990) *Gender and Knowledge: Elements of a Post-modern Feminism*, Cambridge: Polity Press.

Hillyer, S. (2008) 'A Woman's Place is at Home: Women's Perceptions of Playing Fast-Pitch Softball in the Islamic Republic of Iran', *Copenhagen Summer Institute*, Copenhagen, Denmark.

Hillyer, S. (2011) The Iranian women's softball team. Presented at NASSS.

Ibrahim, H. (1982) 'Leisure and Islam', *Leisure Studies*, 1(2): pp. 197–210.

Ingle, S. (2016) 'British Cycling Must Come Clean over Shane Sutton and Jess Varnish'. Accessed online at: www.theguardian.com/sport/2016/dec/08/british-cycling-jess-varnish-shane-sutton

Ismail, H.F. (1999) *Islam and Sport*, Madrasah Arabia Islamia, South Africa.

Johnson, M.R.D. (2000) 'Perceptions of Barriers to Healthy Physical Activity among Asian Communities', *Sport, Education and Society*, 5(1): pp. 51–70

Kassab, E.S. (2010) *Contemporary Arab Thought: Cultural Critique in Comparative Perspective*, New York: Columbia University Press, pp. 91–112.

Kay, T. (2005) 'The Voice of the Family: Influences on Muslim Girls' Responses to Sport', *LSA Newsletter*, 71: pp. 62–71.

Kay, T. (2006) 'Daughters of Islam: Family Influences on Muslim Young Women's Participation in Sport', *International Review for the Sociology of Sport*, 41(3–4): pp. 357–373.

Kremers, S. *et al.* (2010) 'Palestinian Women's National Football Team Aims High', in T. Benn, G. Pfister and H. Jawad (eds) *Muslim Women and Sport*, London: Routledge.

Mahmood, S. (2005) *Politics of Piety: The Islamic Revival and the Feminist Subject*, Princeton: Princeton University Press.

Martin, W. H., and Mason, S. (2003) 'Leisure in Three Middle Eastern Countries', *World Leisure*, 45(1): pp. 35–44.

Matus, R. (2004) 'Islamic USF Player: Dispute over Uniform Led to Dismissal'. Accessed online at: www.prohijab.net/english/USA-hijab-news.htm

Mernissi, F. (1975) *Beyond the Veil: Male–Female Dynamics in a Modern Muslim Society*, Indiana: Bloomington Press.

Moghissi, H. (1999) *Feminism and Islamic Fundamentalism. The Limits of Post-Modern Analysis*, London: Zed Books.

Moghtader, M.M. (2011) 'FIFA Disqualifies Iranian Women's Soccer Team for Wearing Hijab'. Accessed online at: http://globalpublicsquare.blogs.cnn.com/2011/06/17/fifa-disqualifies-iranian-womens-soccer-team-for-wearing-hijab/

Mohanty, C.T. (1988) 'Under Western Eyes: Feminist Scholarship and Colonial Discourses', *Feminist Review*, 30(1): pp. 61–89.

Mohanty, C.T. (1991) 'Cartographies of Struggle: Third World Women and the Politics of Feminism', in C.T. Mohanty, A. Russo and L. Torres (eds) *Third World Women and the Politics of Feminism*, Bloomington: Indiana University Press: pp. 2–47.

Mohanty, C.T. (2002) '"Under Western Eyes" Revisited: Feminist Solidarity Through Anti-Capitalist Struggles', *Signs: Journal of Women in Culture and Society*, 28(2): pp. 499–535.

Mohanty, C.T. (2003) *Feminism without Borders: Decolonizing Theory, Practicing Solidarity*, Durham, North Carolina and London: Duke University Press.

Morgan, W.J. (1998) 'Hassiba Boulmerka and Islamic Green: International Sports, Cultural Differences and Their Postmodern Interpretation', in G. Rail (ed.) *Sport and Postmodern Times*, Albany, USA: State University of New York Press: pp. 345–366 .

Naciri, M. (1993) 'The Islamic Position in Sport', in *Sport in the Modern World. Chances and Problems*. Scientific Congress, Munich Olympics. Berlin: Springer Verlag.

Nakamura, Y. (2002) 'Beyond the Hijab: Female Muslims and Physical Activity', *Women in Sport & Physical Activity Journal*, 11: pp. 21–48.

Patai, R. (1973) *The Arab Mind*, New York: Charles Scribner's Sons.

Pfister, G. (2000) 'Doing Sport in a Headscarf? German Sport and Turkish Females', *The Journal of Sport History*, 27(30): pp. 497–523.

Pfister, G. (2003) 'Women and Sport in Iran: Keeping Goal in the Hijab', in I. Hartmann-Tews and G. Pfister (eds) *Sport and Women. Social Issues in International Perspective*, London: Routledge: pp. 207–223.

Pfister, G. (2010a) 'Outsiders: Muslim Women and Olympic Games', *International Journal of the History of Sport*, 27(16–18): pp. 2925–2957.

Pfister, G. (2010b) 'Women and Sport in Islamic Countries'. Accessed online at: www.idan.dk/vidensbank/downloads/women-and-sports-in-islamic-countries/66143704-113b-41d5-aacc-a39500c1c799

Pye, J. (2008) 'Al-Gassra a Standout in her Hijab'. Accessed online at: www.comcast.net/olympics/story.asp?i=20080819093334411280408&ref=rec&tm=&src=DOLY

Ratna, A., Samie, S.F, Jamieson, K. and Thangaraj, S. (2017) 'Learning Lessons from the Feminisms of Ethnic "Others" ' in L. Mansfield, J. Caudwell, B. Watson and B. Wheaton (eds) *The Handbook for Feminisms in Sport, Leisure and Physical Education*, Basingstoke: Palgrave (in press).

Rodinson, M. (1991) *Europe and the Mystique of Islam*, Seattle: University of Seattle Press.

Rodriguez, E.G., Boatcă, M. and Costa, S. (2010) *Decolonising European Sociology: Transdisciplinary Approaches*, London: Routledge.

Rose, G. (2001) *Visual Methodologies: An Introduction to the Interpretation of Visual Material*, London: Sage.

Said, E. (1978) *Orientalism*, London and Henley: Routledge and Kegan Paul.

Said, E. (1997) *Covering Islam: How the Media and the Experts Determine How We See the Rest of the World*, London: Vintage.

Samie, S.F. (2013) 'Hetero-sexy Self/Body Work and Basketball: The Invisible Sporting Women of Pakistani Muslim Heritage', *Journal of South Asian Popular Culture*, 11(3): pp. 257–270.

Samie, S.F. (2014) 'Heterosexy Self/Body Work and Muslim Women's Basketball', in S. Thangaraj, D. Burdsey and R. Dudrah (eds) *Sport and the South Asian Diaspora*, London: Routledge.

Samie, S.F. (2015) 'Being and Becoming Tomboys: Sport and Muslim Women's Stories', in A. Testa and A. Mahfoud (eds) *Sport, Islam and Muslim Communities*, London, Routledge.

Samie, S.F. and Sehlikoglu, S. (2014) 'Strange, Incompetent and Out-of-Place. Media, Muslim Women and the London 2012 Olympics', *Feminist Media Studies* 15(3): pp. 363–381.

Sfeir, L. (1985) 'The Status of Muslim Women in Sport: Conflict between Cultural Tradition and Modernization', *International Review for the Sociology of Sport*, 20(4): pp. 283–305.

Simmons, M. (1995) 'Muslim Women's Exclusion is Target of New Campaign'. *New York Times*. Accessed online at: www.nytimes.com/1995/01/13/sports/olympics-muslim-women-s-exclusion-is-target-of-new-campaign.html

Smith, L.T. (1999) *De-Colonising Methodologies: Research And Indigenous Peoples*, New York: University of Otago Press.

Sports Plus (2009) 'Swiss Basketball Body Forbids Muslim Headscarf'. Accessed online at: www.womentalksports.com/items/read/15/56271

Toffoletti, K. and Palmer, C. (2015) 'New Approaches for Studies of Muslim Women and Sport', *International Review for the Sociology of Sport*, 52(2): pp. 146–163.

Waljee, A. (2008) 'Researching Transitions: Gendered Education, Marketisation and Islam in Tajikistan', in S. Fennell and M. Arnot (eds) *Gender Education and Equality in a Global Context*, London: Routledge: pp. 87–101.
Walseth, K. (2006a) 'Young Muslim Women and Sport: The Impact of Identity Work', *Leisure Studies*, 25(1): pp. 75–94.
Walseth, K. (2006b) 'Sport and Belonging', *International Review for the Sociology of Sport*, 41(3–4): pp. 447–464.
Walseth, K. and Fasting, K. (2003) 'Islam's View on Physical Activity and Sport: Egyptian Women Interpreting Islam', *International Review for the Sociology of Sport*, 38(1): pp. 45–60.
Walseth, K. and Fasting, K. (2004) 'Sport as a Means of Integrating Minority Women', *Sport in Society*, 7(1): pp. 109–129.

Chapter 3

Theoretical considerations in the examination of African American girls and women in sport

Akilah R. Carter-Francique

Introduction

The purpose of this chapter is to understand the need for critical theories to examine the sporting experiences of Black women. As marginalised persons, Black women in America such as Lucy Diggs Slowe (tennis), Alice Coachman (tennis and golf), and Althea Gibson (tennis) have made an impact in sport as pioneers and Wilma Rudolph (track and field), Venus and Serena Williams (tennis), and Gabrielle Douglas (gymnastics) as champions; however, despite their inroads Black women have also endured the harsh realities of access discrimination (i.e. denied access to sport organisations) and treatment discrimination (e.g. negative media portrayals and experiences of both racism and sexism). Moreover, dominant framings of sport in White Western communities suggest sport is counter to womanhood; and thus, women (White and Black) who play sport are often viewed as mannish and/or lesbian (Cahn 1994; Vertinsky and Captain 1998). For African American women, such gender ideologies impact the ways their Black female bodies are further read as 'naturally' suited to sport and/or too muscular and a threat to acceptable codes of (White) sporting femininities (Cahn 1994; Hanks 1979; Smith 1992).

Green *et al.* (1981) and a decade later, Abney and Richey (1991, 1992), also examined African American women's participation in sport and found that racial and gender barriers impacted their involvement. Abney and Richey (1991, 1992) particularly found organisational structures hindered rather than helped African American women's career advancement. The 'good old boys'' network (see Davis 1999; Hoffman 2011; Salter 1996), isolation, tokenism, and the lack of mentors and role models were all stated in their respective studies as factors impacting the lack of African American women in the field. In 2012, on the fortieth anniversary of Title IX of the Education Amendments of 1972 (Title IX), African American women's sport participation emerged, again, as an on-going topic of discussion. A collective of 20 African American women (i.e. administrators, coaches and athletes) of different generations gathered at the Schomberg

Center for Research on Black Culture to discuss the impact of this legislative act since its inception. They acknowledged that African American women's participation rates and athletic scholarship opportunities had increased, but issues of gender and racial marginalisation remained as African American women (a) were predominantly concentrated in two sports – basketball and track and field, (b) had limited access to a broader range of sports such as lacrosse, swimming, and soccer, and (c) had limited representation as collegiate athletic coaches (Rhoden 2012). The discussion concluded that Title IX, in all of its intents and purposes to address gender inequality, managed to reconstruct societal racial inequalities for African American women and women of colour in sport by not better addressing their needs, experiences and sporting aspirations. Thus, the history, hegemonic ideologies, and institutionalised power structures operating in sport marginalize African American women and often stereotypically frame how we understand their relationships with sport. The purpose of this chapter, therefore, is to overview a number of relevant theoretical frameworks which can help researchers to develop a better understanding of African American women's experiences of sport.

Discerning the African American female perspective

The selection of an appropriate theoretical framework for discerning African American women's experiences in sport is important to developing a richer and fuller understanding of their needs and experiences. Moreover, Collins (2000) argues that the marginalisation of African American women creates a standpoint specific to their experiences. This standpoint is demarcated by a collective resistance to dominant hegemonies or dominant cultures (i.e. Caucasian/White male, middle class, able-bodied and heterosexual) in and across various social and cultural institutions such as sport (Collins 2000; St. Jean and Feagin 1998). Examining African American women's experiences from their unique standpoint has the potential to elucidate forms of empowerment (i.e. the achievements of sporting heroes and sheroes), self-expression (i.e. identities and styles of play) and political activism (i.e. for equal pay, racial integration, and challenging social inequalities) (Edwards 1969; George 1992). Whilst sport may hold similar significance to men and other racial groups, African American women's standpoint must be theoretically 're'presented and framed based on the "cultural, personal, and social contexts" that shape their multiple and complex lived realities (Howard-Hamilton 2003, p. 20). Thus, such theoretical tenets enable the development of counter-narratives which make visible alternative understandings of African American women's sporting needs and desires.

But who is best equipped to tell African American women's stories? bell hooks (2000) explicates that African American female scholars are the best people to research and analyse African American women as they share experiences of being an 'outsider within' institutions such as sport. An 'outsider within' accepts that African American women are Othered, but that their relative positions of alterity enable an insider perspective on structures of exclusion and inclusion. That is:

> Living as we did – on the edge – we developed a particular way of seeing reality. We looked both from the outside in and from the inside out. We focused our attention on the center as well as the margin. We understood both. This sense of wholeness impressed upon our consciousness by the structure of our daily lives provided us an oppositional worldview – a mode of seeing unknown to most of our oppressors, that sustained us [...].
>
> (hooks 2000, preface)

African American women's ways of knowing are not monolithic; however, they are informed by a history cultivated from within Black community life and political actions relevant to their individual and collective senses of well-being. Smith (2000) purports "by telling the story" people in society and sport have an opportunity to understand the experiences of African American women contrary to stereotypes and dominant epistemologies that have historically marginalised their voices, lived experiences, and political realities. Embracing Black feminism and its historical traditions, I am in agreement with hooks' belief that the best people to articulate the experiences of African American women are other African American women, but the feasibility that only African American women will examine and, thus, explicate their reality is not realistic, nor controllable.

For example, Liberti and Smith (2015), both White women, wrote a historical account of the African American Olympian Wilma Rudolph. Their contribution to United States (U.S.) race relations history and sports history more specifically is admirable, but one could conceivably understand that the re-telling of Rudolph's life may be interpreted differently if told by African American women. Therefore, beyond the obvious racial disconnect, Rudolph's life experiences may have been re-told by an African American woman to include the heroic significance of her triumphs *and* traumas and the inspirational value of being and representing the African American community as well as African American women more specifically. This observation suggests the potential of an "outsider within" perspective to "foster new angles of vision and oppression" which may not be captured when written from a dominant, racially colourblind, White perspective (Collins 2000, p. 11). Hence, living as an African American woman in the U.S. begets a marginalised existence based on race, gender, and social class that shapes development, interactions, and perspectives. When non-African American women and men (including those of African

American heritage) attempt to re-tell those stories, they run the risk of inaccurately interpreting the sentiment, cultural nuances, and experiences of African American women; and in some cases chose to overlook the insights and contributions of African American women intellectuals. For example, scholars have discussed the varied attempts – of White men and some African American men (Washington 1990) – to write the experiences of African American women and discerned that those writings were filled with inaccurate, misrepresented, distorted, and/or omitted aspects of African American women's lives as they failed to embody their oppressed vantages (Douglas 1988a, 1988b; Oglesby 1981). To overcome this risk, both African American and other male or female researchers need to employ a critical theoretical framework that recognises African American women's experiences of multiple oppressions. Furthermore, when utilising their framework(s) of choice, recognise its systematic and rigorous capacity to illuminate hegemonic ideologies, oppressive structures, cultures and sporting practices as well as moments of resistance, joy and social change.

However, African American women are not all the same. They are different in terms of ethnic heritage, level and type of education, religion, social class, age, skin colour (e.g. lighter skin and darker skin), geographic residence (e.g. northern and southern cities), and socialization practices that culminate their collective experiences; therefore, different Black feminist discourses (e.g. womanism, Black feminist thought, Critical Race feminism, and Hip-Hop feminism) offer varying perspectives and interpretations of African American women's experiences which should be valued and celebrated. According to Bell (2003)

> Black people must come to realize that our greatest strength, our salvation secret, if you will, is Black women [...] our women have functioned without seeking the limelight or the leadership roles that, so often, they perform from self-imposed subordinate positions [...] Black men must understand that Black women know both what should be done and how best to do it in every aspect of our lives: business, educational, political, religious, economic, social, and personal. Just as we acknowledge women's power to give life, we must come to recognize their power to sustain us in life during critical times to come. Black women have always been the salvation secret of our people. It is time for them to assume formally the positions they have always held [...].
>
> (p. xviii)

Thus, Black feminism is not a single way of thinking, but represents a number of discourses which offer inter-connected yet varying perspectives and interpretations of African American women's multiple, intersectional and complex lived experiences.

Black Feminism, intersectionality, and the contribution of African American women

Black feminism was established in the Black community and nurtured by their issues and experiences of oppression. Living in oppressed communities, Black feminists imagined just societies through incremental and radical activists' efforts fuelled by "humanistic visionary pragmatism" (James and Busia 1993, p. 3). The efforts of Ella Baker, Anna Julia Cooper, Rosa Parks, Mary Church Terrell, Harriett Tubman, Sojourner Truth, Ida B. Wells, and a host of other African American women's experiential oppressions, aided in the development of African American women's way of knowing. Thus, Black feminism as a discourse is a combination of historical activisms, and the social movements of the 1960s and 1970s (e.g. Civil Rights Movement, Black Power Movement).

Black feminist theory initially emerged as a way to illuminate African American women's issues: recognising that as a collective, their issues were not the same but different from African American men's and White women's issues. Similar to the positionings of other women of colour (e.g. Hispanic, Asian, Native American), African American women historically lacked privilege in society and sport based on established race, gender, and often social class hierarchies (Smith 1992). However, women of colour are not a homogeneous grouping either and they must be understood in respect of their own unique histories, traditions, experiences, and perspectives. Key writings about Black feminism consist of Toni Cade Bambara's (1970) *The Black Woman: An Anthology*, Barbara Smith's (1983) *Home Girls: A Black Feminist Anthology*, bell hooks' (1981) *Ain't I a Woman*, Angela Davis' (1983) *Women, Race, and Class*, Paula Giddings' (1984) *When and Where I Enter: The Impact of Black Women on Race and Sex in America*, and Audre Lorde's (1984) *Sister Outsider: Essays and Speeches*. These key writings illuminate Black feminist perspectives through the presentation of historical accounts, personal experiences, poetry and prose, and theorising of social, cultural, political, educational, and religious visions in and through the lived experiences of real African American women. James (1993) passionately argues that:

> Although Black women are often characterized as victims, theorizing is a form of agency that provides them with opportunities to "learn, think, imagine, judge, listen, speak, write and act" (Stimson, 1989) – which transforms not only the individual (from victim to activist, for example) but (also the) community, and the (wider) society as well.
>
> (p. 2)

African American women's writings mark the beginnings of Black feminist interventions that challenged oppressive racial and gendered hegemonies and imagined other more egalitarian ways of living. Hence, theorising offers a way to deconstruct and reconstruct ways of knowing in order to make sense of social phenomena; efforts that can promote ways to react, speak up and speak against, and to reimagine a socially just society.

Black feminist thinking and action have always encapsulated the intersections of a raced, gendered, and classed 'Other'; and, in 1989 Kimberlé Crenshaw coined the term 'intersectionality' and contextualized the theoretical underpinnings of Black feminism. Crenshaw's (1991) *Mapping the Margins: Intersectionality, Identity Politics, and Violence Against Women of Color* is one of the seminal writings that presents the significance of intersectionality and its capacity for transformation of organisational policy and practice. Intersectionality explicates that social categorisations are not independent entities, but must be understood in terms of how they connect and reinforce one another. Discussed in Chapter 1 also, intersectionality examines the intersection of marginalised identities within institutions, or systems of domination, that promote oppression, discrimination, and social inequities. In sport, this is evident through studies that attempt to unveil social injustices based upon a range of diverse categorizations including race, gender and sexual orientation (see Anderson and McCormack 2010; Bandya *et al.* 2014; Hills and Kennedy 2009). Intersectionality has also been used to unveil issues of marginalisation for African American women in sport. These writings include Mathewson's (1995) *Black Women, Gender, Equity and the Function at the Junction* that employs intersectionality to illuminate how policy and practices preference one social marginalisation over another; and, thus, discount the value and multiplicative effects of being both Black and female.

On the following pages, I will present four theoretical frameworks which are grounded in thinking intersectionally: womanism, Black feminist thought, Critical Race feminism, and Hip-Hop feminism. Whilst the four theoretical frameworks are rooted in the intellectual insights of Black women, their conception, definition(s), philosophical stance(s), and ability to articulate the African American woman's experience in sport and society varies. Through explicating the theories, I will delineate how the intersectional nature of African American women's experiences in and through sport can be better understood and unpacked.

Womanist theory

Womanism was a movement birthed out of the exclusion of African American women from within the White middle class feminist movement. The term was coined by Alice Walker, famed author of *The Color Purple*, who stated that "Womanist is to feminist as purple is to lavender" (1983b). Walker's statement intimated that feminist theory did not include the perspectives of African American women and was, thus, deemed to contain some racist elements that bolstered ways of knowing and intellectualising White (frequently middle class) women's experiences, positions and perspectives. Walker (1983b) articulates the distinctions of this framework more clearly with

> Womanism is simply another shade of feminism. It helps give visibility to the experience of black women and other women of colour who have always been at the forefront of the feminist movement yet marginalized and rendered invisible in historical texts and the media.

Therefore, womanism served as an inclusive response to the social and political marginalisations of African American women and women of colour more broadly from the White feminist movement.

In 1983, Walker detailed a four-part definition of womanism, or womanist theory, in *In Search of Our Mothers' Garden: Womanist Prose* that presents it as:

> (a) Womanish [...] the opposite of girlish [...]. A black feminist or feminist of color; (b) A woman who loves other women, sexually and/or nonsexually. Appreciates and prefers women's culture, women's emotional flexibility, and women's strength; (c) Loves music. Loves dance. Loves the moon. Loves the *Spirit.* Loves love and food and roundness. Loves struggle. *Loves* the Folk. Loves herself. *Regardless*; and, (d) Womanist is to feminist as purple is to lavender.
>
> (1983a, p. xii)

This four-part definition presents the origin of the term womanism as steeped in the Black community's notion of what it means to be a grown woman. It suggests a womanist is a lover of women, but does not necessarily advocate for separatism from men. A womanist is a universalist that embraces all women of all races and is dedicated to understanding the wholeness of both women and men. Moreover, a womanist fights to unveil inequalities for all women that have been silenced and invisible in and through the White feminist movement. Ultimately, womanism is an identity; it is a way of life that desires to end overlapping and intersecting race, gender, and social class marginalities through spirituality and ethical practices for African American women, women of colour, and African women across the diaspora. Extending the sentiment of overlapping and intersecting marginalities, womanism inclusively accounts for race, gender, and social class and other positions of difference such as religion, sexual orientation, age and (dis)ability.

Whilst Walker is credited with conceptualising womanism, other women have also contributed to the development of the theory. Clenora

Hudson-Weems and Chikwenye Okonjo Ogunyemi provide similar, yet alternate definitions of womanism. Hudson-Weems' (1993) text *Africana Womanism: Reclaiming Ourselves* explicates the conceptualisation of Africana womanism which she states differs from Walker's womanism. Hudson-Weems' Africana feminist theology aligns itself with Black Nationalist rhetoric that embraces collectivist rather than individualist ideals. Counter to Weems, Ogunyemi's Nigerian roots contribute to her theoretical perspective on womanism. She, like Walker, envisions a space where Black women and men can work in tandem to address racial inequalities; yet unlike Walker, Ogunyemi (and Hudson-Weems') do not foresee any reconciliation nor joining efforts with White feminists to address issues that impact Black women. Unfortunately, these divergent definitions, and their failure to address sexuality more explicitly, create tensions within womanist theoretical standpoints and linked activism. In sport, womanism does not seem to have the same traction as other Black feminist theories (see below). But, to date, womanism has helped to elucidate U.S. sporting activities (e.g. cheerleading; Johnson 2015) as well as sporting activities for African women beyond the U.S. (Burnett 2002; Manyonganise 2010).

For example, in 2010 Manyonganise examined Black African people (15 women, 10 teenage girls, 5 men) in Harare, Zimbabwe to understand their respective involvements in sport. Guided by African womanism, the findings for the women and girls revealed that the concept of safe spaces was a hindrance and a help. In this study, the church as an institution was highlighted as a reserved safe space for women in Zimbabwe; however, its rules (e.g. dictating women's attire) as a religious institution created barriers based on philosophical beliefs about the role of women. Conversely, for the African girls and women, participation in the institution of sport was deemed as an unclean activity that promoted perceived deviant behaviour (e.g. prostitution). Employing womanism highlighted how cultural norms and ethnic traditions marginalised women in Zimbabwe, and it simultaneously unveiled how the girls and women's sport participation served as a site of empowerment through building women-filled social networks that promoted 'voice' and discussion between women on issues that were germane to their cultural, economic, political, and health and wellness needs and desires. Based on this study, the use of womanism as a Black feminist theory demonstrated the benefits of the institution of sport and sport participation, whilst unveiling the ideological barriers that Black African women from Zimbabwe must navigate to gain pleasure and a sense of purpose in and through involvement in sport.

Black feminist thought

Conceptualised by Patricia Hill-Collins in the 1990s, Black feminist thought is committed to social justice, emancipation, and the empowerment of oppressed women of colour (Collins 1986, 2000). Black feminist thought grew out of the Civil Rights Movement, and the movement's inherent focus on African American men, as well as critiques of the White feminist movement (see above). Collins (2000) emphasises three themes to address the intersectional experiences of African American women: (a) the meaning of self-definition and self-valuation, (b) the interlocking nature of oppression, and (c) the importance of African American women's culture (Collins 1986, 2000). Black feminist thought has been widely used to understand African American women's experiences in education (see Howard-Hamilton 2003; Hull *et al.* 1982); law and politics (see Crenshaw, 1989; Simien, 2004); women's studies (see Guy-Shefthall 1995; King 1988); family studies (see Few 2007; Few *et al.* 2003), and adolescent sexual scripts (see Stephens and Phillips, 2003). Despite Black feminist thought's usefulness in contextualising the realities of African American women in society across a number of institutions, as a theory it has also been criticised. A majority of the criticisms toward Black feminist thought come from Hip-Hop feminists, or third wave feminists (see jamila 2002; Morgan 1999; Pough 2002, 2003), who believe proponents of Black feminist thought (a) fail to engage in challenging the politics of pre-dominant Western feminisms (Collins 2006) and (b) decidedly take a standpoint of the victim (Morgan 1999). In rebuttal, Collins (1989) states Black feminist thought is situated in the experiences of African American women in the Civil Rights era and a generation that was viewed as monolithic and fighting for racial equality, abortion rights, and the war on drugs. Despite the criticism and generational debates, Black feminist thought shows merit in demonstrating the complexity of African American women's oppression. Collins (1989, 2000) powerfully reveals the complex operation of racism, classism, and sexism and how this leads to a compilation of negative historical and stereotypical images, or derogatory caricatures (e.g. Mammy, Sapphire, Jezebel, Welfare mother) which render invisible, and silence and control African American women's relationships to their bodies, family, African American men and wider society (see Bogle 2001; Collins 2000; hooks 1981; Pieterse 1992; St. Jean and Feagin 1998). More clearly, scholars note these historical images were created as a means to control and justify the treatment (i.e. rape) and oppression of African American women (Collins 2000; St. Jean and Feagin 1998). Collins (2000) sadly contends,

> As part of a generalized ideology of domination, stereotypical images of Black (African American) womanhood takes on special meaning. Because the authority to define societal values is a major instrument of power, elite groups (e.g., Whites/males), in exercising power, manipulate ideas about Black womanhood. They do so by exploiting already existing symbols, or creating new ones [...]. These (historical)

> controlling images are designed to make racism, sexism, poverty, and other forms of social injustice appear to be natural, normal, and inevitable parts of everyday life.
>
> (p. 86)

Such historical images have persisted throughout the generations, and been reinvented and reaffirmed by the next generation. For instance, Stephens and Phillips (2003) provide a thorough account on the impact of negative historical images and how these images have manifested in present day. Specifically, they argue African American girls and women's contemporary visual representations, or more accurately their sexual scripts as 'Freak', 'Gold Digger', 'Diva', and 'Dike' are rooted to historical images, are absorbed and internalised by African American women, shaping their identities and perceptions of 'self' across their lifespans (e.g. Mon'e Davis, Serena Williams, 2007 Rutgers Women's Basketball team; see Chase 2015; Perry 2015; Rishe 2015; Ryan 2015; Soong 2015).

Black feminist thought, grounded within the lives and voices of different African American women, also recognises their agency and how they find meaning in their existence as well as refute negative historical images and stereotypes. As such, Black feminist thought has been useful to elucidate the multiple and complex structures, discourses and agencies that affect African American women's sporting experiences. In 2005, Bruening, Armstrong, and Pastore (a White and Black female research team) employed Black feminist thought in their study *Listening to the Voices: The Experiences of African American Female Student Athletes*. Bruening and colleagues (2005) sought to understand the sport participation patterns of African American female college athletes. The scholars centred the African American women in their examination and discovered that media coverage, athletic administrators, coaches, and other college athletes' efforts to support their participation were lacking due to emphasis on African American male athletes and revenue producing sports, the majority of which happened to be male. The findings revealed that when allowed the opportunity to be heard, African American female college athletes shared their disappointments in the perpetuation of stereotypes about their physicality, awareness of Whites' dominance in the media and positions of power, and the desire to be treated with respect (i.e. not as sexual objects).

In addition to Bruening's scholarship, other scholars have examined African American women's experiences within historically White institutions of higher education utilising a Black feminist standpoint (see Armstrong 2007; Bruening 2004; Bruening *et al.* 2005; Carter 2008; Carter and Hart 2010; Carter and Hawkins 2011; Carter-Francique 2013; Withycombe 2011; Smith 2000). Within these studies, re-occurring themes of marginalisation based on African American women's interlocking identities are revealed; however, despite identified personal and systemic barriers rooted in racism, sexism, and classism (i.e. limited media exposure, negative coaching relationships, experiences of discrimination in the local community), Black feminist thought illuminated how the African American women consciously and unconsciously relied on various cultural traditions (i.e. use of religion and the church; Jones and Shorter-Gooden 2003) and other forms of resilience (i.e. self-talk, reliance on familial networks like their foremothers did) to navigate themselves in, through, and out of those institutions.

In the U.S., I examined 2012 Olympic gold medallist Gabrielle Douglas's electronic and digital media accounts to understand how her experience was framed. Utilising Black feminist thought, I found that the media, particularly social media, entailed racial and gendered framing when capturing her experiences (e.g. "nickname as a site of exploitation", and "hair as a standard of beauty" (see Carter-Francique 2013). Employing Black feminist thought in this study highlighted that Douglas's mediated experiences were not unique to sport, but rooted in and connected to African American women's social location and interlocking identities. For example, I argued how the theme of 'nicknames as a site of exploitation' (e.g. Douglas given the nickname 'flying squirrel' by famed White female gymnastic coach Márta Károlyi) illuminated the need and importance of African American women's ability to define themselves to present an image that is authentic and reflective of who they are and want to be. Whilst the theme 'hair as a standard of beauty' reflected how notions of race and gender superiority worked together, or interlocked, to derogate African American women and their womanhood for their inability to meet dominant society's beauty standards, which are rooted in notions of White womanhood and include long hair and blue eyes (Collins 2000).

Through these examinations, Black feminist thought provided a counter-narrative that elevated the voice of different African American women and began to situate ways of knowing their realities away from various controlling images.

Critical Race feminism

Critical Race feminism stems from Critical Race Theory (CRT) in the 1990s. In 2005, Yosso presented a visual genealogy of CRT to include varying expansions. These expanded theories of AsianCrit, LatCrit, and TribalCrit explored the effects of an oppressive legal system on racial Others and women beyond the Black/White binary of CRT. Led by women of colour that practise and/or teach law, CRF speaks to African American women *and* Asian, Latina, and Native American women's social justice efforts. Hence, pioneering women like Lani Guiner, Anita Hill, Kimberlé Crenshaw, Mari Matsuda, and Patricia Williams contribute to the development of this framework. And, whilst the names may be familiar, this theoretical framework is not as well known and has been somewhat engulfed by CRT.

Fortunately, Adrien Wing's (2003) *Critical Race Feminism: A Reader* provides a collection of essays that speak to the varying issues, concerns, and themes on women of colour to include debates about (a) essentialism and anti-essentialism; (b) outsiders in the academy and profession; (c) mothering; (d) criminality; (e) domestic violence; (f) working, and (g) bordering identities. Critical Race feminism is closely tied to CRT (e.g. endemic nature of racism, permanence of racism, multidisciplinary approach, use of narratives and storytelling), but Wing (2003) characterises Critical Race feminism as a self-described feminist intervention within CRT. In addition, Critical Race feminism embraces notions of theory *and* praxis as it emboldens engagement with the researched community so that theoretical findings can promote real life change. Praxis in Critical Race feminism can consist of "assisting clients, drafting legislation, serving on Bar Association committees, designing innovative legal strategies, joining in practical coalitions, and mentoring a student or child" (Wing 2003, p. 17).

Critical Race feminism has demonstrated merit though analysing the range of issues in their respective institutions; however, there is a dearth of research that employs Critical Race feminism in the institution of sport. Nevertheless, there is value with employing this framework. Such employment may be in the methodology and how the research is framed. For instance, reviewing Hannon and colleagues' (2009) examination on the role of gender and race with adolescent sport involvement highlighted its use of critical feminist theories; however, specifically employing Critical Race feminism could have provided a deeper and more meaningful analysis of the intersections of race and gender to describe the cultural meanings of sport for different racial groups of girls and boys included within the research. Moreover, illuminating the theoretical and sociocultural significance of sport would have been beneficial to link this to practical resources for teachers to implement with students. For instance, in 2005 Azzarito and Solomon provided practical examples to promote the inclusion of youth that live at the intersections of race and social class. These scholars demonstrated (although not necessarily identifying with) the principles of Critical Race feminism as they aimed to redesign effective curricula programmes to directly engage with marginalised groups through open and honest conversations. Thus, they were using their theoretical knowledge to engage diverse students in and beyond the field of Physical Education.

Hip-Hop feminism

Similar to Critical Race feminism, the fourth and final framework that will be discussed is also not widely used in the study of sport. Hip-Hop feminism is described as Black feminist thought positioned in Hip-Hop culture

(Collins 2006; Durham 2007). Joan Morgan (1999), author of *When Chickenheads Come Home to Roost: A Hip-Hop Feminist Breaks it Down*, coined the term 'Hip-Hop feminist'. Morgan, Gwendolyn Pough (2003), and Rachel Raimist (1999) promote the need for Hip-Hop feminism as a response to contemporary societal issues that marginalise African American women (i.e. misogyny, body politics, mediated images). In *Home Girls Make Some Noise: Hip Hop Feminism Anthology*, Durham (2007) defines Hip-Hop feminism as:

> a socio-cultural, intellectual and political movement grounded in the situated knowledge of women of color from the post-Civil Rights generation who recognized culture as a pivotal site for political intervention to challenge, resist and mobilize collectives to dismantle systems of exploitation.
>
> (p. 306)

Emerging during the mid-1990s, Hip-Hop feminism endorses the notion of social justice and consciousness by using various technological and cultural mediums like film, art, and music to challenge the African American community's and African American men's misogynistic behaviour and ideas (Collins 2006). Accordingly, Hip-Hop feminism challenges African American women's consciousness and understanding of their: (a) relationships to their personal and political histories; (b) relationship to self; and, (c) relationships to African American men (Chambers 1996; Collins 2006; Jones 1994; Morgan 1999; Springer 2002). Due to the contemporary pervasiveness of Hip-Hop, Morgan (2007) conveys that it has an "increasing stronghold in American pop culture" (p. 476); and, as such, the stronghold and commodification leaves young African American women with mixed emotions of affirmation and disempowerment, and no safe space to critically assess those emotions.

Hip-Hop feminists provide a theoretical perspective, 'a way of knowing' that addresses the complex experiences of African American women who are part of the Hip-Hop generation. For instance, as a person considers empowering African American women in the twenty-first century they must consider her generational realities in addition to the management and culture of different societal institutions. Scholars and second wave feminists have criticised Hip-Hop feminism for (a) its inability to approach issues of misogyny from a societal perspective, rather than personal; (b) the lack of social and political strategies to address oppressive realities; and, (c) Hip-Hop feminists articulating the same message as Black feminists regarding the need for social change (Morgan 1999; Peoples 2008; Springer 2002). Ultimately, the critics contend that Hip-Hop feminists are reinventing the proverbial Black feminist wheel. Thus, critics feel Hip-Hop feminists should focus on three issues: (a) discuss sexuality and its complexities, (b) focus on economic well-being, and (c) consider the cultural norms of African Americans.

Ifekwunigwe (2009) employed Hip-Hop feminism to examine tennis greats Venus and Serena Williams. Ifekwunigwe (2009) sought to understand how politics, economics, social class, and the structural status of African American women as well as generational politics affect the media's 're'presentation of the Hip-Hop generation sisters and their celebrity. More pointedly, the examination of the Williams sisters through the mediated imagery of the 'on the court' working-class 'ghetto Cinderella' and the 'off the court' entitled 'Black American Princess' demonstrates the polarising and capitalistic potential of their success. Derivatives of the aforementioned historic images, Ifekwunigwe (2009) denotes that these images reflect the Williams' accessibility to a wider and more diverse audience due to their success, rise to fame, and upward mobility from Compton, California to number one national and international rankings in a sport historically reserved for White elites. Thus, she alludes that the sisters' imagery is justified due to the 'truth' of their socioeconomic beginnings, and ultimately, a truth and history embraced by the sisters for their ability to attract a range of people (e.g. age, race, ethnicity, socioeconomic background) to the sport and acquisition of endorsements.

To the critics' points, Ifekwunigwe (2009) powerfully explicated how Hip-Hop feminism captured the complexity of how being an African American female, athlete, and a celebrity can simultaneously empower and disempower. The illumination of this complexity is significant within this framework as the cultural institution of sport can serve as a site for African American women to enact efforts of social justice to promote social mobility like Venus Williams' quest for women's equal pay at Wimbledon (see Shreedhar 2015). Thus, Hip-Hop feminism can address the current conditions and efforts of African American women. However, Morgan (1999) exclaims, "we are the daughters of feminist privilege [...] . We walk through the world with a sense of entitlement that women of our mother's generation could not begin to fathom" (p. 59). This entitlement is connected to Hip-Hop culture: the concomitant assertion of social rights and life-choice as well as the more confident calling-out of persisting and emerging inequalities.

Acknowledging this sentiment, I appreciate Hip-Hop's spirit of African American, Caribbean, and Latino expression through language (e.g. Black English), art (i.e. graffiti) and dance (i.e. break dancing), and clothing (e.g. FUBU, Cross Colours). That said, I am of the Hip-Hop generation, and am profoundly impacted by the lyrical consciousness of Queen Latifah, Salt-N-Pepa, Mary J. Blige, Jill Scott, and Erykah Badu. The words of these artists and lyrical poets promote feelings of empowerment and achievable dreams. This example reaffirms Morgan's (1999) perspective which conveys, "Sexism may be a very real part of my life but so is the unwavering belief that there is no dream I can't pursue and achieve simply because 'I'm a woman'" (p. 59). Therefore, Hip-Hop feminism and Hip-Hop's voice work to unite women, bridge communities, and connect generations. Accordingly, there are some persons, communities, and scholars that are not appreciative of the cultural notions of Hip-Hop. Still, Alridge and Stewart (2005) assert:

> Hip Hop must be taken seriously as a cultural, political, economic, and intellectual phenomenon deserving of scholarly study, similar to previous African American artistic and cultural movements such as the Blues, Jazz, the New Negro Renaissance, and the Civil Rights, Black Power, and Black Arts Movements.
>
> (p. 190)

Nonetheless, there is a dearth of examinations that employ Hip-Hop feminism in sport; however, Hip-Hop as a cultural tradition has been examined. Harrison, Moore, and Evans (2006) examined male and female college athletes' engagement in a learning community. The premise of the learning community is to encourage education, social support, and faculty interaction through the implementation of two academic courses which employed Hip-Hop, sport, and a race-based curriculum. The authors indicated a positive benefit for some African American college athletes due to social and intellectual engagement and an attention to cultural learning styles (e.g. relational cognitive style, expressive creativity, oral expression) in which Hip-Hop and rap elicited verbal expressions and creativity. Whilst Hip-Hop was not the primary impetus for the learning community, Hip-Hop did prove to be a valuable medium for the emancipation and empowerment of these African American college athletes (Harrison *et al.* 2006). Therefore, Hip-Hop can serve as a possible tool to understand the experiences of African American women.

Peoples (2008) views Hip-Hop feminism as a "generational and culturally relevant vehicle" (p. 25) that has the potential to not only understand younger generations, but also to unveil contemporary spheres of power, provide critical analysis, and empower African American women (Collins 2006; Peoples 2008). Collins' (2006) *From Black Power to Hip-Hop: Racism, Nationalism, and Feminism* discusses Hip-Hop's significance and contributions to Black feminism, and in doing so, she promotes how this framework can support the next generation by giving voice and purpose to women removed from their mother's and grandmothers' feminisms. Moreover, Durham (2007) proclaims, "If Hip-Hop feminism is to move in the minds, hearts, and hands of this generation, we must continue to pose new questions that open up new opportunities for feminist activism across generations" (p. 309). Thus, Hip-Hop feminism as a theoretical framework is still evolving, but it too has the viable potential to explicate the contemporary experiences of African American women in/beyond sports. The opportunity to understand rhetoric from a post-Civil Rights generation that is steeped in present day race, gender, and class cultural teachings and the influence of music, art, and social media can be beneficial to articulating the experiences of young people (i.e. generation X, generation Y, and generation Z). Contemporary researchers addressing issues of African American women's sport participation rates (i.e. youth level, collegiate level), advancement in coaching and administration (e.g. collegiate athletic directors and coaches), and athlete activism (e.g. Black Lives Matter protests, women's equal pay) could attain new and greater considerations through a Hip-Hop feminist lens that aids in actioning social change.

Conclusion

African American women's social locations at the margins of sport and society require re-addressing, yet the failure to effectively acknowledge their realities has the potential to minimise deeper understandings of their everyday lived experiences, devaluing their social contributions, and perpetuating exclusionary practices and forms of discrimination. Therefore, it is imperative that examinations acknowledge the complex, diverse and multiple experiences of African American women. Scholars of all races, ethnicities and gender, who choose to include African American women in their research, must centre African American woman and aim to better understand the nature of intersecting identities and forms of marginalisation that African American women experience and resist. The presentation of the four theoretical frameworks rooted in Black feminism provides an opportunity to interrogate sport from the viewpoints of African American women. Whilst the presentation of an extensive history of the frameworks was beyond the scope of this chapter, the inclusion of referential works was provided to allow scholars and interested persons to further delve into the histories, critiques, and nuances of Black feminist theorising. Arguably, grounded in relation to the theorisings of African American intellectuals, and the need to think intersectionally, the four theoretical frameworks presented in this chapter have similar concerns and divergent areas of focus. Womanist theory recognises the significance of African American women's sisterhood to promote social justice for them, other women of colour, and the African American community more broadly. Black feminist thought acknowledges African American women's historical experiences and traditions as a marginalised group, and encourages use of voice and self-advocacy to promote social justice. Critical Race feminism speaks to the marginalisation of African American women, in addition to Asian, Hispanic, and Native American women as racial and ethnic 'Others', and, likewise, promotes social justice through voice and direct policy-making.

And Hip-Hop feminism attends to the conscious and unconscious realities of the younger generations of African American women that are engulfed and influenced by modern day technology and social media, yet interested in new techniques and strategies to address systemic marginalisations and social injustices. The point of overviewing the different yet connected ways African American women's experiences of sport can be framed and understood is to offer both scholars and practitioners opportunities to re-think and re-develop alternative ways of understanding African American women's relationships with sport. Moreover, these frameworks offer the opportunity to develop counter-narratives that are separate to problematic discourses and images, and are relevant to who African American women are as well as to make visible the myriad of ways that they may choose to express their agency and action social change.

References

Abney, R. and Richey, D. (1991) 'Barriers encountered by Black female athletic administrators and coaches', *Journal of Physical Education, Recreation & Dance*, *62*(6), pp. 19–21.

Abney, R. and Richey, D.L. (1992) 'Opportunities for minority women in sport – the impact of Title IX', *Journal of Physical Education, Recreation & Dance*, *63*(3), pp. 56–59.

Alridge, D.P. and Stewart, J.B. (2005) 'Introduction: Hip hop in history: Past, present, and future', *The Journal of African American History*, *90*(3), pp. 190–195.

Anderson, E. and McCormack, M. (2010) 'Intersectionality, critical race theory, and American sporting oppression: Examining Black and gay male athletes', *Journal of Homosexuality*, *57*(8), pp. 949–967.

Armstrong, K.L. (2007) 'The nature of Black women's leadership in community recreation sport: An illustration of Black feminist thought', *Women in Sport & Physical Activity Journal*, *16*(1), p. 3.

Azzarito, L. and Solomon, M.A. (2005) 'A reconceptualization of physical education: The intersection of gender/race/social class', *Sport, Education and Society*, *10*(1), pp. 25–47.

Bambara, T.C. (ed.) (1970) *The black woman: An anthology* (Vol. 1433), New York: Signet.

Bandya, S.J., Gorib, G., and Jinxiac, D. (2012) 'From women and sport to gender and sport: Transnational, transdisciplinary, and intersectional perspectives', *The International Journal of the History of Sport*, *29*(5), pp. 667–674.

Bell, D. (2003) 'Foreword to the first edition', in A.K. Wing (ed.) *Critical race feminism: A reader*, New York: NYU Press, pp. xvii–xxi.

Bogle, D. (2001) *Toms, coons, mulattoes, mammies, and bucks: An interpretive history of Blacks in American films*, New York: Bloomsbury Publishing.

Bruening, J.E. (2004) 'Coaching difference: A case study of 4 African American women student-athletes', *The Journal of Strength & Conditioning Research*, *18*(2), pp. 242–251.

Bruening, J.E., Armstrong, K.L., and Pastore, D.L. (2005) 'Listening to the voices: The experiences of African American female student athletes', *Research Quarterly for Exercise and Sport*, *76*(1), pp. 82–100.
Burnett, C. (2002) 'Women, poverty and sport: A South African scenario', *Women in Sport & Physical Activity Journal*, *11*(1), p. 23.
Cahn, S. (1994) *Coming on strong: Gender and sexuality in twentieth-century women's sport*, New York: Free.
Carter, A. (2008) Negotiating identities: Examining African American female collegiate athlete experiences in predominantly white institutions. Unpublished Dissertation, University of Georgia.
Carter, A.R. and Hart, A. (2010) 'Perspectives of mentoring: The Black female student-athlete', *Sport Management Review*, *13*(4), pp. 382–394.
Carter, A.R. and Hawkins, B.J. (2011) 'Coping strategies among African American female collegiate athletes in the predominantly white institution', in K. Hylton, A. Pilkington, P. Warmington, and S. Housee (eds) *Atlantic crossings: International dialogues in critical race theory*, Birmingham: C-SAP The Higher Education Network, pp. 61–92.
Carter-Francique, A.R. (2013) 'Black female collegiate athlete experiences in a culturally relevant leadership program', *The National Journal of Urban Education and Practice*, *6*(2), 87–106.
Chambers, V. (1996) *Mama's Girl*. New York: River Books.
Chase, C. (2015) 'Serena Williams ends Indian Wells boycott, 14 years after racist incident', *USA Today*, 4 February. Retrieved from http://ftw.usatoday.com/2015/02/serena-williams-end-indian-wells-boycott-14-years-after-racist-incident
Collins, P.H. (1986) 'Learning from the outsider within: The sociological significance of Black feminist thought', *Social Problems*, pp. S14–S32.
Collins, P.H. (1989) 'The social construction of black feminist thought', *Signs*, *14*(4), pp. 745–773.
Collins, P.H. (2000) *Black feminist thought–knowledge, consciousness, and the politics of empowerment*, London and New York: Routledge.
Collins, P.H. (2006) *From black power to hip hop: Racism, nationalism, and feminism*, Philadelphia: Temple University Press.
Crenshaw, K. (1989) 'Demarginalizing the intersection of race and sex: A black feminist critique of antidiscrimination doctrine, feminist theory and antiracist politics', *University of Chicago Legal Forum*, *1989*(1), p. 139.
Crenshaw, K. (1991) 'Mapping the margins: Intersectionality, identity politics, and violence against women of color', *Stanford Law Review*, *43*(6), pp. 1241–1299.
Davis, A. (1983) *Women, race and class*, New York: Vintage.
Davis, T. (1999) 'Racism in athletics: Subtle yet persistent', *University of Arkansas Little Rock Law Review*, *21*, p. 881.
Douglas, D. (1988a) *Discourses on black women-history of silence: A review of relational analyses in education and sport literatures*. Paper presented at The North American Society for the Sociology of Sport Conference, Cincinnati.
Douglas, D. (1988b) *Race, class and sex: Toward a relational level of analysis of black women's responses to oppression in sport*. Paper presented at the R. Tait McKenzie Symposium on Sport, Knoxville, Tennessee.

Durham, A. (2007) 'Using [living hip hop] feminism: Redefining an answer (to) rap', in G.D. Pough, E. Richardson, A. Durham, and R. Raimist (eds) *Home girls make some noise: Hip-Hop feminism anthology*, New York: Parker Publishing, pp. 304–312.

Edwards, H. (1969) *The revolt of the black athlete*, New York: Free Press.

Few, A.L. (2007) 'Integrating Black consciousness and critical race feminism into family studies research', *Journal of Family Issues*, *28*(4), pp. 452–473.

Few, A.L., Stephens, D.P., and Rouse-Arnett, M. (2003) 'Sister-to-sister talk: Transcending boundaries and challenges in qualitative research with black women', *Family Relations*, *52*(3), pp. 205–215.

George, N. (1992) *Elevating the game: Black men and basketball*, Lincoln: University of Nebraska Press.

Giddings, P. (1984) *When and where I enter: The impact of Black women on sex and race in America*, New York: Morrow and Company.

Green, T.S., Oglesby, C.A., Alexander, A., and Franke, N. (eds) (1981) *Black women in sport*, Reston, Virginia: American Alliance for Health, Physical Education, Recreation and Dance.

Guy-Sheftall, B. (1995) *Words of fire: An anthology of African-American feminist thought*, New York: The New Press.

Hanks, M. (1979) 'Race, sexual status, and athletics in the process of educational achievement', *Social Science Quarterly*, *60*, pp. 482–496.

Hannon, J., Soohoo, S., Reel, J., and Ratliffe, T. (2009) 'Gender stereotyping and the influence of race in sport among adolescents', *Research Quarterly for Exercise and Sport*, *80*(3), pp. 676–684.

Harrison, L., Moore, L.N., and Evans, L. (2006) 'Ear to the streets: The race, hip-hop, and sports learning community at Louisiana State University', *Journal of Black Studies*, *36*(4), pp. 622–634.

Hills, L. and Kennedy, E. (2009) 'Double trouble: Kelly Holmes, intersectionality and unstable narratives of Olympic heroism in the British media', in P. Markula (ed.) *Olympic women and the media: An International Perspective*, UK: Palgrave Macmillan, pp. 112–131.

Hoffman, J. (2011) 'The old boys' network', *Journal for the Study of Sports and Athletes in Education*, *5*(1), pp. 9–28.

hooks, b. (1981) *Ain't I a woman. Black women and feminism*, Boston: South End.

hooks, b. (2000) *From margin to center* (2nd Edition), Boston: South End.

Howard-Hamilton, M.F. (2003) 'Theoretical frameworks for African American women', *New Directions for Student Services*, *2003*(104), pp. 19–27.

Hudson-Weems, C. (1993) African womanism: Reclaiming ourselves, Troy, MI: Bedford Publishers.

Hull, G.T., Bell-Scott, P., and Smith, B. (eds) (1982) *All the women are White, all the men are Black, but some of us are brave*, New York: The Feminist Press.

Ifekwunigwe, J.O. (2009) 'Venus and Serena are "doing it" for themselves: Theorizing sporting celebrity, class and black feminism for the hip-hop generation', in B. Carrington and I. McDonald (eds) *Marxism, cultural studies and sport*, London and New York: Routledge, pp. 130–153.

James, S.M. (1993) 'A possible Black feminist link to social transformation?', in S.M. James and A.P.A. Busia (eds) *Theorizing Black feminisms: The visionary pragmatism of Black women*, London and New York: Psychology Press, pp. 44–54.

James, S.M. and Busia, A.P. (eds) (1993) *Theorizing Black feminisms: The visionary pragmatism of Black women*, London and New York: Psychology Press.

jamila, s. (2002) 'Can I get a witness? Testimony from a hip-hop feminist', in D. Hernandez and B. Rehman (eds) *Colonize this! Young women of color on today's feminism*, New York: Seal Press, pp. 382–394.

Johnson, C.M.E. (2015) '"Just because I dance like a ho I'm not a ho": Cheerleading at the intersection of race, class, and gender', *Sociology of Sport Journal*, *32*(4), 377–394.

Jones, C. and Shorter-Gooden, K. (2003) *Shifting: The double lives of Black women in America*, New York: HarperCollins.

Jones, L. (1994) *Bulletproof diva: Tales of race, sex, and hair*, New York: Doubleday.

King, D.K. (1988) 'Multiple jeopardy, multiple consciousness: The context of a Black feminist ideology', *Signs*, *14*(1), pp. 42–72.

Liberti, R. and Smith, M.M. (2015) *(Re) presenting Wilma Rudolph*, New York: Syracuse University Press.

Lorde, A. (1984) *Sister outsider: Essays and speeches*, Berkeley, California: Crossing Press.

Manyonganise, M. (2010) 'From "safety" zones to public spaces: Women's participation in sport in Zimbabwe', in J. Shehu (ed.) *Gender, sport and development in Africa: Cross-cultural perspectives on patterns of representation and marginalisation*, Dakar: Codesria, pp. 13–26.

Mathewson, A.D. (1995) 'Black women, gender equity and the function at the junction', *Marquette Sports Law Journal*, 6, p. 239.

Morgan, J. (1999) *When Chickenheads come home to roost: My life as a hip hop feminist*, New York: Simon and Schuster.

Morgan, J. (2007) 'Afterword, Joan Morgan', in A. Durham, G.D. Pough, R. Raimist, and E. Richardson (eds) *Home girls make some noise!: Hip-hop feminism anthology*, Mira Loma, California: Parker Pub., pp. 475-480.

Oglesby, C. (1981) 'Myths and realities of black women in sport', in T.S. Green, C.A. Oglesby, A. Alexander, and N. Franke (eds), *Black women in sport*, Reston, Virginia: American Alliance for Health, Physical Education, Recreation and Dance, pp. 1–13.

Peoples, W. (2008) 'Under construction: Identifying foundation of hip-hop feminism and exploring the bridges between second wave and hip-hop feminisms', *Meridians: Feminism, Race, Transnationalism*, *8*(1), pp. 19–52.

Perry, D. (2015) 'College player kicked off team for controversial Mo'ne Davis tweet'. *CBSSports.com*, 22 March. Retrieved from www.cbssports.com/mlb/news/college-player-kicked-off-team-for-controversial-mone-davis-tweet/

Pieterse, J.N. (1992) *White on Black: Images of Africa and Blacks in Western popular culture*, New Haven, Connecticut: Yale University Press.

Pough, G. (2002) 'Love feminism but where's my hip-hop? Shaping a Black feminist identity', in D. Hernandez and B. Rehman (eds), *Colonize this! Young women of color on today's feminism*, New York: Seal Press, pp. 85–95.

Pough, G.D. (2003) 'Do the ladies run this…?: Some thoughts on hip-hop feminism', in R. Dicker and A. Peipmeier (eds) *Catching a wave: Reclaiming*

feminism for the 21st century, Boston: Northeastern University Press, pp. 232–243.
Raimist, R. (1999). Nobody knows my name [Motion Picture]. United States: Women make movies.
Rhoden, W.C. (2012) 'Black and White women far from equal under Title IX'. Retrieved from www.nytimes.com/2012/06/11/sports/title-ix-has-not-given-black-female-athletes-equal-opportunity.html?_r=0
Rishe, P. (2015) 'Does appeal or corporate bias explain endorsement gap between Serena Williams And Maria Sharapova?' *Forbes Magazine*, 6 June. Retrieved from www.forbes.com/sites/prishe/2015/06/06/does-appeal-or-corporate-bias-explain-endorsement-gap-between-serena-williams-and-maria-sharapova/2/#6baf45b03cbf
Ryan, S. (2015). 'Analysis: Why are Serena Williams' curves discussed more than her serves?' *The Chicago Tribune*. Retrieved from www.chicagotribune.com/sports/ct-smack-serena-williams-ryan-spt-0907-20150906-story.html
Salter, D.F. (1996) *Crashing the old boys' network: The tragedies and triumphs of girls and women in sports*, Westport, Connecticut: Greenwood Publishing Group.
Shreedhar, A. (2015) 'The inspiring story of how Venus Williams helped win equal pay for women players at Wimbledon', *Women in the World: Court of Appeals*. Retrieved from http://nytlive.nytimes.com/womenintheworld/2015/07/10/the-inspiring-story-of-how-venus-williams-helped-win-equal-pay-for-women-players-at-wimbledon/
Simien, E.M. (2004) 'Gender differences in attitudes toward black feminism among African Americans', *Political Science Quarterly*, *119*(2), pp. 315–338.
Smith, B. (1983) *Home girls: A Black feminist anthology*, New Brunswick, New Jersey: Rutgers University Press.
Smith, Y.R. (1992) 'Women of color in society and sport', *Quest*, *44*(2), pp. 228–250.
Smith, Y.R. (2000) 'Sociohistorical influences on African American elite sportswomen', in D. Brooks and R. Althouse (eds), *Racism in college athletics: The African American athlete's experience* (2nd ed), Morgantown, WV: Fitness Information Technology, Inc., pp. 173–198.
Soong, K. (2015) 'Serena Williams isn't the world's highest-paid female athlete'. *Washington Post*, 12 August. Retrieved from www.washingtonpost.com/news/early-lead/wp/2015/08/12/serena-williams-isnt-the-worlds-highest-paid-female-athlete/
Springer, K. (2002) 'Third wave feminism?' *Signs*, *27*(4), pp. 1059–82.
St. Jean, Y.S. and Feagin, J.R., 1998. *Double burden: Black women and everyday racism*, New York: ME Sharpe.
Stephens, D.P. and Phillips, L.D. (2003) 'Freaks, gold diggers, divas, and dykes: The sociohistorical development of adolescent African American women's sexual scripts', *Sexuality and Culture*, 7(1), pp. 3–49.
Vertinsky, P. and Captain, G. (1998) 'More myth than history: American culture and representations of the black female's athletic ability', *Journal of Sport History*, *25*(3), pp. 532–561.
Walker, A. (ed.) (1983a) *In search of our mothers' gardens*, San Diego: Harcourt.
Walker, A. (1983b). 'From an interview', in A. Walker (ed.) *In search of our mothers' gardens*, San Diego: Harcourt Brace Jovanovich, pp. 244–272.

Washington, M.H. (1990) 'The darkened eye restored: Notes toward a literary history of black women', in H.L. Gates (ed.) *Reading black, reading feminist: A critical anthology*, New York: Penguin Books, pp. 30–45.
Wing, A.K. (ed.) (2003) *Critical race feminism: A reader* (2nd edition), New York: NYU Press.
Withycombe, J.L. (2011) 'Intersecting selves: African American female athletes' experiences of sport', *Sociology of Sport Journal*, *28*(4), pp. 478–493.
Yosso, T.J. (2005) 'Whose culture has capital? A critical race theory discussion of community cultural wealth', *Race Ethnicity and Education*, *8*(1), pp. 69–91.

Chapter 4

Re-confronting whiteness

Ongoing challenges in sport and leisure research

Beccy Watson and Sheila Scraton

Introduction

As feminist scholars researching leisure and sport, we continue to engage with how we might 'confront' our whiteness, as white women, across the research process. Given our longstanding interest and political commitment to document black and South Asian and BME[1] sport and leisure experiences, confronting whiteness to us means concurrently tackling the "hegemonic discourse of white, middle class, heterosexual and able bodied feminism" (Watson and Scraton, 2001: 275). We use the term 'confront' as an active verb – to us 'confronting' is a necessary response to the question of whiteness – not in a confrontational manner but in our efforts to be responsive in a way that encompasses *both* deconstruction of dominant discourses of whiteness where/when appropriate *and* to highlight processes and actions that researchers are engaged in. Consequently, confronting whiteness is something we attend to as an ongoing process, rather than assuming it as something to be 'accomplished' or as achievable in a completed sense. The focus of our engagement with whiteness remains tied to methodological implications and how we approach researching difference and inequalities.

Some leisure and sport scholars have highlighted different aspects of confronting whiteness, highlighting a number of key challenges that such an endeavour requires (Arai and Kivel, 2009; Hylton, 2005, 2009; Kivel, Johnson and Scraton, 2009; Long and Hylton, 2002; McDonald, 2005, 2009). McDonald (2009, 2014), for example, draws on critical whiteness studies (and the work of Ruth Frankenberg, 1993 in particular) to assert the need to consider power evasiveness and whiteness, normalisation processes and whiteness as intersectionality in leisure and sport scholarship. Her conclusions remind us that whiteness is an ideological process, and she warns that studying it may well mean we are in danger of reifying it and further marginalising black voices and black epistemology. She also implies that some attempts to confront whiteness have produced 'confessional white narratives' that do little to redress power imbalances. McDonald's conclusions resonate with key themes in our efforts to confront whiteness in the research process and we expand on these as the chapter develops. In earlier work (2005) McDonald encourages sport scholarship to challenge the hegemony of whiteness, to recognise whiteness as process and a site of privilege and power relations. Similarly, whilst drawing more directly from Critical Race Theory (CRT), Hylton (2005, 2009) urges leisure and sport researchers to attend critically to the whiteness of their theorising.

In this chapter, we (re-)consider researcher reflexivity, including our "situatedness" as researchers (Frankenberg, 2004) in order to offer our interpretation of reflexivity with responsibility. We draw on debates associated with insider-outsider dualisms in relation to reflexivity, as this issue remains pertinent to our attempts to name and confront our whiteness. We do this in an attempt to destabilise our position as privileged knowledge producers, locating ourselves as white researchers. We are not direct proponents of 'whiteness studies' and nor have we set out to research whiteness as such but we continue to be concerned with the implications of carrying out research that either fails to consider the impact of (our) white identity and/or to account for and hold to task whiteness as a hegemonic standpoint. This ongoing challenge underpins our discussion here and informs our premise that methodological concerns are inextricably bound to wider epistemological questions.

We draw on Ahmed's (2004) critique of naming or 'declaring' whiteness and consider the significance of her review for leisure and sport scholarship. Her declarations of whiteness include an emphasis on 'institutional racism', identified by Ahmed as a common context for the reification of whiteness. We suggest that such a stance is often drawn upon as a means of 'explaining' racism in sport and we consider this further within the chapter. We touch on the potential for thinking intersectionally because we regard confronting whiteness to be a necessary feature of researching identities in the context of inequalities (Watson and Scraton, 2013). That is, we have been prompted to consider confronting our whiteness through our interest and commitment to examining interconnections and interrelationships across and between socio-economic and cultural factors. We weave in accounts of research practice at different points in the chapter and in so doing, want to stress that the process of generating data is a lived experience, that there is no place from which to gather data that is not dynamically constituted by the interaction that takes place as part of the research process (Best, 2003; Watson and Scraton, 2001). In the final section of the chapter, we therefore look in further detail at researcher and researched interactions and offer some critique of 'new' research methodologies. In drawing attention to some of our published scholarship and that of other leisure and sport researchers we extrapolate and lay bare some of the persistent challenges and insurmountable obstacles to confronting whiteness.

Reflexivity and our critical feminist scholarship

Situating 'us' in relation to whiteness

Despite previous attempts to be 'reflexively responsible', we have at times failed to adequately interrogate our whiteness and, in doing so, inadvertently represented ourselves as 'raceless' (Watson and Scraton, 2001: 269). We were and are still not alone in recognising this. We also lament the (continued) paucity of research that directly engages with questions of whiteness in a broader context of 'race' and its intersections with complex social factors, especially in our area of research interest (feminist scholarship of leisure and sport). It is a feminist lens that informs our critical engagement with whiteness. Seeking to confront whiteness is often easier to state as an aim, or rather it is difficult to know how 'best' to enact it methodologically and it is not surprising that at times, engaging with whiteness also has been justifiably referred to as a mere 'speech act' (Ahmed, 2004, 2005; hooks, 1989). After all, white researchers have and continue to retain and maintain power and privilege whether and where we seek to expose and/or name our whiteness (Bilge, 2013). We are influenced by critical black feminist perspectives in our thinking and research practice and continue to strive for what hooks calls "examining the self from a new critical perspective" (1989: 118). As feminists working within a sociological framework the 'self' to us is a conflation of individual subjectivity/ies and external social relations (Brah, 1996). We are mindful that the self in 'science' is generally premised on whiteness, along with maleness (Amos and Parmar, 1984; Collins, 1990; hooks, 1984). In our published work of 2001, we outlined a commitment, albeit a little simplistically, to 'give voice' to women in what we hoped were more egalitarian ways through our research practices; we remain committed to this cause. We also continue to account for processes of difference and their lived, material consequences in relation to gender and its interconnectivity with other social factors. In this regard, Avtar Brah's (1996) work remains directly influential, particularly her conceptualisation of difference across identities and material relations. We grapple with the ongoing challenging of calling into question our positions and perspectives, attempting to unhinge our scholarship from dominant norms linked to whiteness.

When we began to write about confronting whiteness as a fundamental aspect of our role as researchers it was premised (mostly) upon methodological concerns we had about gathering empirical research data whilst we mentioned epistemology in relation to feminist critiques of difference (Watson and Scraton, 2001). Ruth Frankenberg (1993), along with others, usefully established that whiteness is an ideological process that needs to be contextualised both historically and as contemporary practice; whiteness is not a fixed state, rather a configuration of power and privilege. This informs our understanding of our 'positionality' – as white, as middle class (certainly in relation to having established, academic posts), as able bodied and, arguably, as heterosexual. We were and are in a privileged position to select our research foci and to retain influence and (relative) 'control' over our analysis and outputs. Frankenberg's (1993) work was notable in its forthright declarations to expose and to seek to account for whiteness as structure and as a standpoint that reifies and reproduces dominant cultural values. She suggested that despite this dominance, whiteness, as a set of practices, was unmarked and that white retained a status of 'raceless'. As feminist researchers, we are distinctly aware of how a white hegemonic standpoint (along with masculinist, able-bodied and heteronormative positions) goes remarkably unchallenged, both within leisure and sport practice and within leisure and sport scholarship. Scraton (2001) alluded to this point, citing Frankenberg's critique of whiteness as 'raceless', to call for sport as both a white institution and as institutionally white to be more fully scrutinised, and for sports scholars, in particular, to engage more critically with their own whiteness. According to Scraton (2001: 182)

> Analysing the gendered whiteness of sport would identify the structural advantages that are historically located in the institution of sport as well as challenging white women to examine themselves in relation to both black women and men.

At the time, Scraton (2001) also argued that engagement with and *application* of black feminist theoretical approaches was especially crucial to challenging ethnocentric conceptualisations of black and minority ethnic women. Birrell (1989) had previously argued that sport studies needed to engage with black feminist perspectives and her calls for the inclusion of black feminist autobiographical accounts retain their significance. For us, confronting whiteness is necessary if we are to overcome what Frankenberg (1993) referred to as 'power evasiveness' – the phenomenon whereby white women 'sidestep' their position of (relative) privilege. Confronting whiteness therefore begins with recognising that 'race' is as much a feature for white women as it is for black, minority ethnic and all women regarded as 'Other' (Amos and Parmar, 1984; hooks, 1989). This means confronting a legacy of scholarship that both normalises and perpetuates discourses in which a white standpoint constitutes the hegemonic position, and remains 'raceless' (Frankenberg, 1993). It also means questioning and destabilising various aspects of social and cultural life in which white people are depicted as possessing limited 'race cognizance' when compared to black and BME individuals who often have 'race' forced upon them through their very being. Articulations of BME identity are produced within societies that are 'governed' by whites (white males), be that in practice as well as ideologically (Collins, 1990; hooks, 1989, 1990, 1992). We examine this further in the context of reflexivity with responsibility.

In this chapter we are cognizant of the fact that 'seeing whiteness' does not necessarily mean that whiteness can be 'unlearnt' (Ahmed, 2004; hooks, 1989; Sholock, 2012). In attending to Ahmed's (2004) six different 'declarations of whiteness' anyone seeking to confront whiteness is presented with some seemingly insurmountable challenges. The declarations are that: (1) Whites are able to 'see' white and thus critically account for it; (2) Whites propose institutional racism as a/the key explanation of racism (and thus come up with what needs to be done to overcome it); (3) White people feel ashamed of racism and therefore can be apologetic about it; (4) Whites can feel 'happy' about proclaiming an anti-racist stance (in response to guilt); (5) The 'study' of whiteness can somehow undo its privileged status (i.e. by naming and defining 'whiteness studies', whiteness is somehow 'dealt with'); (6) Whites as 'coloured' can achieve diversity (and by implication end discrimination). In short, Ahmed's challenge to whiteness studies, and importantly, whites making declarations about whiteness, is useful for our examination of whiteness in the research process. It serves as a powerful reminder that these types of declarations are made from positions of (classed and ethnic) privilege and hegemonic location (in relation to race at least). Her arguments also remind us that racism is emotive, embodied and not something that can be necessarily objectified or rationalised (and thus overcome via specific actions or 'speech acts'). We seek to engage and explore this further in the remaining sections of the chapter.

In combination the declarations demonstrate, at an epistemological level at least, that trying to 'undo' the privileges of whiteness can all too often also result in reaffirming its hegemonic status. That is, the taken for granted nature of white epistemic privilege and certainty can be reproduced, rather than disputed and disrupted (Sholock, 2012). Certainly this is a pertinent reminder against making rhetorical statements regarding reflexivity. Instead, researchers need to look more critically at what being 'reflexive' entails.

Reflexivity with responsibility

We have always upheld a methodological premise based upon sharing, naming, and being open about our position and location as researchers as far as possible, a position that is informed by feminist debates on research methodology (Collins, 1990; Maynard and Purvis, 1994; Mirza, 1997; Stanley and Wise, 1993). This is encapsulated for us in the phrase 'reflexivity with responsibility' (Watson and Scraton, 2001). We remain 'caught up' in this challenge – confronting the issue that (much) feminist knowledge production has been and continues to be 'by' white women and is often 'about' white women, or certainly it evades difference (as in

Frankenberg's critique). Where difference/s are acknowledged and in some cases deconstructed and analysed, resulting knowledge production often continues to be that which is constituted *through* the eyes of white women. Acknowledging this, particularly in leisure and sport research, remains a fundamental problem (Aitchison, 2000; Arai and Kivel, 2009; McDonald, 2005, 2009). Reflexivity with responsibility therefore necessitates us asking "what can we do" in our role as researchers to change this. We believe we can continue to be engaged in research that helps understand the complexities of social and material relations and we stand by that assertion. Documenting and analysing the experiences of Black and minority ethnic individuals (in and beyond sport) is important if we are to expose and make sense of inequalities (in and beyond sport). We were mindful of Mirza's (1997) warning that white academics can be drawn to the margins as a 'trendy' place to hang out. Not surprisingly there are disjunctures between what makes sense at a philosophical level – that is, to conceptually challenge whiteness as a power based privilege – and how best to uncover and tackle whiteness at a methodological, practical level. Sholock (2012) draws on Harding's (1991) concept of 'traitorous identities' as a means to 'adopt' subject positions that centre black standpoint positions, for instance, drawing on Collins' (1990) thesis on black epistemology and methodology that centres black positionality as knowledge producing, as opposed to writing from white perspectives about black lives. Sholock (2012) advocates attempts to 'strategically deploy' epistemic uncertainty, a part of which might entail white researchers being traitorous towards their white hegemonic positions. It is a form of empathy with the marginalised which may lead to solidarity (if that is the intention) but that is said with Mirza's warning in mind. We are white women writing about black and BME women and that prompted us initially, and prompts us still, to look at how and if we can confront whiteness as researchers. We attempt to carry out research with integrity and openness and in ways we hope achieve some 'authenticity' in relation to various and varying accounts of 'experience' across leisure, sport, and active recreation.

We considered and scrutinised some of our 'shared' leisure experiences with South Asian women in our 2001 publication as an example of reflexivity with responsibility. We claimed a building of trust between ourselves and our respondents and yet, in so doing, we were, and are, mindful of reproducing ourselves, as white researchers, as 'authentic knowledge producers'. That is, our privileged (and potentially powerful) position of 'knowing' what counts in research was and arguably is reproduced from a white standpoint (Frankenberg, 1993; Sholock, 2012). Although we continue to use phrases such as 'give voice to', be 'representative of' and in some circumstances claim aspects of 'belonging' within shared leisure experiences (Watson and Scraton, 2001) we are aware that how we act methodologically, that is, frame research questions, gain access, interact with participants and develop analysis is informed by our whiteness. Our position as researchers is also 'classed' as it is 'raced' and is informed by a whole gamut of other identity issues that emerge (or do not) at different moments. In our research we have often sought to document an under researched area and we have aimed to ask women to talk about their experiences in ways that were meaningful to them. At the same time, however, we are more often than not acting out our role as 'those people from the university' and in the majority of Higher Education Institutions in the UK, certainly in sports related studies, most of 'those people' are white (and middle class). One way we can further unpack some of these research dynamics is to consider the insider-outsider dualism in research settings.

Insider-outsider issues

Our feminist political stance is one based on 'women' (heterogeneously) as an 'Othered' subject position. From this perspective, we believe that there is logic and merit in perceiving gender as a site of power relations that has elements of shared consequences; nonetheless, any notion of 'sameness' is interdependent with difference. From the outset of any project we regard our participants' identities and subjectivities as classed and racialised as well as gendered. Methodologically, we have been keen to place our participants, who tend to be predominantly (but not exclusively) women, firmly at the heart of our research and we regard them to be the crux of our empirical studies. Therefore, we negotiate insider and outsider subject positions and we arguably attempt to legitimise our claims to talk *about and for* 'Others' and to establish empathetic and convincing accounts of different lives. We continue to utilise semi-structured interviews as an effective means of data collection but also question interviews as a research context and place of interaction (and we return to this in the final section of the chapter). In our research we have been informed by questions of sameness and difference in the research process, drawing on feminist critiques of interviewer-interviewee 'matching' (e.g. Bhopal, 1995, 2001; Phoenix, 1994) and broader conceptual questions of addressing difference that have been articulated by black and BME feminists for a considerable time (Brah, 1996; Collins, 1990; hooks, 1990). There is also useful material that does not identify explicitly with feminist critiques. Buford May (2014), for example, usefully summarises insider-outsider issues on the grounds of 'race matching'. Three key advantages are seen to be that those with shared ethnicity based community interests (Nayak, 2006) will be less likely to exploit research participants; second, bonds of emotional engagement and a sense of 'inclusivity' may be developed between researcher and subjects (*sic*); third, sameness on the basis of racialised identity offers more 'authentic' accounts of data, including openness in talking about race. Arguably, these forms of 'sharing' and their perceived benefits reflect the fundamental basis of much feminist methodological debate regarding the value of women talking to other women (Stanley and Wise, 1993). One of the major issues with this has always been the potential homogenisation of women and women's experiences and a failure to acknowledge or engage with intersecting aspects of identity, in particular, racialised identity. There are concerns therefore about potential homogenisation resulting from 'race matching' in research. We raise these issues here because the questions of insider-outsider are not simple ones.

Buford May (2014) highlights potential disadvantages including social class difference where racial identification has little connection between the researcher and researched in their daily lives. This can also fuel frustration and mistrust for participants when they feel that it is researchers who are assuming commonality and/or when researchers try and 'dumb down' their approaches in research interaction contexts. Notions of 'insider-ness' are often designated by researchers and their own assumptions about collectivities and sites of belonging and so forth. Researchers are knowledge producers and as such decide upon boundaries, identities and categories. We attempt to 'define' black and South Asian in our research (Scraton *et al.* 2005; Watson and Ratna, 2011; Watson and Scraton, 2001) and yet more often than not we do not define white. This 'power' to name and define occurs in sport and leisure related research that does not have a feminist focus (Burdsey, 2008, 2010; Fletcher, 2015). We have not, as stated, set out to 'research whiteness' but our attempts to confront it require acknowledgement of the power dynamics of 'naming' our participants. We have pursued a course of self description and self 'labelling' by our participants across our research involvement, be that in relation to identity categories and in relation to pseudonyms and self naming to ensure anonymity. However, whilst this allows our research partners to self name and self identify as far as possible, it still fails to remove our whiteness in terms of power and privilege; race or gender matching is problematic if difference within and across the research process is ignored. We engaged in empirical data collection (Scraton and Watson, 1998; Watson, 2000) that informed the basis for our attempt at confronting whiteness in 2001 and we continued to work through and with tensions that arose in the 1990s. We consciously sought to challenge a lack of research on one hand and respond to generalised stereotypes of South Asian women's leisure experiences on the other. We were convinced by the need to look at interrelationships across gender, race and class and this was informed by feminist conceptual and theoretical debate, as indicated above, and importantly, by being responsive to our research participants. We actively sought to research with women who identified as part of a South Asian diaspora in the UK (informed by Brah's work on this and the work of Afshar, 1994). There was very little work in leisure and sport and that which existed was based around stereotypes of passivity and non activity (Watson, 2000). There is not the room to go into the detail of this work here but what is significant, methodologically, is the 'invitation' to and encouragement of women naming and labelling their racialised and/or ethnic (sometimes one and not the other and sometimes a conflation) identities in their own words. We 'offer up' our identities, across class and 'race' and gender (and other identity markers in other contexts) as part of negotiating access and agreement for participant involvement. In doing so we are well aware that we act as researchers in those contexts and so whilst we might claim openness and reflexivity we are well aware that in relation to whiteness we are in a privileged majority. Watson has been quoted in Hylton's (2009) overview of Critical Race Theory, stating that she knew full well what was meant by an African-Carribean identified 'gate-keeper', stating that she (Watson) was "still a little white girl with a university education" (p. 61). We return to researcher interactions in the final section of the chapter but here, the example is a useful reminder that insider and outsider positions are relative and moveable.

A further disadvantage of becoming an 'insider' for Buford May is that participants might well have feelings of being 'let down' when they realise that researchers, as individuals, cannot necessarily change or improve specific material relations and conditions. What this points to is that issues of insider-outsider 'status' go beyond who is perceived to be an 'insider' in the context of individuals, groups and populations under immediate review. There are bigger questions at stake than perceived areas of shared experience and we have used the term 'meta-narratives' elsewhere (Watson and Ratna, 2011) to question the 'insider' (and exclusivity thereof) popular cultural representations of South Asian populations. This is a further way in which we consider who gets to speak for whom (Frankenberg, 2004) and importantly reminds us that a construct such as insider-outsider is all too often white-centric (Ahmed, 2004; hooks, 1989). Reflexivity with responsibility is therefore about acknowledging how we are motivated to carry out particular research as well as scrutinising how we go about this research. This can include researching under-represented or misrepresented groups and individuals, responding to calls from community groups to establish evaluative evidence about their sport/ leisure provision and more (Scraton *et al.*, 2005; Watson *et al.*, 2013). This opens up possibilities for researchers to 'give back' to research participants in some way, possibly impacting on policy or resource allocation but it is a grand claim and one that should not be made lightly. Our discussion here, however, is not focused on justifying the content and output of our research involvement; rather it is about sharing some reflections on why confronting whiteness, as opposed to claiming that we have 'confronted' it, remains central. If our research involvement prompts us to question inequalities and/or injustices and can inform action to challenge white (and other) hegemonic positions then that is a positive outcome. That is a fairly pragmatic reading of various research outcomes. Epistemologically speaking, if whiteness is not accounted for and efforts made to confront it then there will continue to be a research basis that is white centric and white normalising. Research on non-white women is likely to reproduce further stereotyping and denial of BME women as active knowledge producers. That said recognising whiteness can reinforce white privilege as outlined in the declarations of whiteness that Ahmed and others warn against.

Ahmed's (2004) third and fourth declarations for instance attend to the fact that white people often extend a misguided apologetic tone; shame enables whites to 'feel bad' about being racist and guilt is 'utilised' as a means through which to say sorry (with the implication that the act of sorrowfulness results in change). hooks (1989) warns that guilt is a performance rather than an action. Ahmed and hooks usefully 'put it back onto' white subjects, reminding us that whiteness is embodied and emotive; it is not something that is 'out' or 'over there' in the guise of institutional racism that is somehow not 'us' as white individuals and white bodies. In our research we have explored how we feel as researchers in different spaces, for example, as a white minority in specific leisure sites (Watson and Scraton, 2001). That example refers to our attendance at leisure 'events' that were organised by and for South Asian women. We were invited to attend, rather than assuming we could be present as researchers; being offered access to leisure spaces is a privilege and informs our position of reflexivity. In other research, we have had different roles, on reflection recognising aspects of being in the majority, the 'normalised', institutionally white sporting spaces that we sought to explore (Scraton *et al.*, 2005). In research into 'space for leisure' we have been both present and felt somewhat 'distanced', as observers in different public spaces, as opposed to being involved participants or interviewers (Watson and Ratna, 2011). Being white and non-white researchers in different contexts, along with other identity factors, informs and is informed by the research scenarios in which we find ourselves. We would argue that we do not set out to research the leisure lives of South Asian and Black and minority ethnic women broadly because we 'feel bad' about our whiteness. We do it, partly because there is still little knowledge about different women's experiences, and women's experiences of difference, and partly because there remains little published work by BME women writing about sport and/or leisure (Ratna, 2017).

From our feminist perspective we suggest that 'small acts' are something we argue can have meaning: in the things we do, at 'work', in the community, in our personal relationships, through our research. Small acts relate to political activism in ways that might be regarded with a small 'p' and a small 'a'. This can involve joining committees focused on widening participation (for staff and students in higher education), actively seeking to recruit BME students to higher level study (and supporting them appropriately), working collaboratively with BME colleagues on research projects and 'sharing' our research knowledge in these various contexts. This sharing is not necessarily transferable to 'outputs' and measures of accountability in neo-liberalist, productivity driven contexts, and as highlighted above, we remain sceptical of a paternalistic 'white as do-gooder in promoting diversity' as encapsulated by Ahmed (2004: 200).

Whiteness might be hegemonic but it is not homogenous and that has only been given limited attention in sport and leisure scholarship (see e.g. Long and Hylton, 2002). There are justifiable concerns about positioning whiteness within diversity rhetoric, as in Ahmed's (2004) sixth declaration and in her questionning of diversity based policy in higher education institutions (2012). The concern here resonates to some extent with earlier black feminist concerns such as that highlighted by hooks (1989: 51–52) where she warned that terms such as 'oppression' and 'exploitation' were being replaced, conceptually at least, by terms such as 'other' and 'difference'. It is not feasible to proscribe how to be a 'white conscious' researcher or to be an effective anti-racist researcher any more than it is feasible or possible to outline a distinct 'feminist methodology'. However, let us return for a moment to Ahmed's second declaration of whiteness that seeks to undo white privilege by identifying and defining institutional racism.

Sport, leisure and the institutionalisation of whiteness: some recurring tensions

Our research interests are focused, in the round, on micro level experiences of leisure (and we return to some of the challenges of using the phrase 'experiences of leisure' below). We argue that a key contribution feminist critiques can offer is to take a view of sport as a social and cultural activity that is situated in the context of leisure more broadly and hence the focus of much of our scholarship in that area. We draw directly on individual accounts and the lived, material relations in which sport and leisure is experienced and negotiated. We consistently argue, following Brah's (1996) assertion, that micro level analysis requires 'mapping onto' broader macro relations (of difference and of power). Our inferences to leisure and sport institutions are made because sport and arguably leisure are contexts in which the institutionalisation of whiteness – at theoretical, policy and disciplinary levels – *and* the dominance of white institutions that make up the multiple sites of what we commonly regard as leisure and sport cannot be ignored (McDonald, 2005, 2009). We are drawn to Ahmed's view that 'blaming' racism on institutions keeps the personal responsibility of whites at arm's length. Here she suggests that in depicting racism as 'institutional' we fail to acknowledge the very processes that we set out to expose and explain. She argues that 'institutional' refers to a collective noun of individuals (who are racist) who make up the institution and it is white institutions (made up of white hegemonies regardless of whether there are any BME individuals present or not) who get to state what racism is and how it 'should' be overcome.

As an 'institution' it can be stated that sport is the epitome of normalising whiteness (Hylton, 2009; Long and Hylton, 2002; Long and Hylton, 2014; McDonald, 2005, 2009; Scraton, 2001). These accounts point to the significance of Frankenberg's (1993) critique of the recurring ideological normalisation of white standpoint. This is inextricably linked to discourses that 'blame' race on black people themselves and can be traced in various 'constructions' of the black athlete where the valorisation of black athleticism, for instance, continues to be founded upon racialised stereotypes of physicality (Carrington, 2011), including, albeit differently, the black female athlete (Ifekwunigwe, 2017). Scraton (2001) asserted that white males embody dominant positions in sport, thus requiring critical analysis of the inextricable links between hegemonic whiteness and hegemonic masculinity. Where there are attempts to engage with the complexities of 'race' and racism in sport (Long and Spracklen, 2010), the term 'institutional racism' is often referred to as a key explanatory framework. This has implications in reaffirming a normalised whiteness that limits the potential for confronting white as the dominant standpoint, despite efforts to decentre it. We can consider this further in relation to sport and campaigns attempting to address racism.

The Macpherson Report (1999) is significant in the UK with regards its potential impact on 'anti-racist' campaigns across institutions including sport, for example, Kick it Out (www.kickitout.org). The way Macpherson defined and detailed institutional racism as a failure to recognise the needs of the other and a failure to tackle recurring perpetuation of ignorant prejudices that are informal yet insidious feeds into a 'racism is wrong and we don't want it here' kind of rhetoric that links to Ahmed's declarations regarding white shame and a notion of 'institutional admission'. Her counter approach is that:

> [...] we might wish to examine how institutions become white through the positing of some bodies rather than others as the subjects of the institution (who the institution is shaped for, and who it is shaped by). Racism would not be evident in what 'we' fail to do, but what 'we' have already done, whereby the 'we' is an effect of the doing. The recognition of institutional racism within the Macpherson Report reproduces the whiteness of institutions by seeing racism simply as the failure 'to provide' for non-white others 'because' of their difference.
>
> (Ahmed, 2004, para. 18)

That is, perceived differences and perceptions of those differences are re-inscribed rather than refuted whilst the 'Other' continues to be denied a platform from which to speak and define their own issues on their own terms and as such denied personhood. The 'Other' can, in sporting terms, be offered only assimilationist or integrationist access to sport whereby the white, male sport nexus (Travers, 2008) is not 'de-hegemonised'.

In researching BME women footballers Scraton *et al.* (2005) acknowledge: "We remain mindful of the functioning of Whiteness in our own research" (p. 85). Through their findings they highlight the 'whiteness' of football across the gendered *and* racialised contexts of female players' everyday lives providing evidence of the normalisation of whiteness and gendered hegemonies in sport. Scraton (2001) outlined a need to examine the gendered nature of whiteness and warned that a focus on race either neglects the significance of whiteness as *gendered* or fails to recognise the central role and value of black feminism for informing any attempts to confront whiteness. This view on sport informs our leisure based research; a black feminist standpoint is crucial to feminist analysis and our attempts to approach research intersectionally. Without the theoretical and empirical evidence based 'voices' of BME women then the normalising and institutionalised aspects of white standpoint that Frankenberg exposed (1993) will not be destabilised, nor will the 'race' cognisance of whites be developed and reconceptualised and as such attempts at 'genuine' acts of anti-racism (small or large) will remain shadowed by declarations of whiteness. McDonald (2005) notes that despite attempts to destabilise white sporting bodies, the contributions of feminist critiques and those of and by black and minority ethnic feminists remain lacking. She reminds us, again, that whiteness is a process and its interrogation is "an ongoing interdisciplinary knowledge project" (McDonald, 2005: 247).

Numerous aspects of leisure, including sport, as suggested above, are commonly associated with institutional contexts – 'family leisure', 'sport and recreation', 'outdoor activities'. More experiential and subjective aspects, including notions such as 'freedom to choose', make associations with institutionally based connotations more challenging to account for (McDonald, 2009). Nonetheless they, along with institutionally based activities and temporal and spatial elements, that is, 'time' and 'space' for leisure (that includes sport), continue to commonly be defined and described from white standpoints. In addressing leisure conceptually, specifically in relation to 'leisure experience', Kivel *et al.* (2009) challenge the dominant discourse of categorising leisure and 'race', acknowledging that "researchers have not explored 'whiteness' as the standard for 'difference' and nor have they included an examination of any other categories that were used to differentiate people based on race" (2009: 479). Further, Arai and Kivel (2009) outline a potential 'fourth wave' of race research drawing on perspectives of social justice and CRT (Critical Race Theory) in an attempt to develop a critical approach to whiteness. They assert that "what matters (more) is how researchers contextualise race and the ideological underpinnings that give meaning to this construct" (2009: 463, brackets added) and go on to identify "a need to contextualise discussions of race and racism within theoretical frameworks that examine social and structural inequalities such as racism, power, ideology and white hegemony" (op. cit.: 464). This contextualisation is unfinished 'work' for white leisure and sport scholars and arguably leisure and sport studies still pays scant attention to BME feminist calls for analyses of women's lives from a range of perspectives including standpoint and 'strength in difference' (Amos and Parmar, 1984; Collins, 1990), postmodern blackness (hooks, 1990; Mirza, 1997), intersectional and creolisation theories (Brah, 1996) and feminist philosophy based critiques of essentialism (Spivak, 1987). There are ongoing tensions – part of the process of confronting whiteness – regarding white feminist theorists actively engaging with black perspectives, a legacy of Carby's (1982) 'white women listen' arguments, that retain relevance.

Kivel *et al.* (2009) along with McDonald (2009) and Arai and Kivel (2009) outline numerous ways in which power evasiveness and normalisation are reproduced across and within leisure (and sport) research and this informs their calls for further contextualisation. Arai and Kivel, for example, argue that the categorisation of racialised identities reaffirms rather than challenges stereotypes and Kivel *et al.* demonstrate how a similarly ethnocentric view of categorising and defining leisure experience leads to findings and assumptions that account for 'cultural difference' in ways that perpetuate 'Othering' (Aitchison, 2000). Further, McDonald (2009) concludes that in relation to leisure, engaging critically with whiteness requires analysis of leisure sites and spaces, of policy and legislation and conceptually, by framing 'race' intersectionally. Roberts (2009: 506) asserts that "leisure studies is still seeking its place among dialogues on whiteness" and that arguably remains the case today. And as this chapter demonstrates, naming whiteness can reify epistemic certainties rather than actively challenging them (Jonsson, 2016; Sholock, 2012).

We identified challenges in our 2001 paper, stating that researching difference required us to consider conceptual debates and practical realities of researching those who are 'Other' to us (Watson and Scraton, 2001). Methodologically, it is not easy to say how to go about this and there are (further) dangers of assuming an elevated status as researchers exploring the ongoing challenges of reflexivity and positionality, as researchers in the contexts of whiteness and racialisation We have proposed thinking intersectionally as a viable means of addressing social relations as power relations, helping researchers to see discursive aspects 'in operation' and allowing for accounts that are dynamic, shifting and that can include moments of resistance (Watson and Ratna, 2011; Watson and Scraton, 2013). We remain acutely aware of the challenges of accounting for gender in the complex and multiple contexts within which they are constituted. No sphere or aspect of leisure and sport can be fully explored through a single lens of distinct or singular social relations and thus we continue to draw on Brah's conceptualisation of difference as simultaneously individual and collective in this regard. Levine-Rasky (2011: 247–248) articulates this helpfully as

> [...] identity locations conventionally represented as gender, race, class, ethnicity, culture, religion, and so on, are shaped by material differences and are also lived subjectively and practiced in relations with others. Moreover, they are co-produced through such interactions. The process is thoroughly relational.

Hylton (2009, 2012) recognises that challenging and overcoming racism in sport needs to be considered with other social processes and advocates intersectionality as having potential in that regard. However, although reference is made to the need to challenge the power relations between men and women, feminist theory as a/or the key contributor to this analysis is not identified and arguably little space is given to the centrality of black feminist theorising within a CRT framework. Hylton usefully incorporates Ahmed's (2005) critique of 'speech acts' as non-performative performances that reference earlier black feminist critiques, notably hooks (1989), yet the central role feminism plays in confronting whiteness is given little coverage in this analysis. Black feminist critiques of the interrelationship between race and gender (and class) are well established, if often left unacknowledged in sport and leisure scholarship. Collins' (1990) thesis on interlocking and interconnected systems of oppression, Crenshaw's (1989) initial conceptualisation of intersectionality, Brah's (1996) work on creolisation theory and hooks' (1990) problematisation of postmodern blackness inform our *feminist* position in research and broader academic life. It is beyond the scope of this chapter to detail intersectionality though we note its application in recent articulations that seek to expose the persistent and pervasive whiteness of the postfeminist, neoliberal era (Wilkes, 2015). Wilkes demonstrates how white, white-heterosexual, white-middle to upper class women embody and convey all that is normalised (and celebrated) about women's location in western, capitalist societies in contemporary settings, particularly so in popular cultural representational contexts. Mediated imagery (be that 'mass' and online and 'new' media) remains a fundamental feature of 'leisure' and complex arguments surrounding the representation of female athletes across these media indicate the ongoing significance of feminist debates regarding gendered and racialised imagery (see for example, Ifekwunigwe, 2017; Toffoletti, 2016). Meanwhile, more 'mainstream' feminists raise concerns about the competitive nature of contemporary femininity (McRobbie, 2015), at the heart of which is the worked on, dieting, consumerist, white female body. That is, leisure and sport contexts in which the creation and maintenance of much contemporary femininitiy/ies occurs are central. At the same time, Wilkes points to consistencies in how whiteness is normalised across dominant popular cultural representation whilst black and minority ethnic representations remain absent (hooks, 1992). Here, whiteness is reinforced and reproduced *in practice*, as well as being articulated as process.

Re-confronting whiteness – where do we go from here?

To some extent then we arrive back at the start of the challenge; not so much that whiteness is 'exposed', rather the issue being the ways in which whiteness continues to be centralised despite efforts to deconstruct and challenge it. Sport and leisure scholars need to recognise power in the research process, including whiteness, because they are often (still) colour blind or they essentialise difference on the basis of colour and racialised identities.

As indicated in the chapter thus far, the acknowledgement that all research interactions are racialised (Best, 2003) is a useful reminder to us to reject simplistic oppositional categories of black researchers and white researchers. Linking empirical data to theoretical debate is how we get beyond binaries (Brah, 1996). As researchers we need to be more equipped to account for contexts of differences based on power relations rather than offering up explanations based around a "whiteness studies" rhetoric. We are mindful of our position as researchers and we are conscious of our ability (and as such our privilege) to generate research questions, gather empirical data and construct accounts and narratives about who and what we think our data represents. In that respect, from the moment we begin to frame a research study or set of questions our whiteness is part of that process. In our 2001 paper we examined various ways in which we positioned questions of race and to an extent we were informed, intellectually and pragmatically, by our respondents; we aimed to listen and to represent them 'authentically'. This, as we have indicated, was and continues to be informed by our feminist politics. However, as Ratna (2011: 394) notes, "The process of doing research though, is not always a smooth and friendly exchange of information." In relation to confronting whiteness it is a complex and contradictory aspiration (as demonstrated in our reference to Ahmed's critiques). Best (2003: 909) expresses this usefully:

> I continue to question whether meaningful and open conversations about race are possible within the context of in-depth interviewing, aware that people of color have historically engaged in a form of

> self-censoring in the presence of those with power (largely as acts of self-preservation) and White folks rarely see themselves as racial meaning makers.

Evidently, whiteness still needs displacing (Frankenberg, 1997). We can trace continuities of power evasiveness, the normalisation of whiteness and race, cognizance in Best's account of interviewing, as social interaction. Despite what we claimed as good intentions in 2001 (and elsewhere in our research) we framed and controlled the discussions of race (and other social relations) within our interviews. Best (2003) usefully points out therefore that reflexivity cannot be used in a static way, that is, although we might aim to 'locate' ourselves as researchers (we made reference to Stanley and Wise's (1993) use of 'intellectual biography'), our racialised (and gendered and classed and so on) position is constituted within and through research interactions; they are 'live' situations. We suggest therefore that in claiming the continued significance of reflexivity with responsibility, that all iterations of our research, and any interactions that occur as part of that process, are acknowledged as sites and spaces in which whiteness is constituted and reproduced (as well as potentially confronted and displaced).

An interesting context within which to explore this further is in relation to what we might call the 'methodological appropriateness' of different research techniques in attempts to confront whiteness. The use of narrative analysis is a relevant example in this regard. Jonsson (2016) argues that within dominant discourses of contemporary feminism there continues to be a lack of voice or visibility for black feminist knowledge and/or where it is present it is co-opted (and controlled) by white feminists. This issue is taken up by Ifekwunigwe (2017) in relation to cultural representations of the black female athlete and more broadly in relation to popular cultural representations of black femininity/ies. Ifekwunigwe deconstructs the presence and hypervisibility of Serena Williams (sport/tennis) and Beyoncé (music/popular culture) for instance as signifiers of, on one level, affirmation and resilience of black females in the public domain. Simultaneously, she asserts that multi-level intersectional analysis of embodied difference is required to more accurately locate black female 'success' in wider circuits of epistemic and structural violence in which black women's lives are situated. Jonsson (2016) meanwhile demonstrates that contemporary narratives of white feminism imply a sense of having 'moved on' from racism, based on postfeminist accounts of diversity offered up as the normalised in neo-liberal contexts (McRobbie, 2015). Thus, we can trace continuities with hooks' (1992) earlier thesis on the limits of cultural representations of black and otherness in popular culture.

We realise that there are subtle differences between narrative as technique (method) and the use of narrative as discourse or overarching context, although there are links between the two. The use of narrative methods is commonly a mechanism for detailing the complexity of experience and a means of highlighting material, often via recollection and memory based techniques. The way in which Jonsson describes feminist narrative is to draw attention to its overarching discursive elements, even where fragmentation and nuanced differences are evident, there is, she suggests, a dominant narrative of particular white femininities. McDonald (2009, 2014) demonstrates some wariness towards 'confessional narratives' that reflect an apologetic response to whiteness despite attempts to account for where and how white as norm ideologies are formed and reformed (such as educational and sporting contexts). There have arguably been some worthwhile attempts to adopt narrative techniques in sport, leisure and PE (Physical Education) based research (e.g. Dowling *et al.*, 2012). Kivel *et al.* (2009) propose collective memory work (and the use of narratives therein) as a potentially meaningful way to disrupt notions of leisure experience based on white standpoints. However, these approaches require methodological scrutiny not least in detailing differences between stories, accounts, memories and recollections and how these are used as data. Further, what are the contexts for generating these 'narratives' and in what ways do they represent further ways in which white standpoints are centralised, despite attempts to use them to deconstruct and destabilise those standpoints? Hylton's (2012) calls for CRT informed methodology to account for racism in sport and collaborative work that engages with racialised difference (and similarity) is arguably worthwhile (Spracklen *et al.*, 2010). This was something we stated in 2001. Nonetheless we do need to be more willing to 'unpack' our use of language in *all* research situations if we hope to scrutinise its implications and inferences as we try to make sense of lived experience and everyday lives. Our position is not to turn away from the challenges of accounting for whiteness but to continue to engage with these. However, the tension between describing and outlining whiteness, even in a pragmatic sense of 'doing research', does not, as this chapter demonstrates, undo whiteness. Stark issues of white privilege and the reproduction of white standpoint remain and many methodological dilemmas are ongoing.

We argue, therefore, that confronting whiteness is continual and unfinished. Whilst researching women's (in all their diversity) qualitative, everyday life experiences of sport and leisure remains imperative, this is increasingly difficult in a neoliberal university context that prioritises managerialist and scientific discourse based upon white, masculinist hegemonies. As we have shown, confronting whiteness is part of a broader project to not only engage critically with race and racism but also to work towards an understanding of difference in experiences and theoretical frameworks that disrupts and challenges whiteness as the norm. For us this requires research into existing power inequalities in sport and leisure that utilises a feminist lens that forms allegiances across the many sites of inequality.

Note

1 Black and Minority Ethnic.

References

Afshar, H. (1994) 'Muslim women in west Yorkshire: Growing up with real and imaginary values amidst conflicting views of self and society', in Afshar, H. and Maynard, M. (eds) *Researching Women's Lives from a Feminist Perspective*. London: Taylor & Francis, pp. 127–150.

Ahmed, S. (2004) 'Declarations of whiteness: The non-performativity of anti-racism', *Borderlands* e-journal, 3(2). Available at: www.borderlands.net.au/vol3no2_2004/ahmed_declarations.htm

Ahmed, S. (2005) 'The non-performativity of anti-racism', *Borderlands* e-journal 5(3). www.borderlands.net.au/vol5no3_2006/ahmed_nonperform.htm (last accessed 28 June 2017).

Ahmed, S. (2012) *On Being Included: Racism and Diversity in Institutional Life*. Durham: Duke University Press.

Aitchison, C. (2000) 'Poststructural feminist theories of representing others: A response to the "crisis" in leisure studies' discourse', *Leisure Studies*, 19(3): pp. 127–144.

Amos, V. and Parmar, P. (1984) 'Challenging imperial feminism', *Feminist Review*, 17: pp. 3–19.

Arai, S., and Kivel, B.D. (2009) 'Critical race theory and social justice perspectives on whiteness, difference(s), and (anti)racism: A fourth wave of race research', *Journal of Leisure Research*, 41(4): pp. 459–470.

Best, A. (2003) 'Doing race in the context of feminist interviewing: Constructing whiteness through talk', *Qualitative Inquiry*, 9(6): pp. 895–914.

Bhopal, K. (1995) 'Women and feminism as subjects of black study: The difficulties and dilemmas of carrying out research', *Journal of Gender Studies*, 4(2): pp. 153–168.

Bhopal, K. (2001) 'Researching South Asian women: Issues of sameness and difference in the research process', *Journal of Gender Studies*, 10(3): pp. 279–286.

Bilge, S. (2013) 'Whitening intersectionality: Evanescence of race in intersectionality scholarship', in Hund, W.D. and Lentin, A. (eds) *Racism and Sociology*. Zurich; Munster: Lit Verlag, pp. 175–206.

Birrell, S. (1989) 'Racial relations theories and sport: Suggestions for a more critical analysis', *Sociology of Sport Journal*, 6: pp. 212–227.

Brah, A. (1996) *Cartographies of Diaspora*. London: Routledge.

Buford May, R.A. (2014) 'When the methodological shoes is on the other foot: African American interviewer and white interviewees', *Qualitative Sociology*, 37: pp. 117–136.

Burdsey, D. (2008) 'Contested conceptions of identity, community and multiculturalism in the staging of alternative sport events: A case study of the Amsterdam World Cup football tournament', *Leisure Studies*, 27(3): pp. 259–277.

Burdsey, D. (2010) 'British Muslim experiences on English first-class cricket', *International Review for the Sociology of Sport*, 45(3): pp. 315–334.

Carby, H. (1982) 'White woman listen! Black feminism and the boundaries of sisterhood', in Centre for Contemporary Cultural Studies *The Empire Strikes Back*: Race and racism in 70s Britain, London: Hutchinson.

Carrington, B. (2011) *Race, Sport and Politics*. London: Sage.

Collins, P.H. (1990) *Black Feminist Thought: Knowledge, Consciousness and the Politics of Empowerment*. Cambridge: Unwin Hyman.

Crenshaw, K.W. (1989) *Demarginalizing the Intersections of Race and Sex: A Black Feminist Critique of Antidiscrimination Doctrine, Feminist Theory and Antiracial Politics*. University of Chicago Ugal Forum, pp. 139–167.

Dowling, F., Fitzgerald, H. and Flintoff, A. (2012) *Equity and Difference in Physical Education, Youth Sport and Health: A Narrative Approach*. London: Routledge.

Fletcher, T. (2015) '"Does he look like a Paki?" An exploration of "whiteness", positionality and reflexivity in inter-racial sports research', *Qualitative Research in Sport, Exercise and Health*, 6(2): pp. 244–260.

Frankenberg, R. (1993) *White Women, Race Matters: The Social Construction of Whiteness*. Minneapolis: University of Minnesota.

Frankenberg, R. (ed.) (1997) *Displacing Whiteness: Essays in Social and Cultural Criticism*. Durham, North Carolina: Duke University.

Frankenberg, R. (2004) 'On unsteady ground: Crafting and engaging in the critical study of whiteness', in Bulmer, M. and Solomos, J. (eds) *Researching Race and Racism*. London: Routledge, pp. 104–118.

Harding, S. (1991) *Whose Science? Whose Knowledge? Thinking from Women's Lives*. Ithaca, New York: Cornell University Press.

hooks, b. (1984) *Feminist Theory: Frome Margin to Center*. Boston, MA: Southend Press.

hooks, b. (1989) *Talking Back: Thinking Feminist, Thinking Black*. Boston, MA: Southend Press.

hooks, b. (1990) *Yearning: Race, Gender and Cultural Politics*. Boston, MA: Southend Press.

hooks, b. (1992) 'Representing whiteness in the black imagination' in Grossberg, L., Nelson, C. and Treichler, P.A. (eds) *Cultural Studies*. New York: Routledge, pp. 338 –346.

Hylton, K. (2005) '"Race", sport and leisure: Lessons from critical race theory', *Leisure Studies*, 24(1): pp. 81–98.

Hylton, K. (2009) *'Race' and Sport: Critical Race Theory*. London: Routledge.

Hylton, K. (2012) 'Talk the talk, walk the walk: Defining critical race theory in research', *Race, Ethnicity and Education*, 15(1): pp. 23–41.

Ifekwunigwe, J. (2017) '"And still Serena rises": Celebrating the cross-generational continuities of black feminisms and black female excellence in sport', in Mansfield, L., Caudwell, J., Wheaton, B. and Watson, R. (eds) *The Handbook of Feminisms in Sport, Leisure and Physical Education*. London: Palgrave Macmillan (in press).

Jonsson, T. (2016). 'White feminist stories: Locating race in representations of feminism in the Guardian', *Feminist Media Studies* 14(6): pp. 1012–1027.

Kick It Out www.kickitout.org/ (accessed July 2016).

Kivel, B.D., Johnson, C. and Scraton, S. (2009) '(Re)theorising leisure, experience and race', *Journal of Leisure Research*, 41(4): pp. 473–493.

Levine-Rasky, C. (2011) 'Intersectionality theory applied to whiteness and middle-classness', *Social Identities*, 17(2): pp. 239–253.

Long, J. and Hylton, K. (2002) 'Shades of white: An examination of whiteness in sport', *Leisure Studies*, 21(2): pp. 87–103.
Long, J. and Hylton, K. (2014) 'Reviewing research evidence and the case of participation in sport and physical recreation by black and minority ethnic communities', *Leisure Studies*, 33(4): pp. 379–399.
Long, J. and Spracklen, K. (eds) (2010) *Sport and Challenges to Racism*. Basingstoke: Palgrave Macmillan.
Maynard, M. and Purvis, J. (eds) (1994) *Researching Women's Lives from a Feminist Perspective*. London: Taylor & Francis.
McDonald, M.G. (2005) 'Mapping whiteness and sport: An introduction', *Sociology of Sport Journal*, 22(3): pp. 245–255.
McDonald, M.G. (2009) 'Dialogues on whiteness, leisure and (anti)racism', *Journal of Leisure Research*, 41(1): pp. 5–21.
McDonald, M. (2014) 'Mapping intersectionality and whiteness: Troubling gender and sexuality in sport studies', in Hargreaves, J. and Anderson, E. (eds) *Routledge Handbook of Sport, Gender and Sexuality*. London: Routledge, pp. 151–159.
McPherson, W. (1999) The Stephen Lawrence Inquiry, London: Home Office Publications, accessible at www.gov.uk (last downloaded July 2016).
McRobbie, A. (2015) 'Notes on the perfect: Competitive femininity in neoliberal times', *Australian Feminist Studies* 83(3): pp. 3–20.
Mirza, H.S. (ed.) (1997) *Black British Feminism: A Reader*. London: Routledge.
Nayak, A. (2006) 'After race: Ethnography, race and post-race theory', *Ethnic and Racial Studies*, 29(3): pp. 411–430.
Phoenix, A. (1994) 'Practising feminist research: The intersection of gender and "race" in the research process', in Maynard, M. and Purvis, J. (eds) *Researching Women's Lives from a Feminist Perspective*. London: Taylor & Francis, pp. 203–219.
Ratna, A. (2011) '"Who wants to make aloo gobi when you can bend it like Beckham?" British Asian females and their racialised experiences of gender and identity in women's football', *Soccer and Society*, 12(3): pp. 382–401.
Ratna, A. (2017) 'Black women, Black voices: The contribution of a Spivakian and Black feminist analysis to studies of sport and leisure', in Long, J., Fletcher, T. and Watson, B. (eds) *Sport, Leisure and Social Justice*. London: Routledge, pp. 153–167.
Roberts, N.S. (2009) 'Crossing the color line with a different perspective on whiteness and (anti)racism: A response to Mary McDonald', *Journal of Leisure Research*, 41(4): pp. 495–509.
Scraton, S. (2001) 'Reconceptualising race, gender and sport: The contribution of black feminism', in Carrington, B. and McDonald, I. (eds) *Race and Sport in British Society*. London: Routledge, pp. 170–187.
Scraton, S. and Watson, B. (1998) 'Gendered cities: Women and public leisure space in the "postmodern city"', *Leisure Studies*, 17(2): pp. 123–137.
Scraton, S. Caudwell, J. and Holland, S. (2005) '"Bend it like Patel": Centring "race", ethnicity and gender in feminist analysis of women's football in England', *International Review for the Sociology of Sport*, 40(1): pp. 71–88.
Sholock, A. (2012) 'Methodology of the privileged: White anti-racist feminism, systematic ignorance, and epistemic uncertainty', *Hypatia*, 27(4): pp. 701–714.

Spivak, G. (1987) *In Other Worlds: Essays in Cultural Politics.* New York and London: Methuen.

Spracklen, K., Timmins, S. and Long, J. (2010) 'Ethnographies of the imagined, the imaginary and the critically real: Blackness, whiteness, the north of England and rugby league', *Leisure Studies*, 29(4): pp. 397–414.

Stanley, L. and Wise, S. (1993) *Breaking Out: Feminist Ontology and Epistemology*. London: Routledge.

Toffoletti, K. (2016) 'Analyzing media representations of sportswomen – Expanding the conceptual boundaries using a postfeminist sensibility', *Sociology of Sport Journal*, 33: pp. 199–207.

Travers, A. (2008) 'The sport nexus and gender injustice', *Studies in Social Justice*, 2(1), pp. 79–101.

Watson, B. (2000) 'Motherwork, motherleisure: Researching difference in the context of young mothers' leisure lives'. PhD thesis, Leeds Metropolitan University.

Watson, B. and Ratna, A. (2011) 'Bollywood in the park: Thinking intersectionally about public leisure space', *Leisure/Loisir*, 35(1): pp. 71–85.

Watson, B. and Scraton, S. (2001) 'Confronting whiteness? Researching the leisure lives of South Asian mothers', *Journal of Gender Studies*, 10(3): pp. 265–277.

Watson, B. and Scraton, S. (2013) 'Leisure studies and intersectionality', *Leisure Studies*, 32(1): pp. 35–47.

Watson, B., Tucker, L. and Drury, S. (2013) 'Can we make a difference? Examining the transformative potential of sport and active recreation', *Sport in Society*, 16(10): pp. 1233–1247.

Wilkes, K. (2015) 'Colluding with neo-liberalism: post-feminist subjectivities, whiteness and expressions of entitlement', *Feminist Review*, 110: pp. 18–33.

Part II

Experiences at the intersections of identity

Chapter 5

'Using the pen as a weapon'

The resistance of an outsider within

Aarti Ratna

Introduction

> These images – the angry black man, the angry woman, the angry Arab – are weapons of control. To dismiss someone as angry is to say that she is governed by emotion rather than reason ... and so unworthy of serious engagement. To dismiss someone as angry is to say that she herself is the problem – and not whatever it is that she is angry about.... Many black people are angry. Many women are angry. Many Arabs are angry. Their experience has given them much to be angry about. And this is precisely what these weaponised images obscure: that anger is often a reasonable response to an unreasonable world.... Anger can be a weapon in the hands of the powerless.
>
> (Amia Srinivasan *In Defence of Anger*, aired on BBC Radio 4's *Four Thought*, 2014)

In their historical review of Black women who have worked at predominantly white institutions (PWI) of higher education, Howard-Baptiste and Harris (2014) claim that in 2013, 91 years after the first Black woman began to work in academia, in America, Black women faculty continue to feel excluded and discredited by both their white peers and students. There is an enduring and deeply resonating sense amongst Black scholars that they have always had to confront and transcend their marginalisation. Thus, Black scholars feel anger and this provides the basis for meaningful action (Collins, 2000; hooks, 1989; Srinivasan, 2014). It is important to note, though, that in the United States for instance, Black universities and colleges have provided a more inclusive and empowering space for both Black students and staff (Carter-Francique and Richardson, 2015; Howard-Baptiste and Harris, 2014). In white spaces of academia, though, much of the literature focuses on Black women's need to stay silent or to stand up and speak out (about their negative experiences) and to challenge for better working conditions. In this chapter, I use my 'pen as a weapon' to write about the racialised, gendered and class contours of academia that have constructed and continue to structure my professional career as 'outsider within', in order to expose structures and cultures of inequality as well as to serve as a therapeutic project for people like me who may also similarly feel marginalised.

For me, the process of speaking out is driven by the creative energy to use anger as a form of empowerment in order to interrogate structures, cultures and relations of power, although I acknowledge that writing back can often induce anxiety, as one's lived experiences – my experiences – may be judged, and discredited by people who I both know and do not know in and beyond the academic community of sport and sociocultural studies (see Howard-Baptiste, 2014). 'Writing back' may also involve colleagues and peers who see past situations and incidents from a very different perspective to my own. Nevertheless, I feel that it is important for me to action my pen in order to create spaces of belonging that may benefit my fellow Black peers and Black students – in and through the sociocultural studies of sport – as someone who has experience of navigating this complex space to varying degrees of success and inclusion. This chapter focuses more specifically upon my early experiences in the field and is based on inter-personal stories and incidents. Whilst these reflections elucidate micro-tensions and issues, they are nonetheless symptomatic of the machinations of academia which structure and continue to maintain institutional privileges for different groups of people, in different ways, which have been further questioned by others (e.g. Ahmed, 2009; Arya, 2012; Martinez *et al.*, 2015; Maylor, 2009; Puwar, 2004; Roberts, 2013; Robinson, 2013; Rollock, 2013; Wallace, Moore and Curtis, 2014). Whilst their work is broader than the sociocultural analysis of sport, it bears relevance and has many overlapping points of contention. That is, links between sport and the education system that may connect and/or collide, especially within the collegiate context of sport in the United States. Both fields purport historical ideologies about racialised and gendered bodies; what they can do, cannot do and what they can achieve. Thus, the reproduction of such dominant ideologies, within and across spaces of sport and education, compound through their mutual reproduction false and problematic stereotypes. For Black women, this can result in an expansive and enduring experience of marginalisation across multiple spaces and over time. In my own experiences, mainly playing sport at school and then studying and working through the lens of sport from within an education environment, the two spaces have always been connected. Moreover, gleaning insights from my own sporting research and my own sporting experiences, arguably Black women are positioned as an 'outsider within' across both of these spaces. Therefore, speaking from the outside in, to challenge dominant hierarchies, in this case within the academic sub-field of sport and sociocultural studies, bears relevance to thinking about the participation field of sport more broadly.

In this chapter, I specifically appropriate the work of Black feminists such as Audre Lorde, bell hooks and Patricia Hill Collins, in order to *write back* to the dominant hegemonies that have structured my career. That is, specifically in relation to studying and working from within the disciplinary spaces of the sociocultural analysis of sport. To begin this chapter, I elucidate my epistemological framing by examining the Black feminist notion of 'talking back' (hooks, 1989) (read writing back) before critically exploring my early experiences of being a student on a sport course in the late 1990s, and then specifically considering the role of language within academia more generally. I conclude this chapter by re-asserting the need to work dialogically across different feminist and anti-racist positions, as part of a broader commitment to dismantling structures of exclusion in and through our scholarship within and beyond the study and practice of sport.

The politics of location and writing back

Coming to voice for me has been made possible through the language of Black feminism. The words of Patricia Hill Collins (2000) in particular, although predominantly about the lives of African American women, 'spoke' to me. When I first picked up her book, *Black Feminist Thought*, perhaps in 2003, I could see my own life within and beyond the fields of both sport and academia represented in a way that I had not read in any other feminist literature before. Reading Collins' book was a powerful awakening of my critical consciousness. Her work is central to understanding how speaking from positions of marginality, as an 'outsider within', facilitates the critical interrogation of orthodox practices, and how they function to maintain the privileges of some groups and the exclusion of others. Alcoff (2000: 250) further explains how structures and cultures of inequality are often taken for granted since "there are no contrary assumptions present by which they come into relief". That is, elements of a space are seen to be so natural, that they do not warrant remark or dissection. Yet naming race in academia, and/or arguably the participatory spaces of sport, is so difficult to unpick as they are often valued as meritocratic, colourblind and neutral (Burdsey, 2011; Carrington, 2012; Hylton, 2005; Wright *et al.* 2007). In the sociocultural analysis of sport, for instance, the visibility of Black male and female athletes is often read as evidence of an equitable field of play (Kivel *et al.* 2009). But, arguably, the visibility of Black athletes does not diminish the need to continue to examine this field as reflective of both oppression and pain as well as newfound possibilities and pleasures. As one of a few *female* Black scholars, who grew up in a working-class household, I feel compelled to speak out and back from my position of alterity. Thus, I critique the sociocultural field of sport as a discipline, from within but nevertheless on the peripheries of this academic space. Rollock (2013), referring to a critical mass of work produced by a range of eminent scholars from within the field of education, provides a compelling summary for privileging the standpoint of the marginalised:

> These accounts from the 'liminal spaces of alterity' (Rollock 2012a, p. 65) not only help to highlight the complex, intersectional nature of identities and the centrality of whiteness in informing our understanding of racism and feminism (Ladson-Billing and Donnor, 2008; Wynter, 1992) but also reveal how the centre operates often in subtle yet sophisticated ways to maintain an inequitable status quo.
>
> (Rollock, 2013: 492)

Whilst I agree with the statement that centring Black women's standpoints and voices is important to developing critical insights into the machinations of any cultural space, I would be more wary of other claims made by those who endorse womanist traditions, a strand of Black feminist thinking, which suggests that Black women's insights can only be understood and garnered by other Black women (Sudbury, 1994). This view flattens and ignores differences between Black women – in terms of ableness, class, sexuality, age, and generation – which reifies the notion of an authentic Black positionality that only one who shares that oppression can understand (Collins, 2000). In my own research about British Asian girls and women, I have reflected on the moments of dissonance as well as moments of connectivity that I encountered whilst interviewing women similar to myself – in terms of both race and gender – about their experiences of playing football which were not smooth or friendly exchanges but involved tensions and uneasy dialogues (Ratna, 2007). More broadly, across the subject discipline of the sociocultural analysis of sport and leisure, my own connections with white feminist and anti-racist scholars lead me to believe that people different to the groups that they are researching can and have raised the political and social realities of marginalised Others (e.g. see Burdsey, 2007; Hargreaves, 2000; Scraton, 2001; Watson and Scraton, 2001). Furthermore, they are using their academic privileges to challenge the inequities of sport on behalf of outsider groups in and through their scholarship and research outputs. Thus, standpoint politics fail to recognise how we may all, regardless of our race, experience varying degrees of both privilege and inequality (Collins, 2000). Instead, I advocate for the politics of location which demands for the subject position to be centred in a way that identifies the social, cultural, geographical and imaginary boundaries which orientate people with others (Sudbury, 1994). Thus, whilst the 'outsider within' position is still significant to exploring experiences of marginality, it requires a narrowing of location which resists essentialising subject positionality, and facilitates a relational analysis by linking to the position of others. Thus, I argue researchers do not have to be Black and/or female to express a Black and/or feminist political consciousness. However, as Black women constitute a minority group in the spaces of academia, and sport more specifically, the responsibility has predominantly fallen to them to expose and to challenge white privilege and inequitable structures and cultural practices. And, as already noted, speaking out as a minority scholar is a hard thing to do.

In Audre Lorde's classic text *Sister Outsider* (2007, 1984) she specifically urges Black women to take the pen, to use anger as a tool for resistance, and to write back to omnipresent social forces of oppression and marginalisation. She argues that when we, as a social collective of Black women, turn from anger, about circumstances which have made us angry, sporting or otherwise, we lose the critical insights that stem from this emotion. Lorde acknowledges though that speaking from anger involves risk. Lorde's famous words about speaking out, at a time when she realised she was dying from cancer, best capture this anxiety:

> and when we speak we are afraid
> our words will not be heard
> nor welcomed
> but when we are silent
> we are still afraid
> So it is better to speak...
> (Lorde, 2007, 1984)

bell hooks (1989), in *Talking Back*, also promulgates coming to voice and moving from silence into speech as a revolutionary act: daring to disagree, contend issues with authority figures and express an opinion which may cause tension and/or may not be well received. As suggested, in the fields of both sport and education, this can feel so hard to do as both spaces are already assumed to be neutral and meritocratic. hooks (1989) further suggests that worrying about saying the 'wrong' thing, and the repercussions of that, have in the past immobilised her ability to speak or to write. I often too have kept silent at conferences or events about the socio-cultural analysis of sport even when in areas of my expertise for the fear of sounding inarticulate, being publically berated and/or not feeling able to challenge the views of those more senior/established than myself. For me, this fear became particularly galvanised when another (more senior) British Asian woman at a seminar about popular culture and the South Asian diaspora in the U.K. continued to question/attack me about the terminology I had used to label the diverse British Asian girls and women included in my PhD study. As another Black woman in a predominantly white space, I felt she validated her own supposed expertise by humiliating me. Arguably, whilst this type of exchange is unfortunately probably quite common in academia, between and amongst scholars of various gender, racial, ethnic and class backgrounds, it still nevertheless feels like an assault that, as a developing PhD student, I neither had the confidence nor the language to successfully challenge. Moreover, it undermines arguments which assume solidarities and mutual support are a given between those who share the same gendered, racial, and class histories, and thus to be confronted by another Black academic in a white environment publically made visible this racial disconnect. My fear of speaking out in many ways muted my political agency to voice a different type of more dialogical rather than confrontational intellectual space of sharing knowledge. After many years of publically keeping silent, as a self-preservation mechanism, the need to speak back and out could no longer be suppressed. Recognising that my ongoing and wider frustrations needed to be voiced and heard, like hooks, I now choose to use anger as a creative energy to write back to structures and cultures of exclusion as well as those who un/intentionally propel such an exclusionary system. In the following sections, I further reflect on the politics of writing back in and through more focused reflections about my own academic research and developing career.

Becoming 'raced'

Like Roberts (2013), who critically unpacks her experience of becoming a Black academic, I also did not see myself as 'raced' until I entered the spaces of higher education. As a British Asian, who was born in North-West London, I did not know I was different, as everybody where I lived was racially different. Whilst I was aware of broad racial and ethnic tensions that existed between people from within this area, we were all similarly different and this is what united us. To be white was to be in the relative minority in this space. Although still, all the people who seemed to have power – at least from within the spaces of sport and school – were white. However, I become more aware of my own identity when I went to a PWI (predominantly white institute) outside of London to study sport studies and geography. As an institution that was campus based, first year students lived and attended lectures on campus. The student population was relatively small but at that time (1996–1999) it was clear to me that I was perhaps one of six Black students: five of us women were British Asian and one man was African Caribbean. On my sport studies course (which I majored in), of about 100 students, not only was I the only Black person (the 'racialised Other') but also I felt alienated. At times, lectures and seminar discussions about race and sport privileged the idea that the traditional values and etiquettes of sporting institutions and elite infrastructures of sport were somehow being eroded by changing and adapting their ideals to allow Other races and foreign cultures to freely participate. This notion became more salient during discussions about ethnic minority communities asking for leniency to wear culture and religious appropriate clothing. The ethnic minorities were positioned as the problem, and the exclusionary and colonial legacy of sport was completely ignored. In other lectures, I was troubled, humiliated and ashamed at the perpetuation of stereotypical assumptions about people like me – ethnic minorities to be precise. In one particular lecture about sport and racism, the white woman lecturer spoke of racial stacking, positioning it as a form of "reverse racism against white athletes", whilst failing to confront a plethora of breathtakingly racist ideals that led sports practitioners of the time to believe and accept for instance that Black people were good at boxing because they had thicker skulls. Instead, her choice of words, her examples and her stories made it sound like now the tables had turned: that now, only white people experienced racism, and that sport was now a way for Black people to get out of the 'ghetto'. In that class, and precisely in those moments, I vividly remember wanting to be metaphorically 'swallowed up' by the lecture theatre. Whiteness was the taken-for-granted normative frame of reference, which positioned me and those like me as non-normative bodies, in other words, as social beings out-of-place. What was deemed as 'legitimate knowledge' for students neither spoke of nor recognised the needs and viewpoints of minority groups struggling against diaspora marginalisation. Yet it was taken as gospel by the majority of students in the class. In those moments of being homogeneously rendered as belonging to problematic communities, I wondered how my course peers saw me and what assumptions they might have made about me, my lifestyle and my capacity to be more than the racialised, stigmatised body I was made to be. Today, as I action my pen, I wonder whether these very students questioned their own whiteness, bodies and cultures: indeed whether they were aware of their racial privilege.

During my time at university, those who did ask me questions about my racial and cultural background were always surprised that I did not fit their idea of what a British Asian person was/is. These incidents seemed particularly heightened in/through sporting spaces either as my white peers were surprised that I played sport/studied sport (as a British Asian woman who they imagined was oppressed by her culture, religion and family) or that I was also in socialising spaces of sport, and that I was willing and able to drink alcohol and/or to date men. I ended up becoming the spokesperson for my 'race'. This burden of representation weighed heavy on me, and I did a terrible job of challenging myths. On some occasions, I also typecasted these 'backward' South Asians who were of course nothing like me or any member of my family. In this white environment, playing to the western rhetoric of 'us' as modern and liberal and 'them' as backward and insular was easy. And yet, over time, my assimilation and relative acceptance in these white spaces made me feel like a race traitor. My time at university generally was an unhappy one. I felt quite depressed and developed terrible and ineffective coping mechanisms. Playing netball with other (predominantly white) women, though, at this time, was a source of fun but again was an environment in which I hyped up my gendered, able-bodied, and heterosexual similarities to my team-mates and concomitantly, downplayed my racial difference. An insight, incidentally, which I later used to develop the notion of intersectional plays of identity in my own research about sport (see Ratna, 2013). When as a postgraduate student I read the work of Annecka Marshall, about her desire to research the lives of other Black women, I finally found the words to faithfully capture my own internal self-despair:

> I was outraged by seemingly universal theories that either completely denied the existence of Black people, or just concentrated on the situation of Black men. I was angry that white lecturers perpetuated a racist account of social life and that white students failed to recognize this. Instead of articulating my despair, I internalised it. Often I remained silent in seminars. I felt alienated by discussions that excluded my reality. The creative energy to use the pen as a weapon against such racist and sexist misinformation was suppressed by the fear that I needed to conform in order to survive and ultimately pass my degree.
>
> (Marshall, 1994: 107)

hooks (1989) suggests that we should refuse to assimilate, as this only reinforces white privilege through such cultural rituals. For Black bodies out of place, their tenuous position can be negotiated if they are able to, and consciously or subconsciously choose to, through acts of assimilation (see Puwar, 2004). Though, nevertheless, I would argue that their position is still relatively unstable as their Black bodies can be disenfranchised at any moment, by the ways their bodies continue to be read and fixed as racially 'Other'. I recall one of the participants in my PhD study claimed that she played women's football at elite level, representing a number of the top playing sides during her long career, and that racial micro-aggressions were common place (Ratna, 2007; see also Burdsey, 2011). For instance, at one club, her team-mates jokingly claimed any random South Asian woman walking past the training ground was her sister (Ratna, 2007). This player, nor I for that matter, understood the joke. However, we got the deeper point that a white player would not be racially 'Othered' and joked about in a similar way, for no other reason than her obvious skin colour/visual difference. Indeed, Wright *et al.* (2007) argue that playing it white "can never be anything but a substandard substitute for the capital (power) which is embodied in the white face" (159). As I have argued elsewhere, being 'in' a sporting space is not the same as being 'of' that space: 'outsiders within' have to consciously and/or subconsciously negotiate the complexities and nuances of belonging in order to progress their (sporting) careers if they decide to stay put and make claims to insiderness in those spaces (Ratna, 2007, 2010, 2013).

In terms of my own academic career, even when I began to work as a university lecturer, the way I was culturally 'Othered' by both staff and students meant I had to define myself to them in a way other white lecturers probably did not. A pertinent incident 'sticks' with me (as stereotypes about 'us' usually do) (see Amos and Parmar, 1984) when I was introduced to approximately 100 sport students by a white male colleague in the following way: "She may look exotic but she's not; she's from Wembley". The students in the lecture theatre laughed; I cringed. Upon questioning the colleague about his choice of words, he said it was just to get "a laugh" from the students. Mission accomplished. I did not get the joke. Whilst my other white male peers, who were also introduced to the students at the time, were also mocked about their physical appearance, I was upset that my racial and gender differences in relation to them were being made particularly salient. More than that, though, the terminology used to introduce me reduced me to a minority who was out of place, a sexually erotic/subjugated stereotype rather than an intellectual insider. The contradiction of this incident is that it was the same colleague who was also supportive in my early days of lecturing, and through his affirmation, gave me the confidence to teach on modules about the sociocultural analysis of sport and leisure.

Re/presentations of Black sporting 'Others'

The moments that I have unhinged here, and made sense of through a Black critical feminist consciousness, are both the motivation and insight that have helped me to question the representation of Black women and sympathetically yet critically locate their experiences as someone who has shared similar as well as different feelings of marginalisation. In a predominantly white academic environment, it only alerted me to my racial difference. I continued to feel deeply upset and angry that Black people were so poorly represented in/through the sport scholarship, reinforcing wider media and political debates about the problems with racialised and minoritised ethnic cultural communities. The slow mushrooming of critical literature that also challenged stereotypical representations, and laid bare problems connected to sporting cultures, politics and policies, gave me hope, and bolstered my capacity to speak out and share other ways of knowing Black people's existence, identities and relationships to sport (e.g. Birrell, 1989; Carrington, 1998; Carrington and McDonald, 2001; Fleming, 1994; Raval, 1989; Scraton, 2001). When I first accessed the book *Sporting Females* (1994) by Professor Jennifer Hargreaves, my eyes lit up when I read her reference to a Black women's netball team in South

London – this sounded more like my own experiences of playing sport. The significance of this positive representation in and through such sporting academic text cannot be underestimated. Such a representation revealed the agencies of Black women to make their own sporting choices and as a site of pleasure. This work really sparked my academic imagination.

Inspired by the emergence of this kind of critical writing, I lunged forth into Black feminist activism knowing that being a Black women in this un-open space meant challenging and fighting to reclaim space, voice, representation and authority/powers within both academia and sport. I shouldered the burden of this responsibility, using this corpus of literature to fuel my ability to re-think and unsettle dominant racist epistemologies that ignored, silenced or stigmatised me and 'Other' people like me. In my own teaching, scholarship and research praxis, I value what Olson and Gillman (2013) term transactional friendships, to use the dialogical potential of what can be learnt in/through student–teacher and colleague–peer relations as well as with scholars in and across disciplines, in order to think more critically about the re-presentations of racialised groups of male and female bodies. Fostering transactional friendships and pedagogies is also connected to my deeper desire to encourage people like me to access university programmes including those of sport, and also to provide a curriculum and teaching experience whereby they may feel included, and which critically engages with their histories and (post)colonial heritages. Thus, the need for diversifying and decolonising the curriculum in and through studies of sport in order to challenge whiteness as a norm of being and (often male) subject of enquiry is an ongoing and yet pressing need that must be given serious attention by scholars in the field. Moreover, deconstructing the functionalist rhetoric that privileges and romanticises sports use and role in 'saving' (or rescuing) ethnic Others, especially women, from their own allegedly detrimental and androcentric cultures needs to be further interrogated in and through both research and teaching in order to provide a more complex and nuanced re-presentation of sport as both a site of unity and division (Darnell and Hayhurst, 2011).

Language

hooks (1989) claims that the language we use, as part of the process of speaking and/or writing back to dominant hegemonies that pervade different social times, has deep significance and raises pertinent questions about *how* we write and *who* we write for. For hooks (1989) diasporic groups who may find themselves in spaces and sites of being which are not familiar to them, as English may be their second language, cannot always express themselves in a way that captures the emotion of their points. This is not to argue they cannot speak English, but the language itself is limiting as the words do not exist to adequately explain the sentiments of their feelings (Brah, 1999). In other words, as expressed by Lorde (2007, 1984), *The Master's Tools Cannot Dismantle the Master's House*. Moreover, recognising the class dynamics of the constructions of the English language, Black women may be able to speak English fluently but it might not resonate with 'who they are' and how they have grown up. In relation to my own career, as someone who grew up in a working-class environment, and had an average school experience but perhaps not grounded in the grammatical contours of the Queen's English, I often felt muted; I could not speak as, when I did, it sounded 'wrong'. In my PhD work, thus, the writing of my thesis was painful as I found it hard to claim a language that felt alien to me. Although I confidently interacted with my English-speaking friends who I met whilst studying sport during my undergraduate and postgraduate studies as well as fellow academics at national and international sport and leisure conferences, I lacked confidence with many of these academic colleagues. Indeed, if I spoke any different in my spaces of home, I am sure my friends would have berated me for sounding 'too posh' and not 'true' to who I was/who they saw me as. This burden of representation, across different spaces and over time, involved conscious and subconscious identity work, to ensure my performance in the different sport, academic, home, family and friendship settings that I traversed was deemed acceptable. As previously mentioned, such insight enabled me to see how in my own research, many of my British Asian female football research participants also had to deal with constant surveillance across time and space, and the impacts of this on their own conscious and/or self-conscious identity performances (Ratna, 2013).

On reflection, during my PhD, I was changing and being in an academic environment changed the way I spoke (and wrote) which became more aligned to the demands of an elite scholastic field. However, even now, I feel the pressure to write well or 'be found out' as an imposter to the rules of the academic status quo. More than that though, the better I become at mobilising the English language to express my politics, the more I want to rebel. Going back to hooks, I am also cognisant of 'who' I am writing for. Whilst writing well (and getting published) confers status within the spaces of academia, it was never my ambition to write about the participants of my research out of self-interest, although I recognise that it has served that purpose, and benefitted my career development. I wanted to write for 'my' British Asian girls and women who played sport and who at the time were relatively voiceless; their life stories were relatively invisible and/or fixed to stereotypical tropes within and beyond the academic literature. Furthermore, it could be argued that the sporting sensibilities of many Black women are unknown as they are not written in English. Dart argues, in his research about the role of journal editors, whilst many sport sociology journals invite scholars from non-English speaking countries to publish their work (in English), little else is done to support the publication process. Thus, one editor in his study powerfully asserted that "it's all very well saying that women and minorities are welcome to apply – they all know it's bollocks – you have to do a lot more than that" (Dart, 2013: 16). As I write this chapter, I am acutely aware that I am still peddling the elitist language of the Master race in/through my own publications; I cannot break free. hooks' words explain my epistemological contradiction:

> Language is also a place of struggle. I was just a girl slowly entering into womanhood when I read Adrienne Rich's words: "This is the oppressor's language, yet I need to talk to you". This language that enabled me to finish graduate school, to write a dissertation, to talk at job interviews, carries the scent of oppression.
>
> (1989: 28)

Whilst I cannot break free from the deeply entrenched English colonial systems of writing and publishing, arguably an alternative to this would be to work across language divides by better engaging with research published within non-English outputs, to collaborate with scholars whose first language is not English in order to learn with them through transactional collaborations, and to think more critically about the impact of English translation on knowledge production and the ways in which slippages in meaning can be abused and overcome (Kim, 2013; Olson and Gillman, 2013; Ratna, 2017). Arguably the imperial and class legacy of the English language can be interpreted as a form of domination in and of itself, but yet the mastery of the English language, especially within the spaces of academia, is read as a symbol of the writer's intelligence and authority rather than yet another expression of white, elite, post/colonial power. In making this point, I feel 'quietly subversive' (Ali *et al.*, 2010) even if, inside, I detest complying to the rules of the Master's house to work, earn money for my family, and to forge a career in academia (Lorde, 2007, 1984). When I have heard other more established Black scholars use vernacular which speaks directly to their participants, and expresses their anger, I feel it, and I continue to want to break free from the grammatical shackles of the English language. For example, when Shirley Anne Tate at a conference entitled *Speaking to the Activism of Black Feminism* reflected upon her somatic feelings of pain, which she endures and continues to face as a result of being out of place in academia, her cry "mi vex", resulted in a wave of emotion from the predominantly Black crowd (Tate, 2015). Her voice, her Jamaican accent, her expression of anger, captured a deep emotion that "I am vexed" (read in a 'posh voice') would simply not have covered; the words were felt and understood by the crowd as it reflected their own feelings of being out of place. In my own research, some of the younger second-generation British Asian participants challenged racism in women's football by using a rude gal argot which directly confronted the issue, in their own terms, and in their own ways (Ratna, 2007; 2010). For examples, phrases such as 'back up', 'taking the power back', 'stand up for our rights' and 'we won't be knocked like that' expressed their sense of collective solidarity against racism on and off the football field of play (Ratna, 2010). When I hear language used in this way, I feel affected by what is being said as it also speaks to my reality of studying and working from within the sociocultural field of sport. hooks further reflects on her use of the English language by making the following comment about coming to voice:

> [...] my words were written to explain, to placate, to appease. They contained the fear of speaking that often characterise the way those in a lower position within a hierarchy address those in a higher position of authority. Those passages where I was speaking most directly to black women contained the voice I felt to be most truly mine – it was then that my voice was daring, courageous.
>
> (1989: 15)

The power of language for me feels cursed but it is also a gift; coming to a voice even if in the Master's tongue as "a gesture of resistance" (hooks, 1989: 18) which I have chosen to harness through my own critical writings about sporting cultures, policies and practices.

Conclusion

Studying and working from within the sociocultural studies of sport for the last 20 years have personally been rewarding and challenging. Reflecting on my individual career, I am cognisant of the lives of other Black women who may have also felt and continue to feel out of place in academia, and other spaces of sport more broadly. I have used this chapter as a mechanism to write back and deconstruct problematic racial and gendered ideologies, discourses and practices operating within and across academic and sporting spaces. I have also specifically questioned the re-presentations of Black women in and through the curriculum, and the need to diversify and engage with a greater array of racial and ethnic histories. Moreover, working with others through transactional friendships and pedagogies to enact different ways of knowing the lives of marginalised Black girls and women. But, as Srinivasan states (see opening quote), there is still much to be angry about:

> [...] anger expressed and translated into action in the service of our vision and our future is a liberating and strengthening act of clarification, for it is in the painful process of this translation that we identify

> who are our allies, with whom we have grave differences, and who are our genuine enemies.
>
> (Lorde, 2007, 1984)

Whilst arguably exposing and grappling with inequities is an important aspect of transforming space – from the margins to the centre of various interlocking institutional spaces including those of both sport and academia – complexities of exclusion may nevertheless persist. Indeed, I often feel that all I have really managed to achieve is a place of negotiated belonging that remains fragile and precariously positioned, to say enough but not to say too much, in case I offend colleagues, peers and academic friends. Even the writing of this chapter yields a deep-down fear that writing without restraint may expose my outsiderness to those inside the academic field who have speculated, and continue to speculate on, my insiderness, at any moment in time; hence I feel I must remember to toe the line and not to ruffle too many feathers when I action my pen as a weapon. Yet, I do not want to be read uncritically as the 'happy face' of progress made (Ahmed, 2009). Ahmed (2009) argues that we must stay sore as the points we are making. The challenges I faced more than 20 years ago – at the start of my academic journey as well as connected to my own experiences of playing sport – have undoubtedly changed, it would be insincere to suggest that they have not, but in many ways they have also stayed the same and/or become masked under the guise of a post-racial and/or post-feminist epoch. Thus, heeding Ahmed's call, we must stay sore as the points we are making and use that creative energy to speak out and write back, to action our research and scholarly pens in and through our pedagogical practice and teaching, and to confront both persisting and emerging forms of inequity, using our anger in hope and not just despair.

Acknowledgements

I thank a number of colleagues whose words of support and encouragement gave me the motivation to continue writing this chapter, in particular Viji Kuppan and Jason Arday. I would also like to thank Dr. Samie Farooq Samie for her invaluable insights and critical feedback on earlier drafts of this chapter.

References

Ahmed, S. (2009) 'Embodying diversity: problems and paradoxes for Black feminists', *Race, Ethnicity and Education*, 12(1): pp. 41–52.

Alcoff, L.M. (2000) 'On judging epistemic credibility: is social identity relevant?' in N. Zack (ed.) *Women of Color and Philosophy: A Critical Reader*, Oxford: Blackwell: pp. 235–262.

Ali, S., Mirza, H.S., Phoenix, A. and Ringrose, J. (2010) 'Intersectionality, black British feminism and the resistance in education: a roundtable discussion', *Gender and Education*, 22(6): pp. 647–661.

Amos, V. and Parmar, P. (1984) 'Challenging imperial feminism', *Feminist Review*, 17(1): pp. 3–19.

Arya, R. (2012) 'Black feminism in the academy', *Equality, Diversity and Inclusion: An International Journal*, 31(5/ 6): pp. 556–572

Birrell, S. (1989) 'Racial relations theories and sport: suggestions for a more critical analysis', *Sociology of Sport Journal*, 6: pp. 212–227.

Brah, A. (1999) 'The scent of memory: strangers, our own, and others', *Feminist Review*, 61: pp. 4–26.

Burdsey, D. (2011) 'The joke isn't funny anymore: racial microaggressions, color-blind ideology and the mitigation of racism in English men's first-class cricket', *Sociology of Sport Journal*, 28: pp. 261–283.

Burdsey, D. (2007) *British Asians and Football: Culture, Identity and Exclusion*, London: Routledge.

Carrington, B. (2012) 'Introduction: sport matters', *Ethnic and Racial Studies*, 35(6): pp. 961–970.

Carrington, B. (1998) 'Sport, masculinity and black cultural resistance', *Journal of Sport and Social Issues*, 22(3): pp. 275–298.

Carrington, B. and McDonald, I. (2001) *'Race', Sport and British Society*, London: Routledge: pp. 1–26.

Carter-Francique, A. and Richardson, F.M. (2015) 'Black female athletes' experiences at historically black colleges and universities' in B. Hawkins, J. Cooper, A. Carter-Francique and J. Kenyatta Cavill (eds) *The Athletic Experience at Historically Black Colleges and Universities: Past, Present and Persistence*, Lanhma; Boulder; New York; London: Rowman and Littlefield: pp. 61–84.

Collins, P.H. (2000) *Black Feminist Thought: Knowledge, Consciousness, and the Politics of Empowerment*, Second Edition, London, New York: Routledge.

Darnell, S. and Hayhurst, L.M.C. (2011) 'Sport for decolonization: exploring a new praxis of sport for development', *Progress in Developmental Studies*, 11(3): pp. 183–196.

Dart, J. (2013) 'Sports sociology, journals and their editors', *World Leisure Journal*, 55(1), DOI: 10.1080/04419057.2012.759140.

Fleming, S. (1994). 'Sport and South Asian youth: the perils of "false universalism" and stereotyping', *Leisure Studies*, 13(3): pp. 159–177.

Hargreaves, J.A. (2000) *Heroines of Sport: The Politics of Difference and Identity*, London; New York: Routledge.

Hargreaves, J.A. (1994) *Sporting Females: Critical Issues in the History and Sociology of Women's Sport*, London; New York: Routledge.

hooks, b. (1989) *Talking Back: Thinking Feminist, Thinking Black*, Boston, Massachusetts: South End Press.

Howard-Baptiste, S.D. (2014) 'Arctic space, lonely place: "Mammy moments" in Higher Education', *Urban Rev*, 46: pp. 764–782.

Howard-Baptiste, S.D. and Harris, J.C. (2014) 'Teaching then and now: Black female scholars and the mission to move beyond borders', *The Negro Educational Review*, 65(1–4): pp. 5–22.

Hylton, K. (2005) '"Race", sport and leisure: lessons from critical race theory', *Leisure Studies*, 24(1): pp. 81–98.

Kim, K.J. (2013) 'Translation with *Abusive Fidelity*: methodological issues with translating media text about Korean LPGA players', *Sociology of Sport Journal*, 30: pp. 340–358.

Kivel, B.D., Johnson, C.W. and Scraton, S. (2009) '(Re)theorizing leisure, experience and race', *Journal of Leisure Research*, 41(4): pp. 473–493.

Lorde, A (1984, 2007). *Sister Outsider,* second edition, Berkeley: Crossing Press.

Marshall, A. (1994) 'Sensuous sapphires: a study of the social construction of Black female sexuality' in M. Maynard and J. Purvis (eds) *Researching Women's Lives From a Feminist Perspective*, Abingdon, Oxon; New York: Taylor and Francis: pp. 106–124.

Martinez, M.A., Alsandor, D.J., Cortez, L.J., Welton, A.D. and Chang, A. (2015) 'We are stronger together: reflective testimonies of female scholars of color in a research and writing collective', *Reflective Practice*, 16(1): pp. 85–95.

Maylor, U. (2009) 'It is because I'm Black' A Black female research experience', *Race, Ethnicity and Education*, 12(1): pp. 53–64.

Olson, P. and Gillman, L. (2013) 'Combating racialized and gendered ignorance: theorizing a transactional pedagogy of friendship', *Feminist Formations*, 25(1): pp. 59–83.

Puwar, N. (2004) *Space Invaders: Race, Gender and Bodies Out of Place*, Oxford; New York: Berg.

Ratna, A. (2017) 'Black women, Black voices: the contribution of a Spivakian and Black feminist approach to studies of sport and leisure' in J.A. Long, T. Fletcher and B. Watson (eds) *Sport, Leisure and Social Justice*, London and New York: Routledge: pp. 153–167.

Ratna, A. (2013) 'Intersectional plays of identity: the experiences of British Asian female footballers', *Sociological Research Online* www.socresonline.org.uk/18/1/13.html

Ratna, A. (2010) '"Taking the power back!": the politics of British Asian female footballers', *Young, Nordic Journal of Youth Research*, 18(2): pp. 117–132.

Ratna, A. (2007) 'A "fair game?": British Asian females' experiences of racism in women's football' in J. Magee, J. Caudwell, K. Liston and S. Scraton (eds) *Women, Football and Europe: Histories, Equity and Experiences*, Oxford, UK: Meyer and Meyer Sport: pp. 77–96.

Raval, S. (1989) 'Gender, leisure and sport: a case study of young people of South Asian descent. A response', *Leisure Studies*, 8 (1): pp. 237–240.

Roberts, L. (2013) 'Becoming a Black researcher: reflections on racialised identity and knowledge production', *International Review of Qualitative Research*, 6(3): pp. 337–359.

Robinson, S.J. (2013) 'Spoketokenism: Black women talking back about graduate school experiences', *Race, Ethnicity and Education*, 16(2): pp. 155–181.

Rollock, N. (2013) 'A political investment: revisiting race and racism in the research process', *Discourse: Studies in the Cultural Politics of Education*, 34(4): pp. 492–509.

Scraton, S. (2001). 'Reconceptualising race, gender and sport: The contribution of Black feminism' in B. Carrington and I. McDonald (eds) *Race, Sport and British Society*, London: Routledge: pp. 170–187.

Srinivasan, A. (2014) 'In defence of anger' aired on BBC Radio 4's *Four Thought*, 27 August.
Sudbury, J. (1994) *'Other Kinds of Dreams': Black Women's Organisations and the Politics of Transformation*, London; New York: Routledge.
Tate, S.A. (2015) 'Mi Vex: silencing, anger and institutional pain' paper presented at Speaking the Activism of Black Feminism, Trafford Rape Crisis Centre, 26 March.
Wallace, S.L., Moore, S.E. and Curtis, C.M. (2014) 'Black women as Scholars and social agents: standing in the gap', *The Negro Educational Review*, 65(1–4): pp. 44–62.
Watson, B. and Scraton, S. (2001) 'Confronting whiteness? Researching the leisure lives of South Asian mothers', *Journal of Gender Studies*, 10(3): pp. 265–277.
Wright, C., Thompson, S. and Channer, Y. (2007) 'Out of place: Black women academics in British universities', *Women's History Review*, 16(2): pp. 145–162.

Chapter 6

Confronting the 'whiteness' of women's cricket

Excavating hidden truths and knowledge to make sense of non-white women's experiences in cricket

Rafaelle Nicholson

Introduction

Many feminist scholars have noted that "sport history remains the history of man's involvement in sport" (Vertinsky, 1994: 1; Osborne and Skillen, 2010); yet the extent to which sports history – particularly British sports history – continues to privilege a history of 'whiteness' by failing to interrogate racist *and* gendered ideologies is even more troubling. The absence of documented research on women's historical experiences in sport exposes both the masculinisation of the sport, as well as the maleness of this documented history. As van Ingen (2013: 106) states when investigating the history of women's boxing:

> The lack of critical and nuanced historical inquiry on women's boxing history is not solely the fault of poor historical sources. Rather, scholars have paid insufficient attention to how gender, racism, and white privilege have obscured various accounts of history within women's boxing.

However, the absence of historical research on non-white women is even more problematic, and more pervasive when it comes to the sport of cricket. Despite a wealth of research into 'race', racism and the imperial dimensions of cricket – to the extent that Jack Williams has stated that "[r]ace was at the heart of cricket throughout the twentieth century" (Williams, 2001: 1) – almost all of this literature has focused entirely on the men's game. Experiences of female cricketers have either been sidelined or, worse still, simply ignored. Indeed the whiteness and maleness of historical analyses of cricket in twentieth-century Britain have formed the major rationale behind my own research. Research that focuses on unpacking the histories of English cricket all either deals with the women's game in a brief and perfunctory manner (Williams, 1999) or ignores it completely (Birley, 1999; Bateman and Hill, 2011; Davies and Light, 2012). This is unsurprising given the maleness of both sports history and the game of cricket itself. It remains normal, for instance, for major historically-focused texts on cricket to be published with no reference to women at all, let alone ethnic minority women. What information we do have about the experiences of ethnic minority female cricketers in Britain comes from sociologists (Verma and Darby, 1994; Ismond, 2003), who have generally not been concerned with an interrogation of historical context.

According to postcolonial researchers, failing to acknowledge such information has historically allowed (white) 'colonialist powers' to retain and sustain their hold and power over 'the bodies' of non-white Others (Slemon, 1991: 3). It is a reminder of how the first world metropolis has produced and continues to police knowledge about non-white Others that is circulated, accepted, and embedded in Western "institutions, vocabulary, scholarship, imagery, doctrines, even colonial bureaucracies and colonial styles" of knowledge exchange, as well as knowledge that is ignored (Said, 1978: 2). In the contemporary context, this absent knowledge and history is continuously used to explain away non-white women's low participation in sport via-à-vis cultural myths and stereotypes. It is for this reason that it is important to critically interrogate such material so as to lay bare the many ways in which women's cricket was constructed as white and middle class. From the historian's perspective it also points to the need to utilise less traditional archival material, including oral histories, to broaden the perspective offered.

This chapter aims to uncover the previously hidden history of women's cricket in Britain. The central objective is to expose and deconstruct the racial mythologies which contributed to, if not corroborated, idealised perceptions of the female cricketer as 'white' and middle class. The chapter utilises new sources including tour diaries written by white female cricketers between 1948/9 (the date of the first postwar international women's cricket tour) and 1960/1 (the date of the first ever women's tour of South Africa); oral history interviews with white and non-white female cricketers; and other written documents (prepared by white cricketing officials) found in the archive of the Women's Cricket Association (WCA, the governing body of women's cricket in Britain between 1926 and 1998).

Uncovering hidden sporting histories: feminist desire and objectives

At the time my research was undertaken, this otherwise invisible archival knowledge was stored in the WCA archive, hidden away in several large boxes in a shed in a remote Lancashire hamlet, in the garden of a former (white) England cricketer. In this box I discovered press cuttings of overseas tours and a number of tour diaries written by white female English players in the 1940s and 1950s. More hidden truths, including the minutes of the International Women's Cricket Council (IWCC), the international governing body of women's cricket, which was founded in 1958 by England, Australia, New Zealand, South Africa and Holland and represented almost entirely by white (middle-class) women, were found in a private collection, in the home of a former (white) WCA official. I gained access to these documents by contacting the head of the WCA's 'reunion body', the Women's Cricket Associates, who arranged for me to visit the aforementioned players.

Biographers, historians and literary scholars have long considered diary documents to be of major importance for telling history. More recently, sociologists have also taken seriously the idea of using personal documents to construct pictures of social reality from the actors' perspectives (Plummer, 1983). For my research, I embraced these sources accepting that as relics of the past, they represented "cultural artefacts of the moments that produced them" (Dening, 1996: 43). They conveyed details and information about customs, beliefs and cultures and perceptions of non-white women, especially non-white cricketers, which for me was powerful information that needed to be shared with the academy. Not overlooking the dilemma of ascertaining the legitimacy or authenticity of information contained in these sources, I consulted them knowing that they provided details prepared by privileged historical actors whose perceptions could reveal a lot about the gender, racial and class dynamics of cricket at the time. In this sense, they gave me access to a hidden world of knowledge so that I could gain a snapshot of how non-white female cricketers were depicted by their privileged white counterparts. It is important to clarify that I did not embrace these archival sources, especially the tour diaries, as 'pure data' awaiting interpretation; rather, I used them to make sense of and uncover the sets of racialised ideologies that worked to construct and juxtapose differences on the lines of gender, race/ethnicity and class, both to and for the white gaze.

More importantly, throughout my exploratory excavation phase of 'data collection' from the field, I was mindful of the fact that my own position as a white, middle-class feminist sports historian would impinge upon the various descriptions/interpretations, meanings and connotations I would draw from this archival data. I was conscious that I was writing without an insider understanding of racism in sport (or in society generally). Several researchers claim that using archives or historical relics means researchers interpret the past by relating it to cultural assumptions from today's standards, which can affect the 'distinctiveness' of original sources (Scott, 1990: 57). Recognising this point, I also conducted oral history interviews with 27 female cricketers who had all played either international or county level cricket: only one of these participants was a non-white elite female cricketer of African Caribbean heritage. In this research I privilege both the testimonies of the non-white female cricketer, as well as the testimonies shared by the white female cricketers.

Although numerous historians have asserted that oral testimonies must be treated with care due to the unreliability of memory (Thomson, 1994; Yow, 1997), in this research they allowed me to dig beneath the absence of non-white women from the archive, to attempt to fill the gap left by the lack of images or discussions of non-white female cricketers within the written archives. For instance, since my interview questions were based on interrogating white female cricketers' historical perception and encounters, I was able to gather sufficient information to both inform and enhance my understanding and interpretation of information contained in diaries. That being said, I was always very cautious and reflexive in my approach to interviewing, knowing for instance that my own whiteness could shape the dynamics of the interviews with the non-white participant. Nevertheless, I commit to this research knowing that it is my duty as an historian to interrogate issues of gender, race/ethnicity and class, because as Vertinsky (herself a white researcher) puts it:

> Black feminists have something special to say about their distinctive experiences and about issues related to their bodies, their physicality, and their sexuality, but this does not release white feminists from the responsibility to inform themselves about these issues, to provide affinity, and to dialogue with colleagues of color through the act of 'hearing each other into speech'.
>
> (Vertinsky and Captain, 1998: 536)

By consulting hidden knowledge and truth captured in these documents, the intention is to expose and unhinge this past. The hope is that my research will lay down an agenda which other sports historians – including those of colour – will continue to pursue.

It is important to clarify that the historical focus in this chapter is on the period since the Second World War, since this period marked the onset of mass non-white immigration to Britain (Nicholson, 2015). What is troubling for me as a feminist sports historian is that despite the changing racial dynamic and landscape of Britain, women's cricket continues to remain a bastion of 'whiteness'. The scarcity of historical analyses of grassroots women's cricket in Britain makes it difficult to assess with any amount of precision the extent of ethnic minority participation in the sport, as does the lack of survey data on the subject (Nicholson, 2015). It is telling, though, that to date only one African Caribbean woman (Ebony Rainford-Brent, between 2001 and 2010) and two South Asian women (Isa Guha, between 2001 and 2011, and Sonia Odedra, in 2014) have represented England at international level; Odedra did so on a single solitary occasion. Certainly, the absence of non-white members from grassroots club photographs tells a striking tale: that of the absence of ethnic minority women from the game, or indeed the whiteness of the game that refuses to acknowledge or document the presence of non-whites. The latter point is particularly important given the breadth and depth of institutionalised racism in sport (Ahmad, 2011), especially cricket. Carrington and McDonald's (2001: 49) study of English men's cricket highlighted that "racism is both deeply rooted and pervasive in recreational cricket in England". The implications of this on participation were clear: the culture of 'English' cricket was used as a means of excluding black and Asian clubs from the official leagues, causing many of these clubs to lose their grounds and subsequently cease playing the sport altogether. However, for ethnic minority women, who are doubly marginalised on both racial and gender grounds, one cannot assume that their experiences will be the same as their non-white male counterparts. Given the plethora of research on racism in sport and the extent to which a 'cultural deficit' model is often used to explain away low participation levels amongst ethnic minority women (Hargreaves, 1994: 257), there is certainly a need to expose and examine the hostile processes and dynamics that have, over time, contributed to British ethnic minority women staying away from cricket.

In keeping with the ethical sentiments of the relatively few feminist scholars who have interrogated the history of women's participation in sport to expose deep-seated forms of racial privilege and exclusion, this chapter also seeks to privilege hidden stories to reveal concealed truths and knowledge about a 'coloured' demographic of women who matter to me. Like Vertinsky and Captain (1998: 352) who "trace(d) the complex construction and perpetuation of damaging myths of racial and sexual 'difference'" to uncover the extent to which the bodies of black female athletes had been ideologically coded to both uphold notions of acceptable white and black femininity, and undermine their accomplishments, my work also seeks to re-read and deconstruct the racial mythologies that have contributed to our understanding of non-white women's cricket. For me, the excavation of women's cricketing history is informed by a feminist desire to make visible the complex gender, class and race relations involved in English cricket, while also exposing the enduring inequalities that negatively impacted the sporting experiences of ethnic minority women cricketers in Britain. As will be evidenced throughout this chapter, my discussion points to the different ways in which the women's cricketing community, made up of the constituent clubs of the Women's Cricket Association (WCA), operated in exclusionary ways to both consciously and unconsciously cultivate and uphold an environment that ultimately alienated and excluded non-white women from the sport throughout the twentieth century.

This research is both grounded in and informed by a postcolonial feminist lens. Over the last 30 years postcolonial feminism has made a crucial intervention in postcolonial studies, in its exhortation to consider gender issues and to reinsert women's experiences into the study of Empire

(Chaudhuri and Strobel, 1992; Sharpe, 1993; Jayawardena, 1995). White middle-class Victorian women, it has been shown, played a key role in colonialism as well as in the construction of 'white' identities (Frankenberg, 1992; Brown *et al.*, 1999). However, as Scraton (2001: 178) highlights, this approach has often been lacking in histories of sport; there remains a need to "disclose sport's historical role in the construction of white identities". This chapter therefore seeks to explore the discourses surrounding non-white female cricketers, as expressed through written and oral accounts of touring in the postwar period. The first section examines the constructedness of white superiority during international tours, as presented in tour diaries and newspaper accounts. The second section examines the effect this construction of 'whiteness' had when non-white cricketers were encountered, with a particular focus on the construction of the non-white cricketer as 'masculine' because of her refusal to adopt white dress codes. Overall, an attempt is made to uncover the history of gendered, racialised myths of racial 'difference' that have arguably shaped the experiences of non-white female athletes right up to the present day.

Sport, colonialism and cricket

That the British strongly believed in the 'idealism' found in sport and the 'positive values' it provided to those who played along is well documented in the wider sporting literature (see Mangan, 1981; Sissons and Stoddart, 1984; Sandiford and Stoddart, 1988; Holt, 1989: 204; MacLean, 2010). Sport was embraced and championed as an 'honourable pursuit' that facilitated the construction of the Empire (Mangan, 1986). Colonial governors revered sports like cricket for transferring dominant British beliefs and moral codes regarding social behaviour and standards to the colonies (Sandiford and Stoddart, 1988: 652) as well constructing "European (pseudoscientific) theories of racial and cultural difference", particularly with regards to perceptions of the physical and biological inadequacies of the non-white fe/male physical body (Burdsey, 2007: 20; Mills and Dimeo, 2003). Sport thus became an arena where the alleged flaws and inabilities of 'Other' races were not only manufactured, but further juxtaposed to construct an image of the British as civilised, superior, and capable when compared to their inferior indigenous counterparts (Dimeo, 2001, 2002). Not only did these racial ideologies create racial hierarchies, but they also established and maintained Britain's "dominant patterns of social organisation and [...] power" over 'Other' races (Houlihan, 1991: 10). Between 1875 and 1914 white middle-class men were not only able to gain economic control over the colonies, but they were also able to conceptualise women and men in the colonies in a specific way that legitimated their domination. In many ways these ideologies continued to impact the sport of cricket long after the (formal) era of British imperialism. During the twentieth century, for instance, men's cricket and imperialism "became mutually supporting ideologies", helping to promote a 'white' British national identity (Williams, 2001: 1). Incidents such as the animosity felt towards West Indian pace bowlers in the 1970s and the Pakistani team during their 1987 and 1992 series against England, during which the Pakistanis were accused of cheating, contributed to a continued ideology of white superiority, which permeated men's English cricket decades after the Empire had formally concluded (Williams, 2001). Having already illustrated the extent to which much of the documented literature alludes to men's cricket, I turn my attention to unpacking how these ideas also infiltrated and influenced women's cricket.

A noteworthy place to begin this discussion is to look at the establishment of the WCA in 1926, which at the time was a largely middle-class, white organisation. Generally, the sport required time and financial independence in order for women to purchase the correct equipment, pay club subscriptions, and travel to away matches. My own detailed research into the backgrounds of those women who represented England in the postwar decade suggests that this continued to be the case after 1945 (Nicholson, 2015). For example, of the 26 women who played at international level between 1945 and 1955, only one attended a council-run elementary school. Seven attended grant-aided secondary grammar schools; two attended private Catholic schools; one attended a voluntary-aided Methodist school; and six attended independent day or boarding schools, with five of these falling into the category of large public girls' schools. In terms of occupation, 10 of the 20 women for whom data is available worked as teachers (8 of the 10 taught Physical Education), and another worked for the Central Council of Physical Recreation (CCPR, a national body set up in 1935 to help local authorities with recreational provision). Two worked permanently after the war as officers in the newly-formed women's armed forces; three worked as civil servants; one worked in retailing; two were clerks and one a secretary. Additionally, given that women made up only 24 per cent of the university population by 1958 and only 0.2 per cent of working-class girls were able to attend university in these years (Dyhouse, 2001), the fact that 5 of the 24 gained degrees or diplomas and 7 more attended physical training colleges indicates a certain level of privilege. Those women selected for international tours after 1945 were generally selected on merit, in accordance with their cricketing abilities, but until the 1960s all international women's cricket tours were entirely self-funded by players, and those who put themselves forward for selection thus tended to be from middle-class backgrounds. Having discussed, briefly, the cricketing history, it is to a closer analysis of how these white, privileged women used their cricketing tours to carve out and reaffirm a sense of white superiority on the lines of race, ethnicity and class that the discussion now turns.

'Ignorance of spirit and conventions'

As indicated earlier, many of the white participants of this study ($n=26$) were privileged economically. However, at home they were subject to discrimination on the grounds of gender, suffering from limited access to facilities and a lack of media interest in their sport. It was only when these white women participated in international cricket tours that they got to travel the globe, encounter non-white people, and experience different cultures and different ways of life, that a real sense of racial privilege emerged. This is unsurprising given that middle-class English women's sense of immense and absolute moral certitude, self confidence, superiority and assertion as a class was itself predicated on Empire. There is no denying that the Empire provided many opportunities for English women in areas that were otherwise not open to them in England at the time: opportunities to serve and act as missionaries, educators, nurses, doctors, and women preachers. Even as helpmeets of imperial men – as wives of powerful missionaries, political tract-writers, voyeurs, settlers or domestic workers, English women were no longer just "victims of the bourgeois domestic ideology", but instead pivotal in carving out important niches for themselves in the social, political and cultural domains of the Empire. Through their various missions, they created very specific messages about Other men and women and transmitted these imperialistic messages back home to England and to English men in the colonies.

In my own research, the sense of opportunity that English women obtained from the Empire was apparent. Tour diaries from the early years of international women's cricket indicate that those involved at the top levels of the sports came to share, celebrate and perpetuate imperialist ideologies that were already so present in the men's game. Netta Rheinberg, the tour manager on the 1948/49 and 1957/58 tours of Australia and New Zealand, herself a secretary and the daughter of a wealthy export merchant, provides a good example of this. Her description of the large bungalow owned by the team's British host in Colombo in 1948, where they disembarked for a practice match en route to Australia, was as follows: "beautifully and luxuriantly furnished [...] black Cingalese [*sic*] servants everywhere. One claps one's hands and there they are" (Rheinberg, 1948). Additionally on their tour of Panama City en route to New Zealand in 1957, she wrote:

> Ended up at the Panama Hotel – glory me – what a place. £5 a day for a room in season excluding meals is the cheapest. Maids and servants are ten a penny and get paid about $10–20 a month.
>
> (Rheinberg, 1957)

Given the shortage of domestic servants in Britain in the postwar decade, the sense of envy in both these accounts is almost visceral.

Tour diaries such as Rheinberg's suggest that the act of participating in an international tour could create a sense of racial and imperial superiority, due to the fact that those selected acted as informal ambassadors for Britain while abroad. One player who toured Australasia in 1968/9 suggested that England players were treated "like VIPs" (interview, 2014), and this appears to have been the case throughout the postwar years. The 1948/9 tourists socialised with politicians including the Australian and New Zealand Prime Ministers, and famous cricketers like Donald Bradman, and Rheinberg wrote in 1949 that "High Commissioners seem to be two a penny!" (Rheinberg, 1949). Mollie Buckland, one of the players who participated in the 1960/1 tour of South Africa, wrote:

> After a late night neither Ann [Jago] nor I were anxious to get up early. We woke about 9.0 am, rang down and ordered breakfast in bed. There we were, like two titled ladies, waiting for the coloured waiter to bring up the menu, so that we could order.
>
> (Buckland, 1960)

Within these tour diaries, female cricketers, who otherwise were working women in England, were now positioning themselves as 'titled women' – but only when confronted by non-white women who did not share their privileged position. A sense of power was engendered by the powerlessness apparent in the situation of the non-white women they encountered while on tour. A sense of Englishness was also created and retained in very specific ways as receiving breakfast in bed in a radically different landscape instils a level of gentility and bourgeois decorum. This Englishness provided the index against which colonised women were judged, and against which the white middle-class women judged themselves.

The contrast between the 'VIP' status of the England touring team and other groups which they encountered while abroad is emphasised in one striking passage from Netta Rheinberg's 1948/9 diary, which describes the England team's visit to a migrant camp in Australia in December 1948, whereby the effects of the 'White Australia' immigration policy (Carey and McLisky, 2009) were witnessed first-hand:

> We were driven to an Australian migrant camp – where displaced persons from the Baltic countries are 'processed' and given jobs.... The first thing the people learn is English – and they pick up the necessary in about 6 months. The various offices throughout Australia then apply for groups of workers of various categories and these are sent from the camp as requested. Each person is given certain freedom of choice and the whole thing seemed to me to be done on a democratic and broad-minded basis [...].

> Mr. Rees explained that there were three classes of immigrant required by Australia: (1) British, (2) European, (3) any other white race [...]. We were all treated to free fizzy drink of vivid colours and departed to see the local canning factory.
>
> (Rheinberg, 1948)

Everything about this passage points to the casual way which the England team, as national representatives and as privileged observers, accepted this racial hierarchy, with non-white races excluded as 'undesirable', as normal and natural. The settlers in the Australian camp are seen as benefiting from the civilising mission of the English who in addition to teaching them a civilised language, also give these Others 'freedom'.

From a postcolonial feminist perspective, the notion of an unfamiliar, inferior and uncivilised 'Other' is being strategically constructed by players throughout their diaries, and this discourse legitimates the unequal configurations of power apparent between the colonist and the colonised. 'Orientalising' (i.e. discursively constructing) an irrational and backward 'colony' has been shown by postcolonial theorists and historians alike to have been one of many ways through which the white (or Aryan) European civilisations and cultures were able to position themselves as rational, moral and superior (Jan-Mohamed, 1985). This kind of 'Othering' of non-white women is seen clearly by the end of Rheinberg's tour diary. On the voyage home in 1949, for example, the team dismounted at Curaçao, and Rheinberg wrote an evocative description of the sights that awaited them that is tinged with casual racism:

> These people are very dark skinned – negroid looking [...]. We toured the streets [...] the women carrying baskets on their heads and some holding picanninies in their arms. I attempted to photograph some of them but they ran away every time – probably thinking it was the evil eye!
>
> (Rheinberg, 1949)

Thus African women in Rheinberg's diaries are represented according to racial stereotype as belonging to an 'unenlightened' culture which still believed in voodoo, black magic and non-scientific principles. Additionally, 'Arab' men are represented by Rheinberg as dangerous sexual predators, as evidenced when she tries to prevent any of the English team from disembarking at Port Said on the boat voyage to Australia:

> I am not prepared to take the responsibility for the party unless we are escorted by males [...]. It is dangerous to go too far afield for several reasons – (a) anti-British feeling (b) attractive females among Arabs.
>
> (Rheinberg, 1948)

By contrast, Rheinberg emphasises in her diaries that British people in Australia are viewed as brave, kind and stoic, especially in the wake of the Second World War:

> We constantly get the almost sob-stuff attitude of all we went through in the war and how magnificent we'd been – and they lay it on with gusto.
>
> (Rheinberg, 1949)

Dichotomous notions of us and them, Empire and colony (or Others) were thus made real for these women during tours abroad: they served as 'colonial encounters' that allowed white, middle-class female cricketers to be presented with the deepest, most recurring image of the 'Other', analogous to Said's (1978) analysis of the distortion by British and French colonists of non-European civilisations. Said (1978: 2) also argued that distinctions between the colony and coloniser were made real to the Western empire through a variety of literary, political, fictional, scientific writings, travelogues and artistic depictions of the colony and its indigenous cultures and peoples. Some tour diaries were published when players arrived home (see for example Joy, 1950); others were merely shared informally amongst the women's cricket community, being read by friends and relatives. Along with scrapbooks made by players on tour, featuring postcards, ticket stubs and other 'souvenirs', this kind of written representation of tours served to reinforce notions of 'Other'/cultural difference even once players arrived back home.

Race, ethnicity and 'cultural differences' all operated as significant markers in juxtaposing notions of 'difference' between the European 'Self' (white Empire) and 'Others' (non-white colonies). They also legitimised the mutation of unequal (hierarchical) power relations between 'Empire' and 'colony' (Fanon, 1965, 1967). Within women's cricket, this solidified itself through the formation of the International Women's Cricket Council (IWCC) in 1958, a supposedly worldwide organisation of women's cricket associations, formed "for the furtherance of cricket among women and girls" (IWCC minutes, 1958). In actual fact, it was an organisation of the former white Dominions: four of the founder member associations were those in England, Australia, New Zealand and (white) South Africa, and at the 1960 meeting it was agreed to write to Canada and Ireland to encourage them to join – despite the fact that women's cricket in both these countries was almost non-existent. The process of British decolonisation may have been formally complete, but an informal process of exclusion founded upon 'racial difference' continued to operate in the women's cricket community. India, for example, was not issued with an invitation to participate in the inaugural women's World Cup, held in England in 1973.

Indeed women's cricket associations in India and the Caribbean were not admitted to the IWCC until 1973 and 1976 respectively, and even when they were, the racial-imperialist mentality of difference remained firmly in place. When England sent a team to play a triangular series against Jamaica and Trinidad and Tobago in the Caribbean in 1971, for example, the English players were scathing about the inability of their hosts both to play in accordance with the spirit of the game, and to act as 'civilised' hostesses. After England fell short of victory in the second Test by a mere three runs, England captain Rachael Heyhoe-Flint wrote that: "the frustration of being so near and yet so far from victory made me readily lose my temper with both the opposition and the Jamaican administrators". The implication in her autobiography is that the Jamaican authorities deliberately prevented her side from being able to achieve victory, both on this occasion and later in the series: that England were cheated of the series win which was rightfully theirs (Heyhoe-Flint, 1978). Because players were no longer keeping tour diaries by this time, the 'Othering' process is less visible in written sources, but oral histories from those who were touring help to fill the gap. They reflect the belief that the Caribbean compared unfavourably with the former white Dominions as a place to tour, as in the following interview with one of the players who participated in the 1971 visit:

RN: How did that [the 1971 tour to the Caribbean] compare with the 68/9 tour [to Australia and New Zealand]?

S: Couldn't really compare it at all! I mean in fairness they weren't used to doing tours, and didn't know what was expected. Some of the accommodation left a lot to be desired, certainly in Trinidad. Jamaica was okay. Although having said that there was quite a variety of accommodation. I was very fortunate with another one of our team mates, and we were in a wonderful estate, and we had a maid to look after us. And the owners had just left us with the maid, they went off all the while we were there. So we had a car, a swimming pool, we had a fantastic time. And yet two others were with an Indian family down the road, who were lovely, but they had to eat with their fingers and eat rice! So it was very different.

Once again, the non-white 'Other' in this account is represented as domestic servant and/or as uncivilised beings lacking basic eating etiquette.

Etiquette and 'cultural difference' were central to the WCA's notions of 'them' and 'us'. Hargreaves has argued that when studying ethnic minority women and sport, we need to consider the 'intersectionality' of their identities, with a focus on how multiple different oppressions curtailed their participation in physical activities (Hargreaves, 2000). As Vertinksy and Captain put it, "female athletes are racial *and* gendered *and* classed, with each and/or all of these categories taking on a different importance in certain moments and particular contexts" (1998: 535). All evidence suggests that the WCA was not merely exclusionist in racial terms, but in class ones too. This doubly marginalised African Caribbean and South Asian women, who not only often lived in less affluent circumstances than their white counterparts, but were unable to conform to the WCA's coding of class as a white sensibility, oppositional to the imperialist perception that women of colour simply could not understand the 'correct', 'civilised' way to play cricket.

Class was conceived of by the WCA in behavioural terms, with middle-class coded as 'desirable' and working-class coded as 'undesirable'. One editorial of the WCA's official magazine, *Women's Cricket*, stated:

> Cricket for women, I am sure and thank goodness for it, will never rank among the mass movements of the country's history, because the Association has from its earliest days eschewed stunts and undesirable publicity.
>
> (September 1954)

The WCA's ethos in the postwar years had its basis in an imperialist conception of cricket as being more than just a sport, but a set of rules and behaviours which needed to be followed both on and off the pitch. The WCA, wrote Pollard in 1947, would continue to be guided by the "principles and standards" which had led the organisation through the 1930s, whether or not these might "have made things seem more difficult or slow of development" in the past (*Women's Cricket*, May 1947). Thus, for example, the new WCA handbook contained a section on 'cricket etiquette', and *Women's Cricket* ran article series on 'Courtesies'. Instructions included:

> Play as one of the team.
>
> If the backing-up batsman leaves his crease before you bowl, it is quite legal to run him out, but it is only sporting to warn him the first time.
>
> Avoid sitting in front of the pavilion with your feet up on the rails or on the seat in front, since it shows expanses of leg – if nothing worse.
>
> Do something about your personal appearance for lunch and tea and put on a blazer or other extra garments.
>
> (*Women's Cricket*, 14 May 1954 and 28 May 1954)

To WCA members, non-white women would have been unable to meet the criteria of this kind of imperialist class-based sensibility. The only representations of coloured women in writings on women's cricket during this time were those either in the tour diaries of the players, as uncivilised 'Other'/maid and servant – as with Rheinberg's descriptions of the "darkies" in Curaçao, and the "black Cingalese [*sic*] servants" in Colombo

(1949) – or in the WCA's Tour Reports which presented South Asian women as entirely ignorant of the "spirit and conventions" of cricket (WCA memorandum, 1987). The idea that a non-white 'Other' would be able to participate in cricket was thus rejected in terms of class codes of the game.

This was apparent when the Women's Cricket Association of India toured England for the first time in 1986, a tour which fully reflected the WCA's continued belief in their own racial and cricketing superiority. Tensions between the two nations were rife throughout the tour; during one of the early tour matches against Middlesex, the Indian captain reportedly verbally abused the English umpires, and accused them of cheating. The breaking-point came during the first Test match at Collingham; on the final afternoon of the four-day game, England were chasing 254 in the fourth innings for a victory. The WCA's account is as follows:

> A complaint was made [by the Indians] about the size of the Ground. During play numerous requests were made regarding the sight-screen, the reflection of the sun on various fittings around the ground and parked cars. The assistance rendered by the Ground Authorities to alleviate the problems was exemplary. On the fourth day, the over-rate (7) in the penultimate hour precluded a result being achieved by either side. The acting Captain did not seem to have full authority over her players and the delaying tactics were to be deprecated.
>
> (WCA memorandum, 1987)

According to newspaper accounts, after play was over, the WCA chairman entered their dressing room and told them privately that they would be ostracised in women's cricket unless they changed their ways. Several of the players were reduced to tears and the then Indian captain accused the WCA chairman of 'racial abuse'. A written apology was demanded and eventually granted, after the Indians threatened to return home without fulfilling the rest of their tour commitments. Yet the WCA's account of the tour concluded that:

> Throughout the Tour, the tantrums of the team and flagrant gamesmanship signified an obvious lack of understanding of the Laws of Cricket and a complete ignorance of the 'spirit of the game'.... Their ignorance of the spirit and conventions of touring abroad, namely to accept that one's hosts are doing their best to ensure that things run smoothly, caused antagonism among the membership.
>
> (1987)

One WCA official told the *Daily Mail* that the heart of the problem was that "the Indians are a race who will always find something to complain about" (*Daily Mail*, 5 July 1986). The infantilisation of the Indian team in these accounts is entirely in keeping with the representation of non-whites as too primitive to comprehend the English sport of cricket, an ideological positioning which was also at work in the men's game (Williams, 2001). The constructedness of white superiority and the 'Othering' of the colonial subject so present in player tour diaries may have been crude but it was also effective: it had worked its way into formal relationships between the English WCA and its sister associations in former colonies, and continued to hold sway even by the 1980s.

Mythologies of race: whiteness of sports history

Vertinsky and Captain have highlighted the ways in which the stereotyping of African-American women in the interwar period allowed them to participate in certain sports (namely athletics), yet denied them entry to others:

> Attitudes toward the African American woman's amazonian work capacity, and lack of physical and emotional sensitivity, flowed easily into notions about the natural strength and 'manly' athletic abilities of black women in running, jumping, and throwing activities.
>
> (Vertinksy and Captain, 1998)

How did these kind of racial stereotypes manifest themselves within cricket? The previous section highlighted the way in which non-white female cricketers were presented as not embracing the ethics or the etiquette of good sportsmen. However, mythologies of race also developed in the postwar period around the bodies and athletic abilities of non-white cricketers.

As noted above, players were no longer keeping tour diaries by the time of the inaugural tour to the Caribbean in 1971. Newspaper coverage surrounding non-white cricketers, however, is revealing, such as the following passage from the *Observer* during the inaugural World Cup in 1973:

> The West Indians are an oddly ungraceful lot on the field, prone to fall over when batting and to stumble up to bowl as if they're not sure which foot to put down last. But they do have some big, strong and very handsome cricketers, and nobody was hitting the ball harder at Lord's than the Jamaican batsmen.
>
> (*Observer*, 17 June 1973)

In the cricketing context, describing players as "ungraceful" is extremely significant: cricket has always been represented as a 'gentleman's game', requiring a refined and graceful approach, rather than sheer power and strength. The discourses surrounding women's cricket had particularly emphasised this aspect, because it legitimised female participation in the sport. This is apparent in the following extract from the foreword to the WCA's history of women's cricket, *Fair Play* (Heyhoe-Flint and Rheinberg, 1976), written by BBC cricket commentator Brian Johnston:

> I have always supported the girls and think that they've got quite a lot to teach us men. First-class cricket tends nowadays to be rather dull and scientific or 'professional' as it's so often called. The ladies bring a touch of grace to what is essentially a graceful game.
>
> (Heyhoe-Flint and Rheinberg, 1976: 9)

Compare this with the description of the West Indian female cricketers above and it becomes apparent that African Caribbean bodies are being presented as comically unsuited to the graceful sport of cricket.

There is also an element of masculinisation in the description of Jamaican cricketers as "big, strong and handsome". The idea of non-white bodies as masculine was tied in with their inability to fulfil the correct 'etiquette' required of female cricketers, as outlined above. A good example is the WCA's continued attempts to enforce stringent dress regulations for representative matches. Before 1939, rules had dictated that teams must play in white dresses or divided skirts. While after 1945, the Executive Committee amended the rules to allow for 'shorts', the length – not shorter than four inches from the ground when kneeling – was still carefully controlled, and knee length socks were required wear (WCA Yearbook, 1945). Even by the 1990s, resistance to changing from skirts to trousers remained strong. A vote at the 1998 AGM of the WCA on the issue resulted in a reassertion of the rule that all players in domestic competitions should continue to wear skirts (*Wicket Women*, Spring 1998). Even when the new Women's Cricket Advisory Group, formed when the merger with the England and Wales Cricket Board (ECB) formally occurred in 1998, ruled in 1999 that trousers could now be worn at all levels of women's cricket in England, a compromise was instituted whereby clubs could vote themselves on whether they wished to introduce trousers, and for a few years matches took place whereby sides would play in skirts or trousers according to preference (*Wicket Women*, Summer 1999). It was only as a younger generation of players came through and began to dominate domestic cricket, in the early 2000s, that trousers became the norm. This preoccupation with skirts was founded upon a desire to appear 'feminine', as my interview with a player who joined the WCA in the 1950s confirmed:

> They would never, never have worn trousers then. It was not the done thing ... no way would you wear anything that looked male. No, never ... because you were trying to keep feminine in a man's game.

Arguably, this image of the refined, decorous and 'feminine' female cricketer dressed in a skirt was deliberately cultivated in opposition to the women in India and the West Indies who had always worn trousers to play cricket. Those women who chose to play cricket in trousers were somehow not 'real women', excluded as they were from the construction of the idealised white female cricketing body. An interview with England cricketer Sarah Potter in the *Daily Mail* in 1981, for example, included her description of West Indies Women at the Oval in 1979: "They wore trousers and, at a distance, to my terrified eyes, they looked like men!" The interview concluded with Potter stating: "If cricket made me muscular, I'd jump out of the window. I'd sacrifice a lot for the game, but never my femininity". The wearing of trousers, while represented as an issue of decorum linked to social class, thus became yet another marker of racial 'Otherness'. This was sometimes explicit – the West Indian women who participated in the International XI in the 1973 World Cup were forced to play in white shorts "in order to conform with the other [white] members of the team" (Heyhoe-Flint and Rheinberg, 1976) – but always served as a continuous marker of difference.

As well as textual representations, racial mythologies based on the bodies of non-white women were also present in oral history interviews, such as those I conducted with senior WCA members who worked as PE teachers. The clearest example of this was in my interview with one former England player, who represented England between the late 1960s and the 1980s and taught at girls' grammar schools in London throughout this time:

RN: And were there many black or Asian women playing in this country... when you were playing?

W: Not many. No. Not many. And I still don't think there are many.... At club level no, and England level no ... even at school not many of the black girls – they'd play more netball and do athletics. It was interesting. Swimming, they were not very good at, the black girls, because their bone density, they tended to sink. But netball and athletics they liked. They didn't like tennis very much. And hockey and cricket were not games that they liked. It was really interesting to see that.

Given that a large number of female cricketers worked as PE teachers (Nicholson, 2015), it is concerning to think that this type of pseudo-scientific biological racism may have permeated large numbers of girls' schools where cricket was played in the latter half of the twentieth century. What does seem apparent is that the 'whiteness' of women's cricket was partly founded upon racialised bodily myths, tied in with class-based notions of correct cricketing etiquette.

Racialised myths were also present in my interview with a former player and Chairman of the WCA:

RN: What about if I was to say that there's this perception of women's cricket as quite white?

C: Yep.

RN: Yeah. You'd agree with that.

C: Yes. But you could say that about, well certainly men's cricket internationally [...] we had a lovely black girl called Celia who played a long time ago, an absolute hoot, but it takes a big step for them to come and knock on the door and say 'I'd like to play'. A big step [...]. And I think apart from, well, certain inner-city clubs, I would say outside of the big cities cricket is very much a white sport. It's just when you get into London and I suppose Birmingham and Manchester, a lot of the leagues have got a lot of Asians. But yeah, why isn't men's cricket tapping into that talent? It must be huge.

RN: So it's a cricket-wide problem.

C: I think so, yeah.

'C' argued two things during our interview: first, that the 'whiteness' of women's cricket was simply something that carried over unproblematically from the men's game; and second, that it was felt to be the responsibility of African Caribbean and South Asian girls and women to "knock on the door" of the sport, rather than the responsibility of women's cricket to alter its image and seek to actively recruit women from different backgrounds. Both these attitudes appear to have been pervasive, and this helps to explain why there was never any policy commitment on behalf of the Women's Cricket Association to attempt to increase participation in women's cricket by ethnic minority groups. Additionally, as Mike Marqusee observed, the English men's cricket authorities generally denied claims that racism existed within the game, creating a "culture of complacency and denial" which presumably permeated across into the women's game (1994: 314).

Even more problematic was that this former player, who had a great deal of power in her role as chairman, refused to recognise in our interview that her own deeply-held racial stereotyping may have negatively impacted the ethnic profile of the sport. While she did partially accept the view that white spaces can be exclusionary, her argument that for non-white women participation in club cricket would be "a big step" appears to be based on the ever-present view of South Asian women as both passive and unable to participate in sport due to cultural constraints (Scraton, 2001). Additionally her description of 'Celia', the only African Caribbean woman she had ever played cricket with, as "an absolute hoot", fits only too neatly with the long-established Western idea of African Caribbean women as "inept and comical domestic servant" (Vertinsky and Captain, 1998) – an image that Mae King (1973: 12) describes in the American context as a "loser image" which has served to justify racial oppression. In this context, 'Celia' is being presented in a way that actually serves to reinforce the myth that non-white women are incapable of participating in cricket: much like the Jamaican cricketers described above, she is an object of comedy, not a serious competitor.

Conclusion

Throughout this chapter, I have examined multiple historical sources, including tour diaries, newspaper accounts and oral histories, and drawn upon postcolonial feminist thinking to expose the pervasiveness of imperialist discourses in women's cricket during postwar Britain. In doing so, I have demonstrated the many ways in which 'whiteness' and English middle-class femininity in particular, was predicated on the notion of a backward, inferior Empire. In the absence of detailed accounts of the experiences of non-white cricketers, this research serves to highlight the types of racial mythologies that polluted cricketing spaces, and gave superior meaning to the idealised 'white' female sporting body.

In some ways, the focus on racialised imagery and mythology in this chapter reveals more about those in charge of women's cricket than it does about the reality of African Caribbean or South Asian experiences of the sport: the 'whiteness' of women's cricket was not a fixed reality, but something constructed by its participants. If non-white women were not participating in cricket – and much more work needs to be done into grassroots women's cricket before this issue can be fully understood – the problem was not with non-white communities but with the insidious forms of racism at work within the sport. Future research might usefully examine the experiences of non-white women themselves, to more fully understand the impact of the racial ideologies outlined above.

Ultimately, it is hoped that this chapter will serve as a call to arms for others working within sports history. Women's sport history, as Osborne and Skillen (2010: 189) seek to remind us, "remains a peculiarly neglected area of academic research in Britain"; for historians shaping this new endeavour, there is an imperative to look not just at issues of gender but at the ways in which gender intersected with race (and class) to shape the experiences of women who sought to participate in sport across the twentieth century. We can only produce better histories as a result.

References

Ahmad, A. (2011) 'British Muslim Female Experiences in Football: Islam, Identity and the Hijab', in D. Burdsey (ed.), *Race, Ethnicity and Football*. Oxford: Routledge.

Bateman, A. and Hill, J. (eds) (2011) *The Cambridge Companion to Cricket*. Cambridge: University Press.

Birley, D. (1999) *A Social History of English Cricket*. London: Aurum.

Brown, H., Gilkes, M. and Kaloski-Naylor, A. (eds) (1999) *White Women: Critical Perspectives on Race and Gender*. New York: Raw Nerve Books.
Buckland, M. Tour diary, 1960/61. Private collection.
Burdsey, D. (2007) *British Asians and Football: Culture, Identity and Exclusion*. London: Routledge.
Carey, J. and McLisky, C. (2009) 'Introduction', in J. Carey and C. McLisky (eds), *Creating White Australia*. Sydney: Sydney University Press: pp. ix–xxiii.
Carrington, B. and McDonald, I. (2001) 'Whose Game Is It Anyway? Racism in Local League Cricket', in Carrington and McDonald (eds), *'Race', Sport and British Society*. London: Routledge: pp. 49–69.
Chaudhuri, N. and Strobel, M. (1992) *Western Women and Imperialism: Complicity and Resistance*. Bloomington: Indiana University Press.
Daily Mail (1986) 'Owzat for the Prima Donnas of the Crease!', *Daily Mail*, 5 July.
Daily Mail (1981) 'Wicket Girl!', *Daily Mail*, 12 September.
Davies, P. and Light, R. (2012) *Cricket and Community in England: 1800 to the Present Day*. Manchester: Manchester University Press.
Dening, G. (1996) 'A Poetic for Histories', in Cook, T. (ed.), *Performances*. Chicago: University of Chicago Press.
Dimeo, P. (2002) 'Colonial Bodies, Colonial Sport: "Martial" Punjabis, "Effeminate" Bengalis and the Development of Indian Football', *International Journal of the History of Sport* 19: p. 1.
Dimeo, P. (2001) 'Football and Politics in Bengal: Colonialism, Nationalism, Communalism', in P. Dimeo and H. Mills (eds), *Soccer in South Asia: Empire, Nation, Diaspora*. London: Frank Cass: pp. 57–74.
Dyhouse, C. (2001) 'Education', in I. Zweiniger-Bargielowska (ed.), *Women in Twentieth-Century Britain*. Harlow: Longman: pp. 119–133.
Fanon, F. (1967) *Black Skin White Masks*. New York: Grove Press.
Fanon, F. (1965) *A Dying Colonialism*. London: Penguin Books.
Frankenberg, R. (1992) *The Social Construction of Whiteness: White Women, Race Matters*. London: Routledge.
Hargreaves, J. (2000) *Heroines of Sport. The Politics of Difference and Identity*. Oxford: Routledge.
Hargreaves, J. (1994) *Sporting Females: Critical Issues in the History and Sociology of Women's Sports*. London: Routledge.
Heyhoe-Flint, R. (1978) *Heyhoe! The Autobiography of Rachael Heyhoe-Flint*. London: Pelham Books.
Heyhoe-Flint, R. and Rheinberg, N. (1976) *Fair Play: The Story of Women's Cricket*. London: Angus and Robertson.
Holt, R. (1989) *Sport and the British: A Modern History*. Oxford: Clarendon Press.
Houlihan, B. (1991) *The Government and Politics of Sport*. London: Routledge.
International Women's Cricket Council minutes, 1958–1990. Private collection, Surrey.
Ismond, P. (2003) *Black and Asian Athletes in British Sport and Society: A Sporting Chance?* Houndsmill: Palgrave Macmillan.
Jan-Mohamed, A. (1985) 'The Economy of Manichean Allegory: The Function of Racial Difference in Colonialist Literature', *Critical Enquiry* 12: p. 1.
Jayawardena, K. (1995) *The White Woman's Other Burden: Western Women and South Asia during British Colonial Rule*. London: Routledge.

Joy, N. (1950) *Maiden Over*. London: Sporting Handbooks.
King, M. (1973) 'The Politics of Sexual Stereotypes', *The Black Scholar* 4: p. 6.
MacLean, M. (2010) 'Ambiguity within the Boundary: Re-reading CLR James's *Beyond a Boundary*', *Journal of Sport History* 37(1): pp. 99–117.
Mangan, J.A. (1986) *The Games Ethic and Imperialism*. Middlesex: Viking.
Mangan, J.A. (1981) *Athleticism in the Victorian and Edwardian Public School*. Cambridge: Cambridge University Press.
Marqusee, M. (1994) *Anyone But England. An Outsider Looks at English Cricket*. London: Aurum.
Mills, J. and Dimeo, P. (2003) 'When gold is fired it shines: sport, the imagination and the body', in J. Bale and M. Cronin (eds), *Sport and Post-Colonialism*. Oxford: Berg: pp. 107–123.
Nicholson, R. (2015) '"Like a man trying to knit"? Women's cricket in Britain, 1945–2000'. Unpublished PhD thesis, Queen Mary University of London.
Observer (1973) 'Grace Turns Up at Lord's', *The Observer*, 17 June.
Osborne, C. and Skillen, F. (2010). 'The State of Play: Women in British Sport History', *Sport in History* 30(2): pp. 189–195.
Plummer, K. (1983) *Documents of Life: An Introduction to the Problems and Literature of a Humanistic Method*. Reading: George Allen & Unwin.
Rheinberg, N. Tour diaries, 1948/9 and 1957/8. Private collection, Lancashire.
Said, E. (1978) *Orientalism*. London: Routledge and Kegan Paul.
Sandiford, K. and Stoddart, B. (1988) *The Imperial Game*. Manchester: Manchester University Press.
Scott, J. (1990) *A Matter of Record: Documentary Sources in Social Research*. Cambridge: Polity Press.
Scraton, S. (2001) 'Re-conceptualising Race, Gender and Sport: The Contribution of Black Feminism', in B. Carrington and I. McDonald (eds), *Racism and British Sport*. London, Routledge: pp. 170–187.
Sharpe, J. (1993) *Allegories of Empire: The Figure of Woman in the Colonial Text*. Minneapolis: University of Minnesota Press.
Sissons, R. and Stoddart, B. (1984). *Cricket and Empire. The 1932–33 Bodyline tour of Australia*. London: Allen & Unwin.
Slemon, S. (1991) 'Modernism's Last Post', in I. Adam and H. Tiffin (eds), *Past the Last Post: Theorizing Post-Colonialism and Post-Modernism*. London: Harvester/Wheatsheaf.
Sport England (2000) *Sports Participation and Ethnicity in England: National Survey 1999/2000*. London: Sport England.
Thomson, A. (1994) *Anzac Memories: Living with the Legend*. Oxford: OUP.
van Ingen, C. (2013) '"Seeing What Frames Our Seeing": Seeking Histories on Early Black Female Boxers', *Journal of Sport History* 40(1): pp. 93–110.
Verma, G. and Darby, D. (1994) *Winners and Losers: Ethnic Minorities in Sport and Recreation*. London: Falmer.
Vertinsky, P. (1994) 'Gender Relations, Women's History and Sport History: A Decade of Changing Enquiry, 1983–1993', *Journal of Sport History* 21: p. 1.
Vertinsky, P. and Captain, G. (1998) 'More Myth than History: American Culture and Representations of the Black Female's Athletic Ability', *Journal of Sport History* 25(3): pp. 532–561.
Wicket Women magazine, 1998–1999.

Williams, J. (2001) *Cricket and Race*. Oxford: Berg.
Williams, J. (1999) *Cricket and England. A Cultural and Social History of the Inter-war Years*. London: Frank Cass.
Women's Cricket Association. Yearbooks, 1945–1997.
Women's Cricket Association (1987) Memorandum, 'WCA's Views on Recent Visit of India Touring Team'. Private collection, Surrey.
Women's Cricket magazine, 1946–1967.
Yow, V. (1997) '"Do I Like Them Too Much?" Effects of the Oral History Interview on the Interviewer and Vice-Versa', *Oral History Review* 24(1): pp. 55–79.

Chapter 7

Ladies-only!

Empowerment and comfort in gender-segregated kickboxing in the Netherlands

Jasmijn Rana

Introduction

In the Netherlands, girls and young women, especially those of Muslim (Moroccan-Dutch) descent are increasingly active in kickboxing. Some of these girls engage in mixed-gender sessions, while others do not. The focus of this chapter is on those Muslim females who engage in ladies-only kickboxing, not only because it is contentious, but because it very popular in the Netherlands. According to Frelier and Breedveld (2010), Muslim female engagement in ladies-only kickboxing has doubled in the backdrop of national initiatives to promote, widen access and increase opportunities for Moroccan-Dutch females to engage in kickboxing and other combat sports. Too often, their participation is celebrated as a sign that these women are now empowering themselves. This is because kickboxing is marketed as a necessary tool to empower Muslim women, and equip them with the physical skill and power to rescue, strengthen and save themselves (Rana 2014). Local gyms in the Netherlands and various government officials have championed it as an important self-defence skill that these 'helpless' females need to protect themselves from aggressive, controlling men etc. (ibid.) while simultaneously warning others (from the general public) of its glorification of violence and alleged links with organized crime (Dortants and Bottenburg 2013). A lot of media attention is placed on the type of barriers these women have to overcome to initially participate (i.e. Linda 2013; NPO 2015) than on anything else. At the same time, however, their participation in kickboxing is depicted as alarming, both because it has traditionally always been perceived to be a quintessentially masculine sport, and also because as a physically challenging, combative sport, it requires its participants to be aggressive, and to kick and punch their opponents. This latter image of an aggressive Muslim female, violently striking another, goes against dominant perceptions of how Muslim females are typically understood (read: 'submissive' or 'disempowered'), controlled by men and frequently forbidden to access male-dominated spaces such as sports (Pfister 2000; Kleindienst-Cachay 2011). Whether it is marketing kickboxing for Muslim women, or reporting on the effects of kickboxing on Muslim women, what is clear is that their participation, experiences and journeys are often portrayed through stereotypical assumptions of what Dutch people, and non-Muslims, think such Muslim females need, require and gain from sport. Little attention is paid to understanding Muslim females' connections with the sport in and through their own words.

This anthropological research explores the cultural phenomenon of kickboxing in the lives of Muslim women and girls who competed in ladies-only classes in two gyms in so-called disadvantaged neighbourhoods in The Hague, the Netherlands. Based on three years of intensive fieldwork, in which I trained and participated in ladies-only kickboxing classes, while also interviewing the participants, the findings privilege the participants' voices and stories of how and why they engage in kickboxing and what it means to them. Findings demonstrate how the space of ladies-only kickboxing offers a source of comfort, while embedded in racial, gendered and class structures. Anthropological fieldwork enables zooming in on "ethnographies of the particular" (Abu-Lughod 1999: 157), which allows for a more intimate critique of people who have often been generalized as 'Other' through singular perceptions, reflections, interpretations and analyses of their existence. In this case, it allows me to interrogate how young women confront important aspects of representations on the intersections of their gender, ethnicity and religion. It is anticipated that the ethnographic data, the stories, the voices, and journeys captured here in this research facilitate a critical reflection on 'integrationalist' sport policies in the Netherlands.

Moroccan-Dutch and Muslim youth

After Amsterdam and Rotterdam, The Hague is the third largest city of the Netherlands with half a million inhabitants. While the number of youth is decreasing in the Netherlands, this is not the case in The Hague. The Hague is one of the 'youngest' cities: the number of elderly people is decreasing and the percentage of youth has increased up to 23 per cent. Of the inhabitants in The Hague, 49 per cent are considered to be 'allochtonous', and within that demographic, 168,000 are 'non-Western allochtonous'. Most of them have a Surinamese, Turkish, Moroccan or Indonesian background.

Since the events of 9/11, the killing of Dutch filmmaker Theo van Gogh in 2004 and of right-wing politician Pim Fortuyn in 2002, anti-Muslim and anti-Islamic rhetoric has increased in the Netherlands, just as it has in other European countries (Ewing 2008; Mepschen *et al.* 2010; Murray 2006; Pitcher 2009). Consequently, the labels of 'Moroccan' and 'Muslim' are being used interchangeably more often in negative public discourse.

For instance, there is now an even stronger tendency to criminalize Dutch-Moroccan youth, especially men and boys (De Koning 2016). Muslim girls and women, on the other hand, are increasingly positioned as the passive and weaker sex, and represented as 'victims' of Muslim male tyranny. The extent of this discourse was recently illustrated by the Dutch minister of Health, Welfare and Sports, Edith Schippers, in a lecture on 'The Paradox of Freedom'. She claimed that the girls in these kinds of neighbourhoods in The Hague were vulnerable and not truly free to wear whatever they want (Schippers 2016). Being the youth with a migrant and/or Muslim background makes these 'allochtones' the ultimate 'Other' in Dutch society and they often have to cope with being pigeonholed as *immigrants, foreigners* who do not stand with or for the Dutch way of life, but stand against it.

Calls to improve, and advance, community efforts that facilitate the cultural integration of these 'foreign' 'allochtones' has been increasing and, more often than not, are underpinned by a desire to empower the weaker sex amongst these communities (namely, Dutch-Moroccan Muslim females). And yet, the wider perception is that these diverse communities live segregated or insular lives.

Sport, kickboxing and Muslim Moroccan-Dutch females

Sport is widely accepted as providing a symbolic means of representing the nation and constructing national identities (see Brownell 1995; Alter 1992). This idea extends across Western Europe and is evident in France (Silverstein 2000), Germany (Braun and Nobis 2011), Denmark (Pfister 2011) and the United Kingdom (Coaffee 2008), where amateur sports are promoted for stimulating the cultural and social integration of minorities. In the last two decades, sport policies in the Netherlands have shifted in the same direction (Elling *et al.* 2010; Vermeulen and Verweel 2009). Whereas sports policies in 1996 encouraged immigrants to participate in sport in order to "emancipate within their own group" (VWS 1996: 33), policies in 2005 saw sports as "a perfect meeting-point", meaning, sports were now being encouraged as a way to create possibilities for binding, integration and social cohesion (VWS 2006: 17). Today, participation in sports is still glorified as a gateway to participation in wider civic (Dutch) society. Citizens with an immigrant background are particularly encouraged to participate in a variety of sports because of the belief that they provide access to physical health, social bonding and belonging in Dutch society (Elling 2002; Rana 2014). In addition to the health benefits and possibilities for physical, psychological and organizational self-development, the *socio-integrative value* of sports is also recognized as benefiting minority communities (ibid.). And, since participation of migrant female youth is often reported as being significantly lower than that of Dutch youth in general (53 per cent compared to 85 per cent (VWS/WWI 2007)), migrant females, especially those who are Muslim, are considered to be in a 'disadvantaged position' (ibid.: 10) both because they are seen as not having access to an activity from which they can reap the social and other benefits of participating, and because they are seen as being held back from freely engaging in sport. There is a wealth of scholarly literature and journalistic reporting on the barriers that Muslim females face when entering sport that has strengthened these claims and allowed it to be accepted as a 'truth' in Dutch society (Badshah 2014; Gubuan 2015; Linda 2013; NPO 2015; Sanghani, 2014; Pfister 2011; Kleindienst-Cachay 2011). Efforts to promote sport thus often rest on a rhetoric of empowering this otherwise 'disadvantaged' group, and this is most evident in kickboxing.

Kickboxing and Muslim Moroccan-Dutch females

Unlike many other popular sports in the Netherlands, such as field hockey and tennis, that have failed to increase mass participation in ethnic minority communities, combat sport has proved to be successful in drawing in ethnic minorities (e.g. Carrington 2013; Heiskanen 2012; Van Sterkenburg and Knoppers 2004). Contemporary research alludes to the historical 'ethnic' roots of combat sports as one reason for this appeal (Heiskanen 2012). Kickboxing is an umbrella term for contact sports based on kicking and punching with several variations around the world. "Dutch kickboxing", the style that is mainly practised in the Netherlands and internationally known, is developed from boxing, Muay Thai and karate (Harinck 1988; Coenen and De Ruiter 2012). In this chapter I speak of kickboxing, while some gyms I have studied also refer to their practice as Muay Thai or Thai boxing. There is just a thin line between the different techniques in these sports, the use of knees and elbows being the main difference. Several trainers I spoke with in this research indicated that their style of kickboxing is further influenced by their own training in Tae Kwondo. As in other sports, participation in kickboxing is constructed along racial, class and gender lines, but in this research, religion is also taken into account. More recently, research on Muslim women and boxing has pointed to the presence of gender Orientalism, since the freedom and liberation narratives align women's rights with Western cultural standards (Kipnis and Caudwell 2016).

Kickboxing trainers in my research narrated how kickboxing has been a popular sport among Moroccan-Dutch youth for decades. More recently, the sport has been increasingly promoted and funded to target female youth from these communities for a number of reasons. In mainstream media outlets, participation of young Muslim women and girls in kickboxing is frequently celebrated as feminist liberal agency and empowerment (i.e. Linda 2013; NPO 2015) and recognized as a transformative force: one that allows them to be strong and dominant in their own lives. This assumption stems from a liberal feminist belief that engaging in physical exercise (traditionally a male-dominated pursuit), especially in a practice that teaches strength and self-defence, allows females to acquire traits that are typically only associated with physically strong subjects in society. This is unsurprising given that dominant notions of 'masculine' identity, both within and beyond the sporting context, were traditionally borne out of and compounded by images of strength, aggression, and muscularity, obtained in and through sport, thereby implying that physical prowess and physical power are not only dominant and domineering traits, but that sport is a vehicle to obtain power, and having power (instead of not having power) allowed one to be empowered (read: to be strong, etc.). In this sense, women's empowerment is about females gaining domineering skills that men are revered, often glorified, for possessing. This not only solidifies the notion of a link between strength, aggression and power, but also reaffirms "the centrality of the (physically strong) body" in acquiring and having transformative power (Theberge 1987: 390).

Additionally, Moroccan-Dutch Muslim female participation in kickboxing is understood to be empowering because it rests on otherwise religion-bound individuals engaging in what is typically believed to be a secular practice. Modern sport has long been positioned as a practice invented by 'modern European' civilizations, even though various forms of physical activity and sport were embraced in Muslim heritage (Al-Hassani 2012). Instead, Muslim women who participate in sport are depicted as 'breaking from tradition' (Pfister 2011). It is not merely that sport participation was initially depicted as being forbidden, but the narrative shifted to position Muslim women as not being empowered or free to participate in sport under the same conditions as non-Muslim women (i.e. because of religious dress code stipulations, etc.). This stereotype presumes that Muslim females are not already empowered agentic beings, that Islam does not encourage female participation in (combative) sports and that being less connected to Islam makes them empowered. As with media reports about Muslim women in sport more generally, media representation about Muslim women who engage in combat sports also over-emphasizes how much these women have to struggle to compete freely. Pakistani-British Ambreen Sadiq, for example, reported to be one of Britain's first Muslim female boxers, is often depicted as having had to "overcome opposition in her community" to participate in kickboxing (Gledhill 2010). In a recent article in the *Telegraph*, Ambreen was asked to talk about "what it's like battling prejudice and racism from her community – and even her family" (Sanghani 2014). Likewise, Bengali-British Ruqsana Begum, the current British female Atomweight (48–50 kg) World Kickboxing Association Muay Thai champion and captain of the British Muay Thai Team, is reported as the only Muslim woman who is a national champion in her sport, while there were actually national and world champion titles from competitions at other associations won by female Muslims before her. Begum is depicted as having to "break down" (Badshah 2014) or "kick down" barriers (Gubuan 2015), whereas details about her accomplishments are sidelined. Researchers also employ a rhetoric that evolves around barriers and challenges (i.e. Pfister 2011; Kleindienst-Cachay 2011). Although it is good that researchers illustrate women's agency to overcome certain struggles, too often this kind of research is produced simply to show that such Muslim women's experiences lag behind those of their 'Western' counterparts: a point illustrated by Ratna *et al.* (forthcoming) when Samie states

> [Muslim women's] agency is celebrated only in so far as it confirms and solidifies the metanarrative that [they] are always controlled or always resisting being controlled. [Their] agency is a reactionary resistance to the systems of control that [they] have [or are expected] to fend off and navigate around. [They] are depicted as pushing back, struggling against, fighting for, or reclaiming agency as opposed to being depicted in ways that celebrates [them] as embodied subjects who already possess active, controlling, proprietary power over [their] lives and bodies.

This essentialist representation of Muslim sportswomen is unsurprising. Samie and Sehlikoglu (2014) make this point when unpacking the media representation of Muslim women at the London 2012 Games. The fact that various media sources relied on and perpetuated discourses of fear and suspicion to transmit messages about sporting Muslim female subjects' "strangeness" and "incompetence" illustrates how pervasive negative thinking about Muslim women is (ibid.: 14). Nevertheless, while the earlier research on Muslim sportswomen indicated that such women were leading a double life, "trapped" in between modernity and tradition, global and local (Hargreaves 2007: 91), more contemporary research suggests that Muslim sportswomen are able to strike a "balance between two cultures" (Kleindienst-Cachay 2011: 102).

In political discourses, sports like kickboxing are championed as a tool for 'empowering' Muslim women. Empowerment in this setting is presented as a tool for the emancipation of the powerless. In the Netherlands, the English term empowerment is mostly used when talking about ethnic minorities and women, especially those from ethnic minority communities (Boumans 2012), but not necessarily to imply that they possess this trait, but that they lack it which inadvertently implies that white communities and white women are empowered. Empowerment, as a part of citizen participation, has been related to the rise of neoliberalism, and turned into a method for governmental intervention and withdrawal (Zandbergen and Jaffe 2014). Even if sports are understood as part of public welfare, it is promoted and marketed to/for ethnic minorities as a vehicle that will enable them to become a particular kind of (revered) citizen. Meaning ethnic minority communities are always seen as being in a position of 'lacking' something which, through Western intervention, they can acquire. The governmental tool of empowerment is therefore often critiqued as a marketization of social identities and relations (Kamat 2003). The empowerment paradigm legitimizes and reproduces neoliberal practices (such as responsibilization and self-esteem) and subjects and therewith conceals the subordination of actors (Wright 2012). The promotion of empowerment through kickboxing presupposes a submissive, backward, underdeveloped group of people that are in need of being transformed into modern individuals. The discourse of breaking down cultural barriers markets the identity of liberated, emancipated Muslim women. Furthermore, it demonstrates a remarkable focus on gender and ethnicity, as in the following combat sport promotion newsletter:

> Moroccan boys and girls are an important target group in many of the projects of Tijd voor Vechtsport. [...] [W]e equip the trainers and associations to be able to get started with this target group. Many teachers are trained already through various trajectories. Within these training trajectories, the aims of regulation of aggression for boys and empowerment training for allochthonous girls are addressed.
>
> (Tijd voor Vechtport 2008)

The target group for the promotion of kickboxing is in this case defined by ethnic background. The characteristics of aggression and submission are directly linked to Moroccanness while Dutchness is not even mentioned. The gender differentiation in the quotation essentializes the characteristics of Moroccan girls' identities as submissive passivity, and the characteristic of Moroccan boys' identities as unbridled aggression. Remarkably, the same sport is presented as a tool that can do the contradictory work of both decreasing aggression in one and increasing it in the other. To analyse this discourse, we have to recognize the intersectionality (Yuval-Davis 2006) of race, gender, class, and religion within this specific context of ladies-only kickboxing in the Netherlands. It is telling that in Dutch sport policies, religious and ethnic backgrounds of young women and girls in the Netherlands form the precondition to be in need of empowerment. The dichotomy of a perceived powerless girl and such a powerful sport is an important reason for the assumption that kickboxing is a form of feminist agency for young Muslim women. Their empowerment is assumed to need physical force that cannot be gained from other popular sports in the Netherlands, like field hockey or tennis. Muslim girls and young women are assumed to be in need of fighting skills to defend and emancipate themselves. This reproduces ideas of Muslim women and girls as submissive subjects that lack physical power and agency, and that are in danger or under threat. The danger is that agency is primarily read in terms of resistance, and self-defence. There is a tendency among scholars to look for expressions and moments of resistance that may suggest a challenge to male domination (Mahmood 2011: 8). Mahmood confronts this idea by arguing that agency does not always fit within the Western liberal discourse, and can only be understood from within the discourses and structures of its enactment (ibid.: 15).

The creation of gender-segregated kickboxing training, and especially those classes that are specifically aimed at Muslim women, demonstrates how feminist agency is not a challenge to male domination per se, but can be within and alongside patriarchal and heteronormative structures. The trend of practising sports in a gender-segregated setting could include forms of pious self-improvement that highlight the religious practices of the young women and girls. It is not necessarily the sort of liberal, secular practice Western-centric minds may assume to accompany sporting practices, let alone 'empowerment'. That said, a singular focus on the pious characteristics of Muslims neglects the discrepancy between the 'grand scheme' and 'lived practice' of Islam (Schielke and Debevec 2012).

It is important to underscore the fact that gender separatism is not solely a Muslim practice. In almost all team sports and many individual sports, male and female competition and training is segregated. Kickboxing, as a relatively new sport, started as a male sport and still is very much male dominated. Thus, the first women to take up combat sports trained with the men, consequently creating a gender-mixed training environment (Lafferty and McKay 2004; Mennesson 2000). However, the rise of women in kickboxing produced a demand for segregated training sessions for men and women. Kickboxing classes in gyms and community centres that specifically cater for women, so-called 'ladies-only' classes, in fact seem to have increased the popularity of kickboxing among women and girls. Too much of the existing scholarship on Muslim women in sports sensationalizes the religious aspect of this process, when in reality the performance of a religious identity is just one of many expressions of belief and value and symbolism that someone reveres. The fact that another gym, where a man teaches the ladies-only training, is also very popular among young (Muslim) females, highlights the fact that for some women, it is the comfort of women being amongst each other that is more important than the strict religious separation of men and women. Although ladies-only may not go against patriarchy, it does not invalidate the growth that may be encouraged within the space of ladies-only kickboxing.

Participation in kickboxing by Moroccan-Dutch youth can appear to be a self-perpetuating cycle. That is, it is promoted for 'Moroccan' and 'Muslim' youth because it has already proved to be a popular sport among them, and kickboxing, more often than not, is also the sport that most of these adolescents have the most readily available access to, due to how neighbourhood athletic arrangements are currently implemented (Rana 2014).

Comfortable without men

Sporting females who engage in so-called masculine sports are often confronted with clear tensions about their gendered female identity, their femaleness and their heterosexuality. Many female fighters feel combat sports are often seen as a male type of sport. Some of them fight in spite of the prejudice, others because of it. The young women and girls in this research demonstrate various ways of negotiating their gender-identifications during and through kickboxing. Sport facilities for women only have become increasingly available in the Netherlands. Very often they come from grassroots initiatives in neighbourhoods, but sometimes they are also funded by the government, as I indicated earlier. From 2006–2010 many kickboxing gyms in the Netherlands were funded because of their promotion of sports for migrant girls, including gender-segregated training sessions. In all of the ladies-only classes I witnessed, only women and girls were allowed to train in the class, and most often, the trainer was female too. In some classes, I witnessed that both Muslim and non-Muslim women competed, whereas in others, I noticed that Muslim women made up the majority of participants. In some gyms, and especially in gyms where Muslims were the majority, doors were closed and windows were blinded to avoid male eyes. Although religious considerations often influenced some Muslim women's decision to choose to participate in this gender-segregated space, it certainly was not the sole reason, nor was it the dominant reason to choose ladies-only training. Very often, the comfort of engaging in sports within one's own gender-group and the sociability that comes with it were mentioned as a reason to choose separate classes. For these women, it was the difference in physical strength between men and women, or the reluctance of men to fight hard enough with or against women, thus making them unsuitable sparring partners, that many felt disadvantaged their competitive training. Others felt that men would punch and kick too hard, making it an uneven fight. As one ambitious Muslim woman told me:

> I tried kickboxing with men before. In the beginning I was a bit scared that they would be too rough with me, but after half a year of training I was actually experiencing the opposite. Some guys would just not

> punch me in the face, or my stomach, because they felt sorry for me or something. They said things like: 'I'm sorry, I can't really hit you because you're a girl'.
>
> (Naima, 24 years old)

For beginners in kickboxing, the difference in (perceived) physical strength is a reason to start in ladies-only training. For more advanced beginners, the reluctance of men to fight women is a reason to switch to ladies-only classes. Hence many participants felt that the right training buddy could be more easily found in a gender-segregated setting. For others, it was the supposedly relaxed environment of being with other women that participants enjoyed. One participant told me,

> It's just easier you know, with only women. You don't have to worry about... I don't know, maybe it sounds stupid, but I don't have to care about what to wear. When I give a high kick and you can see my underwear, I don't really care. But that's different when there are men. Also, the atmosphere is just better. Women are kind to each other, we laugh, we gossip, we help each other.
>
> (Marieke, 32 years old)

In other words, *comfort* is a reason for women and girls to train amongst each other and not with men. This quote of Marieke demonstrates that the experience of comfort among women and girls is very much a bodily matter. Seeing and feeling other bodies is for many (young) women more comfortable when those other bodies are female too. Separate sports sessions offer possibilities of social bonding through helping, laughing and gossiping and provide them with a sense of control and autonomy (Hargreaves 1994; Walseth 2008).

Nevertheless, scholars have also recently argued that separate sport sessions do not lead to equality in sports, because segregation would ultimately be a function of patriarchal logic (McDonaugh and Pappano 2008; Travers 2008). When it comes to combat sports in particular, Channon (2014) argues that the implication of mixed-sex training might challenge orthodox Western constructions of gender and create more inclusive environments. In the long run, gender-subversive physical practices such as martial arts might instigate a shift towards fairer and freer bodily discourse. It has to be noted, however, that his research was among white, middle-class British women. His research, like many other sport feminist scholars, assumes that the perceptions and experiences of what gender equality or female empowerment entails or means to one group, may not necessarily or equally apply to women (or indeed men) from other social, ethnic and racial or religious groups. A number of my participants claimed that mixed-sex sport settings could prevent them from practising combat sport at all, because they would not feel at ease training among males. Instead, my participants felt strongly that it was the gender-segregated atmosphere of combat sports that had attracted them and many of their friends to participate. The increase of female fighters in the Netherlands demonstrates that gender-segregated spaces lower the threshold for young women to become active in combat sports (Elling *et al.* 2010). It is because of this increase in women's participation in sports that scholars such as Hargreaves (1994) and Messner (2011) argue that reverse segregation in sport might be counterproductive. Strategic categorialism (Messner 2011) still seems necessary in fighting for equality in sports, and it might be the case even more for Muslim females in certain neighbourhoods in the Netherlands.

Closeness and proximity as reasons for participation

Most young women and girls in my research chose the gym that was the closest to home, like the one they come across when going to school or to the supermarket. In some cases, this happened to be a gym that catered for religious considerations, even if it was not the main reason for girls to engage in kickboxing at that gym. Jamila and Hind, for example, two sisters of 14 and 16 years old, only lived three streets away from their gym. Their high school was in the same area as the mosque they visited for Quran classes on Saturdays. Several ladies-only kickboxing classes started as neighbourhood initiatives by local women. One of the most popular gyms of The Hague, which was facilitated by the sister of the owner, initiated ladies-only classes. While her brother was initially hesitant to pursue this suggestion, he eventually agreed to try it because of his sister's persistence. Speaking to me, she stated:

> We especially wanted to have the gym in this neighbourhood, because my brother and I experienced ourselves how there was no chance to participate in sports when we were young. We know that we mean a lot to the children here in the neighbourhood. And for the ladies as well! When my brother opened this school, I told him: 'You need to offer ladies-only training as well'. I personally knew so many women who would attend this training if it existed. So he said OK, but only if I organised it myself.
>
> (Salima, 32 years old)

Salima explains that the initiation of a new kickboxing gym with ladies-only training sessions was carefully planned, and from 2011 to 2015, the gym expanded to three locations throughout the city. While profit at the gym in this specific neighbourhood is low, the location was still important to these siblings because of their feeling of social responsibility towards their own neighbourhood. Even though travelling distances are relatively short in this small city, for some of the participants, it was difficult (financially) to travel to other neighbourhoods. On average 20 ladies attended the training sessions and most of them were mainly of Moroccan-Dutch descent. Many of the young women and girls were related to each other and/or were friends. They already went to the same school, mosque or hairdresser in this neighbourhood. However, two participants who were also cousins, who did not live in or near this neighbourhood, travelled quite a distance to get to the gym. Raja said, "There is really nothing at all in our part of town! If we want to practise sports, we have to come all the way here." Amina: "And we are also the only Moroccans there." Raja: "Yes, and there is no kickboxing, so that's why." They travel a relatively long distance to practise sport in a setting where they feel comfortable. That they do so suggests sport participation is understood as a neighbourhood matter, and that participation in neighbourhood sports is often bound to ethnic groups.

The active engagement of Raja and Amina in sports demonstrates the positive results of gender-segregated sports. If it were not for ladies-only kickboxing training sessions, these two girls would probably not have been actively involved in sports. However, that the girls are also the odd ones out implies that racial segregation in sports facilities across neighbourhoods in The Hague is common. Amina and Raja instantly refer to their Moroccan background when speaking about their decision to travel to this neighbourhood to practise kickboxing.

The intersection of race, religion, gender, and *geography*, as portrayed by the women, is part of a larger discourse of sports participation on neighbourhood level in the Netherlands. It may seem that this ethnic segregation in The Hague is not beneficial to the integration of second generation migrants, and that the multicultural endeavour of the government is failing. It is also the case, though, that the kickboxing gym is used by young Moroccan-Dutch women and girls as a safe space, as they are comfortable there with each other. In this sense, it is not so dissimilar from high-class, 'white' sports, such as field hockey and tennis associations, where municipal funding does not rely on the prerequisite to practise sports in a 'multicultural' setting.

Raja and Amina make a detour to practise a sport they like with a group of people they feel at ease with. While most young women and girls choose a gym as close as possible to their own neighbourhood, a (strict) ladies-only arrangement is also a reason to make a detour:

> The first time I wanted to try kickboxing training, I went to another gym than this one because they had ladies-only too, and it's closer to my house. But during the first training, one of the trainers tried to

> convince me of training with the guys. He asked me if I wanted to be a fighter and I said yes. That's why he wanted me to train with the guys. But I didn't want that. I wanted to train with other girls, and I also told my father that I would go to women's training. So that's why I came to this gym. And whatever, it's only one street farther away.
>
> (Sanae, 16 years old)

Sanae takes a 10-minute bike ride to get to the gym she likes best. She chose to not visit gender-mixed classes, and does not mind travelling a longer distance to train at a gym where she can participate in ladies-only training. While this girl does not mention religious reasons for this change of gyms, other girls and young women choose (a strict) ladies-only setting more explicitly for religious reasons.

Performance of the pious self in sport

Some of the young women and girls in my research considered activities such as sports as irrelevant to religious identity, either because religion was relatively unimportant to them, or because they considered religion to be an inner state of being. To others however religion was an important factor in their everyday practices, including combat sports. It was clear that my participants held a variety of points of view on this issue, ranging from rejection to celebration. There were ample examples of Islamic arguments used to legitimize Muslim women's participation in combat sports. This has been documented for sports such as archery in Iran (Pfister 2006) and in Europe, where young women employ religious lines to gain access to sports (Walseth and Fasting 2003; Kay 2006). They do so by referring to the importance of exercise for taking care of the body, and by using examples from the *hadith*, descriptions of the words and deeds of the prophet Muhammad. Some of the young women and girls I trained with told me that they used Islamic arguments to explain to their parents why it should be no problem for them to do sports. The young women and girls who have taken the step to become active in combat sports do not follow up that discussion in the locker room or during the training. Their concern is less a question of whether to engage in such sports, but *how* to do so. These women and girls discuss their dressing habits and, if applicable, how to behave with a male sparring partner or trainer. Gender-segregated classes are, however, an important qualification for feeling comfortable in a training setting.

One gym I studied changed its policy while I was doing research there. When I started training, there had been a female trainer and a closed room during the ladies-only training, but the owner decided that he wanted his gym to be open to everyone, and to have an equally open character. Some parents, including fathers, wanted to watch their daughters practising kickboxing. Responding to this request, the training was not 100 per cent ladies-only anymore. The window blinds also stayed open to show to the outside world what was happening in this gym. Furthermore, the owner stopped allowing women to wear headscarves during training. In an interview, he compared wearing headscarves to wearing caps. Neither item is part of kickboxing attire, and therefore should not be permitted. Besides, he did not want to give "a wrong impression to the outside world". The outside world, to this gym owner, apparently did not include immigrant or Muslim neighbours, but consisted of his potential 'Dutch' viewers. Again, here he referred to the 'open' character he meant to proclaim. This resulted in a distinct change in clientele. Many Muslim women and girls, and all of those wearing veils, left.

For some Muslim women and girls in The Hague, sport is only an option when gender segregation is taken very strictly: having male trainers or onlookers would not be appropriate or comfortable. One of the two clubs I researched, where both the owner and his sister, who initiated the ladies-only classes, are Moroccan-Dutch and Muslim, maintains a strict gender segregation when the women are training. This is also how they promote their training sessions. While mainstream Dutch flyers of kickboxing often portray women in only a tank top and pink sportswear, the promotional material for these ladies-only classes opts to market kickboxing in a different way. For instance, text that mentions where and when training takes place, the flyer includes a small picture of the two female trainers in clothes that cover the whole body. Furthermore, it lists the special characteristics of these classes: blinded windows, the absence of men and the absence of music. The first two points relate to the full segregation of men and women. Male eyes will not be able to view female bodies. The third bullet-point on the list, the absence of music, is a prerequisite for Muslims who believe that most kinds of contemporary music are considered *haram* (forbidden) (Otterbeck 2008). The list of prerequisites is accompanied by a picture of a halal-stamp, like the ones that are used in the certification of halal food products. Although there is no certification for "halal sports", the symbolic meaning of the stamp is used to highlight the Muslim character of the kickboxing classes. Consequently, the ladies-only training sessions were visited by more Muslim women and girls than in other gyms that I researched. Whenever the male group finished its training and left the room, the female trainer closed the door and put a sign on it that reads "no men allowed". Most women and girls have often already changed into their training gear by this point. The veiled ladies waited until that moment to take their veils off. In these sessions, self-improvement was not only related to building strength, losing weight and learning how to fight, but also always intersected with Muslim subjectivities, since this gym catered specifically to Muslim women. Modesty, often described as a female Muslim characteristic, was a recurrently negotiated theme in the dojo and the locker room in conversations on clothing and behaviour. Many young women and girls wore leggings underneath their shorts and long sleeved shirts. Finally, hitting or punching someone in the face was negotiated. Some participants did not want to be hit in the face because of the pain; others tried to avoid head injuries and visible bruises, but a group of pupils were also concerned that hitting in the face was inappropriate by Islamic standards. Even some of the competitive fighters shared this opinion that outright fighting was not appropriate for Muslims because one should not do harm and avoid striking the face according to the teachings of the prophet. Hence, women were negotiating the terms and conditions under which they engaged in kickboxing, making it relevant and 'halal' enough for them to participate and have fun. While some of the participants trained without aiming for competitive fighting, others trained while avoiding hitting in the face or only did technique exercises, not sparring in any way that would simulate a fight.

The choices the young women and girls made to become kickboxers and where and how to participate in kickboxing were embedded in the bodily dispositions that are related to different fields of power, such as gender and religion, and geographical space. The choices of attending ladies-only training, wearing long clothes and conducting oneself in a modest manner are all examples of this. These dispositions are also cultivated at the setting of the gym, both in ladies-only training and mixed training. Work on the body in the gym was intimately connected to working on the self, and this was important for the participants. The active, agentic voice of the young women and girls tells us how they negotiate their lives in broader social and cultural schemes.

Conclusion

The traditional focus on sport participation, according to the Dutch government's sport policies, has been on wanting to integrate minorities in society, and more specifically empower Muslim females from minority ethnic backgrounds. This has often culminated in certain sports activities, like kickboxing, being marketed to ethnic minority communities with bold claims about what participation can do to transform the individuals. 'Empower' and 'liberate' are terms that are frequently used. However, in this research I have delved a little deeper to make sense of what Moroccan-Dutch Muslim females want and get out of kickboxing. My findings have shown that young Muslim women and girls take up kickboxing in different ways and for different reasons. The ladies-only sessions were often compounded by racial, gendered and class structures; they were not necessarily pursued for the same reasons that are widely portrayed in the media. Instead, I found that some women much preferred the relaxed social setting of being with other women. For many of the participants it was a space that offered a source of comfort. This was also true for those women who had also trained in mixed settings before joining ladies-only sessions. In other cases, women simply enjoyed the freedom to compete in their ways, negotiating what was acceptable and what was not as opposed to following rigid top-down rules about how kickboxing should be taken up and what it should mean to the fighters. It is important for sports campaigns to take seriously these reasons when marketing sports to those from minority ethnic communities. The danger of not taking into consideration these findings is that the voices of real people who are engaged in these programmes at a grassroots level will not only be lost or neglected when facilitating new sports campaigns, but often their real needs will be ignored and replaced by needs that the dominant privileged group think these communities should have. When the needs of local people are taken into consideration, sports campaigns can be set up and provided in ways that have genuine lasting impact on those who engage. Moreover, by recognizing these complexities and nuances in why and how young Muslim females engage in kickboxing, the government and other entities can move beyond its rigid heavy-handed 'integrationalist' rhetoric and lacklustre implementation. Currently, many athletic programmes initiated and financed by the Ministry of Health, Welfare and Sports in the Netherlands promote participation in sports as a gateway for participation in society. The intentions are often good, emphasizing how the programmes will bring social benefits to the participants, by improving health, enhancing social bonding and strengthening a sense of belonging. However, these campaigns also rest on the assumption that people from these communities, especially Muslim females, are somehow 'deprived' of these things already. This discourse reinforces stereotypes of Muslim females as needing help to be rescued, as being submissive and lacking agency to take up sports on their own terms in their own ways.

My research has also paid attention to the subtle (or double) contestations of ladies-only kickboxing. On the one hand, it is perceived as an emancipatory, liberal practice, precisely because of the racial and religious backgrounds of the women and girls. On the other hand, the effects of gender-segregated sport settings might also reinforce heteronormative gender roles. Although this research demonstrates that while the gender binary is indeed upheld within this recreational kickboxing training, it challenges the male-dominated space of kickboxing at large. Both in the Dutch context and worldwide, ethnic femininity is constructed as antagonistic to physical activity in general. Young Dutch Muslim women and girls who take up kickboxing confront important aspects of representations of the intersection of gender and ethnicity. They participate in a form of exercise that is widely perceived as aggressive and offered to them as a way of 'empowering' youthful minority femininity. Young women and girls challenge the notion of a so-called 'masculine' sport by turning it into a source of casual comfort for themselves, at least within the walls of their gym during their ladies-only sessions. While there might be an intention to 'save' young Muslim women and girls through participation in sports, they determine for themselves what form their participation will take and what role it will play in their lives.

Acknowledgements

I would like to thank Jessica Alice Rivers and the editors Samaya Farooq Samie and Aarti Ratna for their careful reading and productive editorial suggestions on earlier versions of this chapter.

References

Abu-Lughod, L. (1999) *Veiled Sentiments: Honor and Poetry in a Bedouin Society*, Berkeley: University of California Press.

Al-Hassani, S. (2012) Sports in Muslim Heritage, Issue 369, *Runnymede Bulletin*. Available from www.muslimheritage.com/article/1000-years-amnesia-sports-muslim-heritage

Alter, J.S. (1992) *The Wrestler's Body: Identity and Ideology in North India*, Berkeley: University of California Press.

Badshah, N. (2014) 'Kickboxer Ruqsana Begum battles against illness and cultural barriers', *Sky Sports*, 5 December 2014. Available from www.skysports.com/watch/tv-shows/sportswomen/news/9593952/kickboxing-champ-ruqsana-begum-battles-back-to-beat-illness [1 July 2016].

Boumans, J. (2012) *Naar het hart van empowerment; Een onderzoek naar de grondslagen van empowerment van kwetsbare groepen [To the Heart of Empowerment: A Research on the Foundations of the Empowerment of Vulnerable Groups]*, Utrecht: Uitgeverij Anraad.

Braun, S. and Nobis, T. (2011) *Migration, Integration und Sport*, Wiesbaden: Springer Fachmedien.

Brownell, S. (1995) *Training the Body for China: Sports in the Moral Order of the People's Republic*, Chicago: University of Chicago Press.

Carrington, B. (2013) 'The critical sociology of race and sport: The first fifty years', *Annual Review of Sociology*, 39: pp. 379–398.

Channon, A. (2014) 'Towards the "undoing" of gender in mixed-sex martial arts and combat sports', *Societies*, 4(4): pp. 587–605.

Coaffee, J. (2008) 'Sport, Culture and the modern state: Emerging themes in stimulating urban regeneration in the UK', *International Journal of Cultural Policy*, 14(4): pp. 377–397.

Coenen, A. and De Ruiter, M. (2012) *Dutch Old School Kickboxing Icons*, Rotterdam: Trichis Publishing.

De Koning, M. (2016) *Een ideologische strijd met de Islam. Fortuyns gedachtegoed als scharnierpunt in de racialisering van Moslims [An Ideological Battle with Islam. Fortuyn's Ideas as Pivot in Muslims' Racialisation]*, Uithoorn: Karakter Uitgevers.

Dortants, M. and van Bottenburg, M. (2013) *Aanzien en overleven in een sport vol passie: Over regulering van full contact-vechtsporten [Respect and Survival in a Sport Full of Passion: On Regulation of Full-contact combat Sports]*, Uithoorn: Universiteit Utrecht, Departement Bestuurs- en Organisatiewetenschap/Arko Sports Media.

Elling, A. (2002) *'Ze zijn er (niet) voor gebouwd'. In en uitsluiting in de sport naar sekse en etniciteit,* Nieuwegein/Den Bosch: Arko Sports Media/Mulier Instituut.

Elling, A.H.F., Wisse, E. and van den Berk, H. (2010) *Beloften van vechtsport [Promises of Combat Sports]*, Den Bosch: W.J.H. Mulier Instituut.

Ewing, K.P. (2008) *Stolen Honor. Stigmatizing Muslim Men in Berlin*, Stanford, California: Stanford University Press.

Frelier, M. and Breedveld, K. (2010) *Meedoen Alle Jeugd Door Sport, 2-meting 2009 [Participation of All Youth in Sport, 2-measurement 2009]*, Den Bosch: W.J.H. Mulier Instituut.

Gledhill, R. (2010) 'Ambreen Sadiq, Muslim girl boxer, aims to combat prejudice to succeed in the ring', *The Times Online*, 21 January. Available from www.thetimes.co.uk/tto/sport/boxing/article1839935.ece. [12 March 2016].

Gubuan, M. (2015) 'Kicking down barriers', *Shirzanan Global Edition*, Winter 2015,. Available from: http://issuu.com/shirzananglobal/docs/shirzanan_mag_no1_digital?e=14218234/10687345 [1 July 2016].

Hargreaves, J.A. (1994) *Sporting Females: Critical Issues in the History and Sociology of Women's Sport*, London: Routledge.

Hargreaves, J.A. (2007) 'Sport, Exercise and the female Muslim body' in J.A. Hargreaves and P. Vertinsky (eds) *Physical Culture, Power, and the Body*, London and New York: Routledge, pp. 74–100.

Harinck, T. (1988) *Muay Thai or Thai Boxing*, Eindhoven: Nikko Toshugo Press.

Heiskanen, B. (2012) *The Urban Geography of Boxing: Race, Class, and Gender in the Ring*, London and New York: Routledge.

Kamat, S. (2003) 'NGOs and the new democracy', *Harvard International Review*, 25(11): pp. 65–69.

Kay, T. (2006) 'Daughters of Islam: Family influences on Muslim young women's participation in sport', *International Review for the Sociology of Sport*, 41(3–4): pp. 357–373.

Kipnis, H. and Caudwell, J. (2016) 'Boxers of Kabul: Women, boxing and Islam' in C.R. Matthews and A. Channon (eds) *Global Perspectives on Women in Combat Sports: Women Warriors around the World*, London and New York: Palgrave Macmillan, pp. 41–56.

Kleindienst-Cachay, C. (2011) 'Balancing between the cultures...: Sports and physical activities of Muslim girls and women in Germany' in T. Benn, G. Pfister and H. Jawad (eds) *Muslim Women and Sport*, London and New York: Routledge, pp. 92–108.

Lafferty, Y, and McKay, J. (2004) '"Suffragettes in satin shorts"? Gender and competitive boxing', *Qualitative Sociology*, 27(3): pp. 249–276.

Linda (2013) Gevaarlijk Vrouwen [Dangerous Women], in *Linda*, August 2013.

Mahmood, S. (2011) *Politics of Piety: The Islamic Revival and the Feminist Subject*, New Jersey: Princeton University Press.

McDonaugh, E. and Pappano, L. (2008) *Playing with the Boys: Why Separate is Not Equal in Sports*, Oxford: Oxford University Press.

Mepschen, P., Duyvdendak, J.W., and Tonkens, E.H. (2010) 'Sexual politics, orientalism and multicultural citizenship in the Netherlands', *Sociology* 44 (5): pp. 962–979.

Mennesson, C. (2000) '"Hard" women and "soft" women: The social construction of identities among female boxers', *International Review for the Sociology of Sport*, *35*(1): pp. 21–33.

Messner, M (2011) 'Gender ideologies, youth sports, and the production of soft essentialism', *Sociology of Sport Journal*, 28: pp. 151–170.

Murray, G. (2006) 'France: The riots and the republic', *Race & Class* 47(4): pp. 26–45.

NPO (2015) 'Islamitische Kickbokster knokt voor vrijheid' ['Muslim female kickboxer fights for freedom'], *NPO Spirit*. Available from www.npo.nl/nihad-wil-vrij-zijn/30-03-2015/WO_NCRV_818218www.npo.nl/nihad-wil-vrij-zijn/30-03-2015/WO_NCRV_818218 www.npo.nl/nihad-wil-vrij-zijn/30-03-2015/WO_NCRV_818218

Otterbeck, J. (2008) 'Battling over the public sphere: Islamic reactions to the music of today', *Contemporary Islam*, 2(3): pp. 211–228.

Pitcher, B. (2009) *The Politics of Multiculturalism. Race and Racism in Contemporary Britain*, Basingstoke: Palgrave Macmillan.

Pfister, G. (2000) 'Doing sport in a headscarf? German sport and Turkish females', *Journal of Sport History*, 27(3): pp. 497–524.

Pfister, G. (2006) 'Islam and women sports', *Sang Saeng*, Summer 2006, pp. 12–15. Available from http://apceiu.org/bbs/files/pdf/2006/sangsaeng/060906_ss_p012-p015.pdf [12 March 2016].

Pfister, G. (2011) 'Muslim women and sport in diasporas: Theories, discourses and practices – analysing the case of Denmark' in T. Benn, G. Pfister and H. Jawad (eds) *Muslim Women and Sport*, London and New York: Routledge, pp. 41–76.

Rana, J. (2014) 'Producing healthy citizens: Encouraging participation in ladies-only kickboxing', *Etnofoor*, 26(2): pp. 33–48.

Ratna, A., Samie, S., Jamieson, K. and Thangaraj, S. (2017) 'Learning lessons from the feminisms of ethnic "Others"' in L. Mansfield, J.C. Caudwell, B. Watson and B. Wheaton (eds) *Handbook of Feminisms, Sport, Leisure and Physical Education*, Basingstoke: Palgrave MacMillan (in press).

Samie, S.F. and Sehlikoglu, S. (2014) 'Strange, incompetent and out-of-place: Media, Muslim sportswomen and London 2012', *Feminist Media Studies*, 15(3): pp. 363–381.

Sanghani, R. (2014) 'Meet the female Muslim boxer "bringing shame on her family"', *Telegraph*. Available from www.telegraph.co.uk/women/womens-life/11046093/Female-Muslim-boxer-bringing-shame-on-her-family-has-play-at-Edinburgh-festival.html

Schielke, J.S. and Debevec, L. (2012) *Ordinary Lives and Grand Schemes: An Anthropology of Everyday Religion*, Berghahn Books, New York and Oxford.

Schippers, E. (2016) 'HJ Schoo-lecture: De Paradox van de Vrijheid' [The paradox of freedom], *Elsevier*. Available from www.elsevier.nl/nederland/achtergrond/2016/09/hj-schoo-lezing-edith-schippers-de-paradox-van-de-vrijheid-353734/

Silverstein, P. A. (2000) 'Sporting faith: Islam, soccer, and the French nation-state', *Social Text*, 18: pp. 25–53.

Theberge, N. (1987) 'Sport and women's empowerment', *Women's Studies International Forum*, 10(4): pp. 387–393.
Tijd Voor Vechtsport [Time for Combat Sports] 2008, *Nieuwsbrief Extra '08 – Marokko Editie [Newsletter Extra '08 – Morocco Edition]*. Digital mailing list.
Travers, A. (2008) 'The sport nexus and gender injustice', *Studies in Social Justice*, 2(1): pp. 79–101.
Van Sterkenburg, J. and Knoppers, A. (2004) 'Dominant discourses about race/ethnicity and gender in sport practice and performance', *International Review for the Sociology of Sport*, 39(3), pp. 301–321.
Vermeulen, J and Verweel P. (2009) 'Participation in sport: Bonding and bridging as Identity Work', *Sport in Society*, 12(9): pp. 1206–1219.
VWS (1996) *Wat Sport Beweegt [What Moves Sport/What is Moved by Sport]*, Ministry of Health, Welfare and Sport.
VWS (2006) *Samen voor Sport: Uitvoeringsprogramma van de Kabinetsnota 'Tijd voor Sport' [Together for Sport: Implementation of the Policy Note 'Time for Sport']*, Ministry of Health, Welfare and Sport.
VWS/WWI (2007) *Warmlopen voor meedoen: Integratie allochtone jeugd door sport [Warming up for Participation: Integration Allochtone Youth Through Sport]*, daM Deventer: Uitgeverij.
Walseth, K. (2008) 'Bridging and bonding social capital in sport – experiences of young women with an immigrant background', *Sport, Education and Society*, 13(1): pp. 1–17.
Walseth, K. and Fasting, K. (2003) 'Islam's view on physical activity and sport: Egyptian women interpreting Islam', *International Review for the Sociology of Sport*, 38(1): pp. 45–60.
Wright, A. (2012) 'Fantasies of empowerment: Mapping neoliberal discourse in the coalition government's schools policy', *Journal of Education Policy*, 27(3): pp. 279–294.
Yuval-Davis, N. (2006) 'Intersectionality and feminist politics', *European Journal of Women's Studies*, 13(3): pp. 193–209.
Zandbergen, D. and Jaffe, R. (2014) 'Participation. Citizenship, democracy and responsibilization', *Etnofoor*, 26(2): pp. 7–10.

Part III

Everyday struggles and transformative practice

Chapter 8

Lorena 'La Reina' Ochoa

Disidentifying toward brown solidarity

Katherine M. Jamieson and Yeomi Choi

In this chapter, we analyse key moments in the career of US-Ladies Professional Golf Association (US-LPGA) golfer, Lorena Ochoa. Utilizing a broad analytic lens that José Esteban Muñoz (1999, 2006) called a 'sense of brown', or sometimes popularly referred to as a 'brown commons', we trace key *movidas* or agitative tactics deployed by Ochoa in order to draw attention to the ways that representations, ideas and language pertaining to minoritized/brown communities and subjects is typically over-produced and contained by modernist sport institutions such as the US-LPGA. Tracing Ochoa's career movidas through a sense of brown reveals her attunement to brown communities, as well as her positionality as a 'global girl subject' long before the US-LPGA could make claims on having created the path toward and public desire for her global subjectivity. In this context, 'global girl subject' refers to the neoliberal framing of the brown girl-child as one in constant need, facing a limited set of resources, and best assisted by Non-Governmental Organizations promoting lifestyle goals of Western over/developed nations (Grewal, 2005, 2007; Hayhurst, 2011). This 'global girl subject' could be read as the girl-child represented in the UN reports and initiatives, the future professional golfer imagined by the US-LPGA in their self-branding as the 'global tour', and/or the local transnational girl subject invited to overcome global economic conditions of inequality through a proper programme of sport for development (Grewal, 2005, 2007; Hayhurst, 2011). Neoliberal consumptive goals of valuing privatized markets, believing in individual responsibility for overcoming losses in the welfare state, and identifying white, Western forms of encounter (language, lifestyle, aesthetics) as the path out of local, two-thirds world conditions of poverty, racism and sexism, all come together to produce and animate this 'global girl subject' (Grewal, 2005, 2007).

Given the economic resources and prominence of her family (see *Grupo Ochoa and Ochoa Sports Management*, 2016) and her elite athletic skill, Ochoa was identified early in her career as one who might put her native country, Mexico, on the Western sport and popular culture landscape. The fact that Mexico does not have a women's professional golf tour, coupled with her proximity to the United States and US-Collegiate career, meant that Ochoa would most likely join the US-LPGA, although, to be clear, there are other professional tours she could have joined (see Rolex Rankings, 2016). We argue that Lorena Ochoa's presence on the tour was imagined by the US-LPGA as part of that organization's far-reaching project in calling forth a global girl subject for the benefit of neoliberal consumptive goals (Grewal, 2005, 2007). Ochoa, however, had other ideas about her presence on the Tour, and never allowed the sport organization to co-opt her image, actions, or career trajectory. In line with the editors and fellow authors in this collection, we aim to work far beyond additive and universalist models of difference as we analyse selected career movidas of Lorena Ochoa as examples of an agitative brownness, and an attunement to a brown commons even while working in and through the very white/ned sport of golf.

Ochoa as/and the global girl subject

Lorena Ochoa Reyes was born on 15 November 1981 in Guadalajara, Mexico to a real estate developer father and an artist mother (Radford, 2008). She began playing golf at the age of five with an omniscient goal to become number one in the world. To date, she is the only Mexican golfer to have held the World number one spot in golf, and is a prominent member of a short list of extremely successful Mexican female athletes, most of whom are track and field athletes, such as Ana Guevara (runner) and Fabiola Corona (triathlete). She is also perhaps one of the most popular Mexican athletes, male or female, evidenced by her presence on the cover of *Women's Health Magazine* (Mexico) (January, 2011), her status as the first, current LPGA professional to grace the cover of *Golf Digest* (2008), and her receipt of Mexico's National Sports Award (Bradley, 2008). In addition to her outstanding junior career, Ochoa amassed 12 collegiate victories, NCAA Player of the Year Awards in 2001 and 2002, and the Nancy Lopez Award for best female amateur golfer. Ochoa officially joined the professional ranks in May 2002, and earned an exemption to play on the US-LPGA tour during the 2003 tour year. Ironically, part of Ochoa's legacy on the US-LPGA tour is deeply tied to her early retirement in May 2010. Her departure left her two years short of the ten-year requirement for admission to the Hall of Fame, a set of requirements she far exceeds in all other categories. Ochoa had a stellar eight years on the US-LPGA tour, from 2003 to 2010, winning two Majors, and 27 overall tournaments, capturing the Rookie of the Year Award, earning both the Vare Trophy and Player of the Year Awards in four consecutive years, and held the Rolex Rankings World number one spot from 2007 through to her retirement. Most striking is the fact that Ochoa missed only four cuts in 172 tournaments, had 108 top-10 finishes, and 63 top-3 finishes. Her breakthrough moment was her first Major victory at the Ricoh British Women's Open in 2007, where she became the first woman ever to earn a tournament title at the famous Old Course at St. Andrews. This is an important win for many reasons, not the least of which is the status of the Royal and Ancient Golf Club of St. Andrews as a "men's cultural centre" (Kidd, 1990: 31), admitting its first seven female members in February 2015, long after Ochoa's win (Chibber, 2015). Ochoa's win at the Old Course momentarily situates a two-thirds world girl subject as the pre-eminent performer in a one-third world sporting space that has been carefully and deeply interwoven into legacies of white, male privilege (Bairner, 2001).

Her career statistics alone make her deserving of our analytic attention, and yet, it is her agitative brownness that most invited this chapter. Notably, Ochoa regularly drew media attention to her home country's contributions to the US-LPGA through skilled labour among the grounds crews. These acts of outreach are cited as integral to her charm and popularity, especially as she expresses a love for humanity and a pride in her fellow Mexican citizens. Given these acts, fans and journalists at times alter her name Lorena to indicate her exalted status as La Reina, the queen, and some have claimed these actions as a Catholic-inspired respect for human dignity (McCarthy, 2009) which adds another layer of cultural meaning around the nickname 'La Reina', possibly referring to a transfiguration of la Virgen de Guadalupe (Yarbro-Bejarano, 1995). A deep analysis of Ochoa's family history and staunchly Catholic upbringing falls outside of this analysis, except to attend to the fact that even her imagining of herself as a devout Catholic offered a point of disidentification when she chose to marry Aeroméxico CEO, Andrés Conesa, a divorcee. Rumours of family dissention and sadness about the loss of her relationship with the Church circulated during her poor golf performance following her marriage to Conesa (Crouse, 2010). The depth and contours of Ochoa's religiosity and faith are surely meaningful and worthy of analysis, but beyond the scope of this chapter.

This analysis pays close attention to the ways that Ochoa actively refuses efforts to Latinize, Americanize, and erase her deeply felt Mexicanness, while also refusing to be put into contention with her brown peers on the tour. To a certain extent, Ochoa more directly exhibits the post-title IX liberation supposedly made available to the global girl subject called forth through modernist sport organizations like the US-LPGA. Such an agitative brownness can easily be missed if the analytic focus remains on ethnicity, or gender, or sexuality, or nationality, without attending to these as intersecting axes of power with varied material effects for Ochoa, her fans, and her golfing peers. Agitative brownness can also be missed if our focus remains on access to circuits of consumption, rather than opportunities to imagine and change one's social world. Throughout this chapter, we rely on Muñoz' (1999) analyses around the brown commons, and more specifically, his concept of "disidentification", or the process of actively refusing an identification strategy and set of conditions in order to choose something different, not only for one's own striving but for the survival of whole communities. Other scholars have described similar *movidas en diferencia*, including Gloria Anzaldúa's (1987) concept of '*la facultad*' and Chela Sandoval's (2000) concept of 'differential consciousness'.

In fact, Chicana feminisms and border studies continue to hold significant, largely untapped, intellectual promise for sport studies scholars (Adams *et al.*, 2016; Birrell, 1990; Ratna *et al.*, 2017). At their core is always a strategy for decolonizing spaces, places, and traces of 'difference', a set of practices that aim to recalibrate historical reckonings, value processes of ongoing entanglements and conditional encounters, and situate brown communities and experiences within these communities at the centre of analytic projects. Muñoz clearly argues that a 'brown commons' is not merely a portal to calcified Latina/o identities; rather it is an articulation of encounters with multiple forms of brownness. In the same way, perhaps, that Lugones (1994) describes coalescence, and Sandoval (2000) articulates a transnationality among and across Latina/o identities, and Moraga (1993) calls for a queer *aztlan* or a homeland that includes all brown people, Muñoz (1999) calls our attention to the already here and not yet present brown communities.

Border Studies and Chicana feminist analyses of sport and physical activity invite and, one might say, require crucial dialogue between sport studies and all-too-often de-linked cultural studies, area studies, and feminist studies. While feminist-informed sport and leisure scholars must actively interrogate the seeming irrelevance of sport and physical activity in projects of Chicana/o Cultural Studies, we must also actively deploy Border Studies and Chicana feminist sensibilities toward questions about the nuances of multi-community and transnational memberships and the role of sport/leisure involvement in brown communities. Similar to other border scholars, Muñoz (1999) describes brown knowingness as a brown commons – a collective reckoning of the simultaneity of the individual and public that links pre-settler colonial relations to the most current set of political conditions that work against brown subjects and publics. Such publics are seldom considered as sport teams or leagues, but rather as a type of gathering that transcends specific places, sites, or events. For example, the Black Lives Matter movement may be seen as a counterpublic, while the current of agitative community developing in and through the movement, including NFL player Colin Kaepernick's protest during the US National Anthem, may also be seen as an emergent 'public', an agitative gathering in multi-sited, worldwide venues. In a classic sense, a public represented a civil society response to conditions of life by a group that could not only gather, but also could expect to be heard and responded to by those occupying positions in governance structures. A brown commons is a uniquely situated public, and perhaps always begins as a counter-public to the extent that there is little precedent for brown communities being heard, let alone not already being spoken for. For Muñoz it is critical to recognize the agitative, not merely oppressed component of the brown commons – it is a space of survival and striving in the face of state-sponsored discounting, removal, taxing, and surveillance of brown bodies. In this manner, a brown commons invites pondering beyond stories of an Old English commons, a static resource that needs protection, and instead toward an understanding, encounter, and sense of brownness itself as a public good that actually creates resources in its survival and striving. Thus, according to Muñoz, a brown commons is a vibrant, historical commons space – a transient place of encounter.

Muñoz also frames a brown commons as a queer ecology – not simply a shared victimhood, but also a shared resistance and an active refusal of the violences and indignations of the quotidian for/with/among brown subjects. When WNBA teams use post-game press conferences to discuss the Black Lives Matter movement, and WTA players Serena and Venus Williams boycott a tournament site, and when world-class runner Dutee Chand refuses to let sport governing bodies over-govern her own physiology, they simultaneously offer a new encounter for each of us – a new encounter with everyday conditions of displacement, marginalization, and suspicion that animates Muñoz' reframing of the commons, as well as his deployment of disidentification to invite an encounter with middle spaces (Anzaldúa, 1987). The visible presence of Lorena Ochoa on the US-LPGA tour and beyond illuminates this brown commons, especially as a set of entanglements that cannot be controlled, cannot be catalogued, and cannot be mastered or enclosed (Muñoz, 2012). It is our contention that Lorena Ochoa is both attuned to and agitates from within a brown commons.

This is where we wish to specifically take up Muñoz' sense of disidentification in sport/performance spaces. To be sure, we must understand fully what is at stake when subjects actively queer sporting spaces or disidentify within the sporting commons, toward a brown sporting commons. While not studying sport per se, Muñoz offered deep analyses of various queer performance artists and projects, each toward its potential to disrupt so-called 'straight time'. In opposition to 'straight time' or structures of domination, Muñoz' sense of a queer futurity featured critical performance art as an imagining of a utopian world through an intentional queering of its most self-regulating features.[1] Disidentification may be read as a survival strategy for minoritized subjects. Muñoz argued:

> Let me be clear about one thing: disidentification is about cultural, material, and psychic survival. It is a response to state and global power apparatuses that employ systems of racial, sexual, and national

> subjugation. These routinized protocols of subjugation are brutal and painful. Disidentification is about managing and negotiating historical trauma and systemic violence.
>
> (1999: 161–162)

Considering minority positionalities as having limitations in enacting identifications in a dominant public sphere, he focused on the possibility of "working on and against" that disidentification value (ibid.: 46). Similar to other border scholars who have analysed middle spaces and third space sensibilities, Muñoz (1999: 11) describes disidentification as "the third mode of dealing with dominant ideology, one that neither opts to assimilate within such a structure nor strictly opposes it; rather, disidentification is a strategy that works on and against dominant ideology". Through a process of transformative restructuration "disidentification is a step further than cracking open the code of the majority; it proceeds to use this code as raw material for representing a disempowered politics or positionality that has been rendered unthinkable by the dominant culture" (ibid.: 31). With these practices of disidentification, we illuminate Lorena Ochoa as a sort of disidentifying subject who transfigures her presence by negotiating and managing with dominant ideological practices.

To read Lorena Ochoa's careers as disidentificatory performances has the potential to effectively interrogate the imperialistic nature of US-centred sport and media, and uncritically embrace stereotypes of minoritarian subjectivities by audiences. We believe this approach to cultural analyses of sport and physical activity fits well within a broader set of analytic sensibilities informed by Chicana and border feminisms. This approach offers a useful insight that connects often strictly disconnected disciplines of cultural studies, area studies, and feminist studies (Ratna *et al.*, 2017). Foregrounding the multi-positioned stance, this approach has a significant value for exploring complex power relations around transnational communities and subjectivities, and the role of sport in day-to-day productions of human relations (ibid.). By critically analysing Lorena Ochoa and the sense of brown with a Chicana feminist sensibility this chapter contributes not only to reveal newly racialized sporting practices with/in brown and queer communities but to produce counter-narratives possessing resistant political possibilities (McDonald and Birrell, 1999). Ultimately, our aim is to deploy disidentificatory readings as an agitative catalyst for readers to carry out and expand their own readings of conditions for minoritized communities in sport. Toward this aim, we analyse specific ways that Lorena Ochoa engaged in practices of disidentification in order to draw attention to structures of domination, and in order to generate newly imagined worlds, or social worlds that work beyond the neoliberal and consumptive aims of the US-LPGA and typical 'post-title 9/11' sport organizations (Jamieson, 2015).

A post-title 9/11 analysis links a framing of gender as globalized and globalization as gendered (Enloe, 2004) with a postcolonial and critical transnational reading of women's sport, and requires a reckoning with the role of global sport in enforced, public performances of US multiculturalism and alignment with white/ned, 'American' exceptionalism. For example, the US 'war on terror', following the attack on the US World Trade Center of September 11, 2001, invited a set of new alliances in the name of safe, productive, industrialized nations and lives (Moreton-Robinson *et al.*, 2008; Winant, 2004) with sport playing an active role as a cultural site for acting out this new national in/security (Grewal, 2007).[2] Working within this post-title 9/11 framework, and focusing on key moments in Ochoa's entry, mid-career, and post-retirement, we collected and reviewed a selective set of media texts that illuminate agitative engagements that we read as 'disidentificatory' practices. For the most part, Ochoa's career has been culturally read as a 2/3 world success story, if given any attention at all. Our aim here is to reorient this narrative, putting her in a role of intentionality and agitation as she navigates the white, Western, post-title 9/11 site of the US-LPGA. In this sense, we are practicing a counter-narrativizing (McDonald and Birrell, 1999) and are less invested in making authenticity claims about her identity or personal goals. We contend that Ochoa and her career activities occupy a significant cultural space in much the same way as do the performance artforms that Muñoz analysed. We further contend that her encounters in this world of global golf deserve our analytic attention from a variety of framings. For this analysis, a variety of cultural texts which include English-language newspaper, magazine, and online golf periodicals were chosen as substantive and representative sources by keyword searches on Ochoa's 'rookie season', 'British Open win', and 'retirement'. These moments offered opportunities to read Ochoa's global sport encounters through the lens of disidentification. We consider our reading of these three career moments as our own practice in becoming attuned to brownness and perhaps to reimagine sporting spaces through the experiences and tactics of agitative, brown, global girl subjects.

In the sections that follow, we attempt to deploy Muñoz' logic as we analyse three components of disidentification throughout Ochoa's professional golf career. Our central aim is to illuminate the ways in which she re-forms the components of subjectivity and practices strategies of resistance. We refer to these components as naming and refusing codes of difference, co-producing counterpublicities, and acting on a communal sense of brown.

Naming and refusing codes of difference

Throughout Ochoa's professional golf career, she remakes not only herself but also a broader public that includes other brown subjects. That is, more than simply counter identify or reject pre-determined identity structures, her various actions of *tactical misrecognition* demonstrate a naming and refusal of "the representational protocols of identity" that are regularly enacted by the US-LPGA, the US media, and US–Mexican politico-economic relations, to name a few (Muñoz, 1999: 175). For example, when the US-LPGA attempted to enact an English proficiency policy with a penalty for not meeting the standard within a specified time-period, Ochoa was one of few current US-LPGA professionals to speak against it, simply stating that it seemed to be a drastic measure (Navarrette, 2008). In this moment, Ochoa could have seized upon her privilege as an English-speaking 'foreigner', but she aligned herself with a sensibility that traversed the boundaries and borders of the US-LPGA's brand of 'global tour'; a tour for those who are willing to assimilate to Western versions of globality. This is a decidedly brown agitation that is not merely rooted to Latino/a heritage, but meant to articulate entanglements of difference. Ochoa's disidentificatory performance through tactical misrecognition unveils oppressive dominant ideologies that shape relations among all of her professional peers, fans, and home community members – she refuses to participate and refuses to disengage – she offers a sense of brown that needs no alibi and will not be erased.

In an example more specifically related to her entry to the US-LPGA, Ochoa was ideologically hailed by the US media and global US-LPGA media in a commonly unspoken, yet expressed, refrain of 'Hey, you, Nancy Lopez[3] reincarnated!'. Ochoa responded with several forms of tactical misrecognition, or ways of refusing to perform the Other for the US-LPGA and refusing to *closet* her multiple identities. Ochoa being intentionally Mexican when the US-LPGA expects her to be an oversimplified, conforming US-LPGA/global citizen, or even a reincarnated (Mexican-American) Nancy Lopez, illuminates a tactical misrecognition. In contrast, mainstream sports journalists and the US-LPGA regularly described Lopez's close ties to family as well as the limits of her working class, Mexican father's ability to usher her into her new professional career (Jamieson, 1998). From the very beginning, Ochoa was clear that she would not be separating from any of her Mexican roots in order to manage her golf career, and in fact, her various Mexican resources, including family, were explicitly part of her preparation for her professional golf career.

Additionally, throughout her career, Ochoa was enthusiastic in conveying a value for and belief in a collective Mexican-ness. Rather than advocating Mexico as a mere replica of the US, she often envisioned autonomous and independent Mexico which is empowered by the home community members themselves, emphasizing Mexican ethnicity as a source of pride. Ochoa regularly encouraged Mexican fans to bring the national flag to Tour events, and the colours of the Mexican flag – red, white, and green – were also obviously displayed through her putter grip (Mell, 2006; Schroeder, 2007). Rather than affirming that Ochoa has vehemently denied or renounced her identity as promoted and manufactured by the US-LPGA, in our notion, the repetitive and spontaneous revelation of herself as Mexican (e.g. saying "don't forget your roots" (*Border Heritage*, 2015: n.p.)) may be considered a sort of 'euphemistic refusal' of being falsely or simply identified in the concept of reincarnation or US centralism. Through these nuanced, yet wilful enactments of her own sense of identity and belonging, Ochoa neither chooses to assimilate within the dominant structure nor completely opposes it (Bagnato, 2007). Not only as a talented US-LPGA golfer but as a deliberate Mexican who has global fame, Ochoa's disidentificatory career works on and against strict and oppressive dominant cultural ideology and the strategic performativity guides spectators to newly envision who she is and where she belongs.

In addition to refusing invitations to distance herself from Mexico, Ochoa also amassed major endorsements without adopting the US-LPGA branding strategy, especially the components focused on sex-appeal (Douglas and Jamieson, 2006). In fact, Ochoa's endorsements included global companies such as Ping, Audi, FootJoy, LaCoste, Rolex, as well as Mexico-based companies Aeroméxico, Banamex and Selther – all business deals made with a focus on her golf skill and global likeability, not on her willingness or ability to sell a sexy image (Rubenstein, 2008). As such, using the resources of identification which are defined by the majoritarian public sphere as raw material, Lorena Ochoa engaged in the project of new world-making that empowers herself and the broader brown public through practices of tactical misrecognition, or naming and refusing codes of difference (Muñoz, 2012; Sandoval, 2000).

Co-producing counterpublicities

Another significant point of disidentification is that "the strategies and practices that constitute disidentification are, for the most part, more readily available to subjects whose class privilege gives them access to systems of representation" (Muñoz, 1999: 164). Ochoa is certainly one of these subjects as her family is quite well-resourced economically. Elite athletes, like performance artists, may be especially able to access systems of representations and thereby act in ways that are generative of strong-ish *counterpublics* and *counterpublicity*. Muñoz defined counterpublics as "communities and relational chains of resistance that contest the dominant public sphere" (ibid.: 146). As a representational and political act, counterpublicity defies the discriminatory ideologies, such as white/American/English normativity, within the majoritarian public spheres. Thus, as Ochoa regularly meets and dines with Spanish-speaking and Mexican course maintenance crew members, she is actively entangled with a range of brownness to which she is affectively and critically engaged throughout her career. Her wilful representation functions as an agitative subject in the brown commons engaged in a practice of counterpublicity, or generating not only a counter narrative of minoritized communities and subjects, but also simultaneously naming the practices that relegate these communities and their members to subjugated social positions. Surely, the counterpublicity gains power in part through Ochoa's celebrity but at the same time, her practice of disidentification generates a space of solidarity among differently situated brown people. As a Mexican-identified golf course crew member shared,

> [...] we get up at two or three in the morning in order to be here early. You have to give it your all because it has to be in perfect conditions and more than anything because of Lorena Ochoa and for her to see a pretty golf course and so she feels proud of her countrymen like we are proud of her.
>
> (Vitiello, 2008)

Here, Lorena Ochoa's presence functions as a sort of rigid string connecting herself, Mexican workers at golf courses, and members of brown communities all together. At the same time, the agitative subject in US-LPGA works as an agent who invites Mexican golf course crew members to defy the predominant white/ned ideologies in the US through the voluntary assiduousness in their professional location. The subjugated positionality of workers can be re-envisioned as an empowered subjectivity and thus the new public status contributes to sustain and undergird a brown counterpublic. The engendered bond among employees of Mexican heritage was often more externally performed. Singing and chanting in Spanish, the workers used to follow Ochoa at a golf course on their day off (Sirak, 2010). These encounters that transcend the place of the golf course represent Muñoz' 'uncontained space' of the brown commons where recognition matters but not in a way that excludes or exonerates. That is, the subjugated subjects autonomously intervene in the white/ned public sphere and strategically construct their selfhood by themselves through the vivid practices such as speaking Spanish. Appearing to various publics as a different mode of identification, cohesiveness becomes forceful among the Mexican people in the counterpublics. Through this uncontained property and the self-actualization, disidentification as a survival strategy is re-echoed against racial, sexual, and national subjugation from global power apparatuses.

Acting on a communal sense of brown

According to Muñoz (1999: 168), "disidentificatory performances resist the social matrix of dominant publicity by exposing the rhetorical/ideological context of state power". As the ability to cultivate the part of the self that transcends the self, the transformative disidentifications make counterpublics become imaginable and visible and it enables subjugated subjects to envision a possibility for freedom. Given this point, Muñoz might read Ochoa's disidentification with the US-LPGA identity structures as a desire to love brown people – to contribute to the sustenance of brown counterpublics and to envision a queer potentiality through a communal sense of brown.

Lorena Ochoa's retirement from the US-LPGA while holding the number 1 spot in the Rolex Rankings may be initially and superficially read as yet another story of female athlete choosing to start a family. An attunement to a brown commons would illuminate a purposeful yet uncontainable set of entanglements with intimate-public and public-public desires, and with a refusal to see her presence on the US-LPGA in a scarcity frame (Mickey, 2013). In fact, Lorena Ochoa's post-retirement activities render the brown commons moveable, constantly travelling, making visible the affective connections that Muñoz describes in disidentifications. Thus, Ochoa's brownness does not only exist in relief to the white/ned American and European golfers on the US-LPGA, but she keeps it active or *live* as she literally walks away from the US-LPGA with much of their capital and puts it to use for Mexican citizens. Specifically, Ochoa accomplishes this through hosting a US-LPGA tour event in her hometown of Guadalajara, Mexico, a site that was not on the radar of the US-LPGA, with its growth projects aimed directly at South Asia and future Olympic venues. The Lorena Ochoa Foundation aims to enhance educational access in under-resourced communities in Mexico and operates La Barranca school, where she puts golf to use to enrich the full development of young people in Mexico. Ochoa affirms their mission this way,

> I love to see the kids, that they are really taking advantage of the opportunities [...] You can see that you are changing their lives, either with golf or no golf. It's about giving them the right education so that they can prepare for the future and help people around them.
>
> (Rubenstein, 2008)

As a host of the Lorena Ochoa Invitational, the only US-LPGA tournament played in Mexico, Ochoa's effort to make a brown commons visible is exemplified through the celebratory sombrero and the Talavera-style pottery trophy. At the same time, it echoes a nature of co-existence in disidentification that is consequently linked to the politics of resistance and empowerment. A powerful image of Korean American female golf player Christina Kim with the sombrero and the Talavera-style pottery trophy, marking her as the winner at the 2014 Lorena Ochoa Invitational, illuminates Muñoz' sense of brownness as "a co-presence with other modes of difference" (Muñoz, 2012: n.p.). More specifically, Muñoz declares, "brownness is a co-existence with blackness, Asian-ness, and other terms that have manifest descriptive force to render the particularities of various modes of striving in the world" (ibid: n.p.). Through this re-imagined, larger, collective mapping of minoritarian subjectivities, a force of transcendence constitutes across mixed visual signs in the new image, bringing about a possibility of resistance against uniform identity politics. Ochoa's disidentificatory subjectivities through her career thus not only fortify a communal sense of brown and the counterpublicity within it but also offer a lens to visualize new global power in sport enacted by minoritarian subjects.

The global girl subject as queer futurity

Despite an ongoing disciplinary distance between Chicana and Border Studies and largely European-informed Sport Studies, decolonial projects around human movement(s) and bodily practices are slowly becoming visible (Chabram-Dernersesian and de la Torre, 2008; Cordova, 1998; Hernandez and Rehman, 2002). Regardless of faulty disciplinary boundaries, analyses of iconic public performers, such as Ochoa, offer their most productive ends when aimed not at uplifting a single, inspirational tale, but when focused on the temporal and contextual conditions under which such a performer sustains their whole brown self while re-worlding or reimagining a social world where the alibi of whiteness no longer legitimizes erasure and violence against brown communities. To be sure, disidentification is not a complete or redemptive practice, nor is it a strategy that is readily available to all subject positions. Our reading of Lorena Ochoa's career movidas suggests she deploys practices of disidentification with cultural and material impact. It seems important and timely to observe her intentional practices of solidarity with minoritized and transnational, brown communities. Ochoa acts with a clarity of mission that is confounding – it is as though she is unaware of her externally imposed subjectivity as a third-world subject who ought to be grateful to the first world empire and its agents, including the US-LPGA.

Given Muñoz' 'sense of brown', it is clear that global girl subjects do not exist 'out there' to be identified, corralled, and studied. Global girl subjects are already present in their ties to Ochoa as fans, as students in her grade school, to the golf course grounds crews, to the displaced communities in the wake of golf community development projects, and in the transnational economy that promotes investments in elite performance abroad as a 'good risk'. Make no mistake, in the very White/ned space of golf there exists already a brown sporting commons, ripe with queerly brown encounters – encounters that may be missed unless we learn to be attuned to their presence in our daily lives. This analysis of selected career movidas by Lorena Ochoa raises the question, "What does it take for sport studies scholars to become attuned to the brown commons, or to the brown sporting commons?" We see three core components of such an attunement including respecting brown communities and members as holders/agents of knowledge, learning to see agitative affect beyond practices of resistance, and recalibrating the worldly possibilities for sport and physical activity in struggles for social and spatial justice.

1 Attunement to a brown sporting commons requires a firm belief in the existence of crucial knowledge in brown communities. Not merely a celebration of the ethnic other and mystical-grounded ways of knowing, attunement requires an historicized recognition of legacies of knowledge and expertise that have been erased or falsely claimed by dominant groups. Taking Muñoz' notion of brownness as more than victimhood into account, an authentic attunement to a brown sporting commons would ensure that brown girls and women are expected and invited to serve as active agents in knowledge production. This sort of gathering, through a brown commons, positions diverse members of the community as agitative subjects for meaningful discussion within a system of knowledge production that transcends simple modes of shared victimhood and instead turns into a communal resistance. This is not a neoliberal call to 'community engaged scholarship', rather it is a requirement to actually engage in issues affecting brown communities and partner with agents already working toward re-worlding with brown communities in mind. An attunement to a brown commons requires a scholarship that is always "for us, not about us" (Know Her Truths, 2016: n.p.).
2 In order to partner, not merely with people who fit within calcified identity categories but, rather, with issues that affect specific communities, we must differentiate between singular resistance or survival and agitative affective practice in the everyday. Resistance is one component of a more fully engaged and ongoing set of politics that agitate for more just communities. Attunement to this agitative affect requires each of us to act to alter unjust conditions within our communities, regardless of our ability to avoid their consequence. Valuing the shifting cultural forces and potentialities, agitative affect induces intensive, meaningful, and palpable brown comingling in the service of varied projects of human striving and challenges. In the uncontained space of a brown commons, various modes of agitative interventions function as a component of counterpublics or newly envisioned minoritarian space.

3 An attunement to a brown sporting commons would also require a reimagining of the role of sport and physical activity in the dailiness of transnational lives. That is, sport and physical activity would be observed as a conduit of meaningful human encounters, not merely from a performance or outcome perspective. The non-spectacular contours of sport and physical activity would be analysed alongside the spectacular. The borders of sport spaces would be considered diffuse, thus the brown sporting commons will not reify a scarcity frame of stagnant sporting places, but would, instead, focus on sporting spaces that both produce and are produced by local and translocal inhabitants. In the vernacular of pedagogical practice, sport studies scholars will 'flip' the question and the sporting space in order to see more clearly the contingent relations making the space possible. Thus, when a journalist calls and asks "Why aren't Latinas participating in sport?" or "Why are South Korean women dominating the US-LPGA tour?" – two prominent questions about women's sport for the past 10 years. An attune sport-social scientist might flip the question to "When and where are persons who identify as Latinex or various Asian ethnicities engaging in sport and physical activity?" and "What role is professional golf playing in the production and control of transnational sporting spaces and inhabitants?" (Kwon and Kim, 2006).

Our reading of Lorena Ochoa's career as agitative in the everyday underscores the fact that an attunement to a brown commons cannot merely make brown communities more readily decipherable and legitimized through/for Western scientific methodologies. Developing a sense of brown, becoming attuned to a brown commons, and learning to see disidentificatory practices, ought to offer new orienting points from which to pose new questions about transnational sporting spaces. Certainly, Lorena 'La Reina' Ochoa engages in her agitative actions from an economically privileged position, but not necessarily from a politically advantaged subject position, thus she skilfully navigates middle spaces throughout her career. While she may face less harsh consequences to her subsistence as compared to her compatriots who work on the grounds crew at the tour golf courses, she is still always a Mexican citizen navigating the one-third world. As stated previously, it is not the intent of this analysis to locate Ochoa in some authentic progressive narrative of her career 'success', including resistance to White/ned framings by the US-LPGA global tour, nor is it our goal to locate her in a specific identity frame once and for all. Ochoa's career offers key moments from which we may practice our own emergent attunement to brownness and to brown commons toward a reorienting of our encounter with the 'global girl subject'. To the extent we are constantly invited to co-create and collectively animate this 'global girl subject' through consumption and uncritical identifications, an attunement to a brown commons becomes a crucial tool for both targeted resistance and expansive recognition in everyday encounters of transnational sporting spaces.

Notes

1 Jean-Michel Basquiat's artwork is one of the projects that Muñoz explicated as a mode of disidentification. Reading Basquiat's Famous Negro Athletes images, for example, Muñoz considered the use of the word *Negro* as an intentional racial signifier that Basquiat used in order to disidentify with the racist cultural history in the US. The frequently inserted crown image is another device for Basquiat to illuminate the rich history of African/Americans, while disrupting the racist imaginings of famous black athletes as a mere commodity for trade. In a sphere where visibility is overwhelmingly controlled by white privilege, Muñoz reads Basquiat's disidentificatory impulses and practical tactics as work that critically examines the racist US society, reimagines black representations, and strategizes survival within it (Muñoz, 1999).

2 Specifically, new immigration policies, definitions of marriage, pay equity laws, repeal of legislation disallowing open homosexuality in US armed forces, along with sport-related gender equity policies (e.g. IOC policy requiring women on all 2012 Olympic teams), all come together to generate the possibility of current US nativist desires for familiar, sovereign, global, 'American' sporting spaces (see Aldama, 2002; Lugo-Lugo and Bloodworth-Lugo, 2010; Lugones, 2007; Moreton-Robinson *et al.*, 2008; Puar, 2006; Winant, 2004).

3 Nancy Lopez is a US-LPGA Hall of Fame member, who had a huge fan base, rivalling that of the most prominent PGA professionals. Lopez was also a prominent working-class, Mexican-American success-story through her elite performance on the US-LPGA.

References

Adams, M.L., Davidson, J., Helstein, M.T., Jamieson, K.M., Kim, K.Y., King, S., McDonald, M. and Rail, G. (2016) 'Feminist cultural studies: Uncertainties and possibilities', *Sociology of Sport Journal*, 33(1): pp. 75–91.

Aldama, A.J. (2002) 'Millennial anxieties: Borders, violences and the struggle for Chicana and Chicano subjectivity' in A.J. Aldama and N. Quinonez (eds) *Decolonial voices*. Bloomington, Indiana: Indiana University Press: pp. 11–29.

Anzaldúa, G. (1987) *Borderlands/La frontera: The new mestiza*. San Francisco: Spinsters/Aunt Lute.

Bagnato, A. (2007) 'Lorena Ochoa rallies to win safeway', *Washington Post*, 25 March. Available from: www.washingtonpost.com/wp-dyn/content/article/2007/03/25/AR2007032500889_pf.html [Accessed 10 April 2016].

Bairner, A. (2001) *Sport, nationalism, and globalization: European and North American perspectives*. Albany, New York: Suny Press.

Birrell, S. (1990) 'Women of color, critical autobiography, and sport' in M.A. Messner and D.F. Sabo (eds) *Sport, men and the gender order: Critical feminist perspectives*. Champaign, Illinois: Human Kinetics Publishers: pp. 185–201.

Border Heritage Magazine (2015) 'Lorena Ochoa', *Border Heritage Magazine*, 23 April. Available from: www.border-heritage.com/lorena-ochoa/ [Accessed 16 April 2016].

Bradley, T. (2008) 'From top of the trees to top of the golf world', *Associated Press*, 29 April. Available from: http://theresabradley.squarespace.com/lorena-ochoa/ [Accessed 1 April 2016].

Chabram-Dernersesian, A. and de la Torre, A. (eds) (2008) *Speaking from the body: Latinas on health and culture*. Tucson, Arizona: University of Arizona Press.

Chibber, K. (2015) 'Hits like a girl: These are the first women to be allowed into the Royal and Ancient Golf Club of St. Andrews', *Quartz*, 11 February. Available from: http://qz.com/342520/these-are-the-first-women-to-be-allowed-into-the-royal-and-ancient-golf-club-of-st-andrews/ [Accessed 5 June 2016].

Cordova, T. (1998) 'Power and knowledge: Colonialism in the academy' in C.M. Trujillo (ed.) *Living Chicana theory*. Berkeley, California: Third Woman Press: pp. 17–45.

Crouse, K. (2010) 'Ochoa has hard day on the course, but a Good One', *New York Times*, 2 April. Available from: www.nytimes.com/2010/04/03/sports/golf/03lpga.html?_r=0 [Accessed 2 April 2016].

Douglas, D.D., and Jamieson, K.M. (2006) 'A farewell to remember: Interrogating the Nancy Lopez farewell tour', *Sociology of Sport Journal*, 23(2): pp. 117–141.

Enloe, C. (2004) *The curious feminist: Searching for women in a new age of empire*. Berkeley: University of California Press.

Golf Digest (2008) 'The power issue: How does she do it? 5′6″. 127lbs. 290yds Lorena Ochoa', *Golf Digest*. Available from: www.golfdigest.com/ [Accessed 1 July 2016].

Grewal, I. (2005) *Transnational America: Feminisms, diasporas, neoliberalisms*. Durham, North Carolina: Duke University Press.

Grewal, I. (2007) '"Security moms" in the early twentieth-century United States: The gender of security in neoliberalism', *Women's Studies Quarterly*, 34(1/2): pp. 25–39.

Grupo Ochoa (2016) 'Grupo Ochoa'. Available from: www.grupoochoa.com.mx [Accessed 3 April 2016].

Hayhurst, L.M.C. (2011) 'Corporatising sport, gender and development: Postocolonial IR feminisms, transnational private governance and global corporate social engagement', *Third World Quarterly*, 32(3): pp. 531–549.

Hernandez, D. and Rehman, B. (2002) *Colonize this!: Young women of color on today's feminism*. New York: Seal Press.

Jamieson, K.M. (1998) 'Reading Nancy Lopez: Decoding representations of race, class, sexuality and gender', *Sociology of Sport Journal*, 15(4): pp. 343–358.

Jamieson, K.M. (2015) 'Making the global turn: The US-LPGA, commissioner rhetoric of difference, and "new imperialism"', *Journal of Sport and Social Issues*, 39(6): pp. 501–520.

Kidd, B. (1990) 'The men's cultural centre: Sports and the dynamic of women's oppression/men's repression' in M.A. Messner and D.F. Sabo (eds) *Sport, men, and the gender order: Critical feminist perspectives*. Champaign, Illinois: Human Kinetics Books: pp. 31–44.

Know Her Truths (2016) Personal communication with conference presenters. Julia Cooper Center, Wake Forest University, Winston-Salem, North Carolina, USA. April 2016.

Kwon, S.Y. and Kim, B.C. (2006) 'Globalizing USLPGA, the international division of sports labor, and golf in Korea', *Korean Journal of Sociology of Sport*, 17(1): pp. 95–108.

Lugo-Lugo, C.R. and Bloodworth-Lugo, M.K. (2010) '475° from September 11: Citizenship, immigration, same-sex marriage, and the browning of terror', *Cultural Studies*, 24(2): pp. 234–255.

Lugones, M. (1994) 'Purity, impurity and separation', *SIGNS: Journal of Women in Culture and Society*, 19(2): pp. 458–479.

Lugones, M. (2007) 'Heterosexualism and the colonial/modern gender system', *Hypatia*, 22(1): pp. 186–209.

McCarthy, C. (2009) 'With Ochoa, golf has a giving side', *National Catholic Reporter*, 27 April. Available from: www.ncronline.org/news/people/ochoa-golf-has-giving-side [Accessed 2 April 2016].

McDonald, M.G. and Birrell, S. (1999) 'Reading sport critically: A methodology for interrogating power', *Sociology of Sport Journal*, 16(4): pp. 283–300.

Mell, R. (2006) 'Pride of Mexico', *SunSentinel*, 16 November. Available from: http://articles.sun-sentinel.com/2006-11-16/sports/0611151272_1_lorena-ochoa-putter-happy-birthday [Accessed 16 April 2016].

Mickey, L.D. (2013) 'Ochoa's legacy casts a shadow over Mexican aspirants to her throne', *New York Times*, 6 December. Available from: www.nytimes.com/2013/12/07/sports/golf/ochoas-legacy-casts-a-shadow-over-mexican-aspirants-to-her-throne.html?_r=0 [Accessed 11 April 2016].

Moraga, C. (1993) 'Queer Aztlán: The re-formation of Chicano tribe' in C. Moraga (ed.) *The last generation: Prose and poetry*. Boston, Massachusetts: South End Press: pp. 145–74.

Moreton-Robinson, A., Casey, M., and Nicoll, F. (2008) *Transnational whiteness matters: Myth understanding*. New York: Rowman & Littlefield Press.

Muñoz, J.E. (1999) *Disidentifications: Queers of color and the performance of politics*. Minneapolis: University of Minnesota Press.

Muñoz, J.E. (2006) 'Feeling brown, feeling down: Latina affect, the performativity of race, and the depressive position', *Signs: Journal of Women in Culture & Society*, 31(3): pp. 675–688.

Muñoz, J.E. (2012) 'Brown commons' [presentation]. *Duke Feminist Theory Conference*. 23 March 2012. Duke University, Durham, North Carolina, USA.

Navarrette, R. (2008) 'LPGA backing off English-only policy', *Tucson Citizen*, 10 September. Available from: http://tucsoncitizen.com/morgue/2008/09/10/96215-navarrette-lpga-backing-off-english-only-policy/ [Accessed 8 April 2016].

Ochoa Sports Management (2016) *Mission* [online]. Ochoa Sports Management. Available from: http://ochoasports.com.mx/es/quienes-somos/mision/ [Accessed 3 April 2016].

Puar, J.K. (2006) 'Mapping US homonormativities', *Gender, Place, and Culture*, 13(1): pp. 67–88.

Radford, R. (2008) 'Mexican star Lorena Ochoa's sunny outlook', *The Virginian-Pilot*, 5 May. Available from: http://pilotonline.com/sports/other/golf/

mexican-star-lorena-ochoa-s-sunny-outlook/article_d39c866b-1890-570e-904a-ec1323ac6117.html [Accessed 2 April 2016].

Ratna, A., Samie, S.F., Jamieson, K.M., and Thangaraj, S. (2017) 'Learning lessons from the feminisms of ethnic others' in L. Mansfield, J. Caudwell, B. Watson and B. Wheaton (eds) *The handbook for feminisms in sport, leisure and physical education*. Palgrave (in press).

Rolex Rankings (2016) 'Overview rankings: Women's world rankings'. Available from: www.rolexrankings.com/en/rankings/?help [Accessed 1 July 2016].

Rubenstein, L. (2008) 'Ruling the fairways', *The Globe and Mail*, 3 May. Available from: www.theglobeandmail.com/sports/golf/ruling-the-fairways/article1324829/?page=3 [Accessed 11 April 2016].

Sandoval, C. (2000) *Methodology of the oppressed*. Minneapolis, Minnesota: University of Minnesota.

Schroeder, G. (2007) 'Ochoa is indeed Numero Uno, LPGA Tour: SemGroup Championship, all of Mexico seems to be in love with LPGA's newest star', *NewsOk*, 5 May. Available from: http://newsok.com/article/3049532 [Accessed 11 April 2016].

Sirak, R. (2010) 'Reflections on Lorena: Connecting with countrymen', *Golf Digest*. 19 April. Available from: www.golfdigest.com/story/golf-ochoa-retirement-reflections [Accessed 13 April 2016].

Vitiello, C. (2008) *Lorena Ochoa Documentary Trailer* [video]. 30 January 2010. Available from: www.youtube.com/watch?v=WDDTWUD6gkM [Viewed 12 April 2016].

Winant, H. (2004) 'The new imperialism, globalization and racism' in H. Winant (ed.) *The new politics of race*. Minneapolis, MN: University of Minnesota Press: pp. 129–149.

Women's Health Magazine (Mexico) (January 2011) 'Lorena Ochoa: Como su vision de vida le dio el exito personal y professional' [Lorena Ochoa: How your life vision may offer you personal and professional success]. Available from: www.womenshealthlatam.com/ [Accessed 1 July 2016].

Yarbro-Bejarano, Y. (1995) 'The lesbian body in Latina cultural production' in E.L. Bergmann and P.J. Smith (eds) *¿Entiendes?: Queer readings, hispanic writings*. Durham, North Carolina: Duke University Press: pp. 181–197.

Chapter 9

Do women get the offside rule?

Female fans, labelling and stereotypes in Turkey

Itir Erhart

Turkish sports papers are filled with the stories of male fans who harass people, damage property on their way to the games and when inside, insult the opponents and throw various objects on to the pitch (*Hürriyet*, *Hürriyet Daily News*, *Milliyet*). This public display of hegemonic masculinity is often explained away with reference to 'male nature'. Female fans (or 'pseudo-fans' as they are typically depicted) are stereotypically represented as perfumed ladies who do not get the offside rule, or bickering aunts who care more about the well-being of players than the game (*Habertürk*, *Mynet*, *Ekşi Sözlük*, Pope 2010). An additional representation is that of the tomboys who are depicted as belonging in the stadia with their (alleged) endorsement of hegemonic masculinity, celebration of toughness, aggressiveness and sexist and homophobic chanting. In this chapter these mediated mis/representations of Turkish female football fans across traditional Turkish media such as *Hürriyet* and *Habertürk* and popular social networking sites are explored, deconstructed and unhinged. The extent to which these stereotypical mis/representations are informed by the natural difference discourse, which is pervasive in Turkish culture and political language, will also be examined.

The natural differences discourse which is often used to support the status quo of gendered structures constructs woman as emotional, delicate, fragile, gentle, soft-spoken, domestic, loyal, and as such, the better caregiver (Butler 1989). Men, on the other hand, are constructed as brave, tough, strong, angry, competitive, determined and, as such, a better fit for the public sphere (Erman 2001; Ayata and Tütüncü 2008; Güvenli and Tanrıöver 2009). The chapter will explore how the mis/representations of Turkish female fans are constructed, fuelled and strengthened in reference to the natural difference discourse. For this purpose, online articles and various entries posted to the largest social media platform in Turkey, *Ekşi Sözlük*, by men and women, were scanned for keywords related to the topic of female fans in Turkey. The keywords were 'female fans', 'female football fans' and 'lady fans'. All 136 news articles and 417 social commentaries where the aforementioned keywords appeared were collected and read twice. An inductive analysis method was adapted to search for patterns of meaning in the data, allowing the texts to help me elaborate on the framing of female fans in/through the Turkish media, rather than adopting specific stakes beforehand to shape the interpretation of the data. The emerging themes and dominant narratives – the tension between authentic fandom and femininity, the alleged difficulties men go through while trying to explain the offside rule to the women in their lives, the metaphors used to define female fans, the attitudes approved by male fans – were then defined. From this initial analysis, three key stereotypes were identified and interpreted.

Natural differences discourse and Turkish gender politics

The natural differences discourse constructs biological dichotomies which attempt at justifying "the 'naturalness' of gendered behaviours and gendered social status" (Lorber 1993, p. 568). These biological 'facts' are internalized as truths, transmitted across and within generations, familiarized and recreated through bodies, actions and represented in language and media. These 'natural' features are portrayed as feminine attributes. Yet, another social process of othering can also be observed. This process inferiorizes (often older) femininity and subsumes it under the discourse of complaining, bickering, disagreeing women who grumble, whine, nit-pick, bicker, murmur, and nag (Direk 2013). Being 'soft spoken', 'gentle' and 'loyal' may seem almost antithetical to being depicted as disagreeable whiners. However, as in the case of the Mary (mother of God)/Eve (mother of lust) dichotomy (Mulvey 1993, p. 51; Linville 1998, p. 135) society sees no contradiction in moving us from stereotype A (the gentle, soft-spoken woman) to stereotype B (the hard to please, argumentative woman). These stereotypes coexist and sometimes even identify the very same woman – the former when she is younger, the latter in older age.

Bourdieu (1977, p. 206) discusses the arbitrariness of naturalness and argues that power structures need the appearance of naturalness to assure their power. That is to say, concepts of 'nature', 'natural differences', and 'creational differences' help to re-create gender roles within patriarchal structures. Scientifically (and religiously) framed 'natural' gender discourses (Foucault 1991) are a central dimension of power relationships, and as Matthews (2014, p. 101) underlines, these processes then become a foundation for building and maintaining patriarchal social hierarchies. As Dick and Nadin (2006) argue, this is fundamental in subordinating women and establishing the notion that inequality between the sexes cannot be avoided.

When we consider the feminist movements in Turkey we can see that neither the Kemalist (secular) nor the Islamic feminists have questioned this 'natural gender' discourse. During the 1920s, imbued through 'state-led feminism', women's most important role was considered to be as mothers (Öztamur 2004). The woman of the new republic was not constructed as an emancipated individual but, instead, as the self-sacrificing mother whose mission is to raise future generations endowed with republican values like modernism (Tekeli 1979). Islamic feminists who have become increasingly visible in regards to debates about the public sphere and the right to wear hijab – and who have mobilized university students in the 1980s – have not questioned the role of women within the family and society (Marshall 2008) either. Thus, both discourses have compounded and glorified the hard working mother, hence re-establishing the appearance of substance and the naturalness of these roles. Smith (1979) argues that the naturalness discourse in which women have clearly defined roles because of their innate qualities and characteristics is also dominant in contemporary Muslim writing. However, to avoid misconceptions such as "all women under Islam are treated in a certain way or other" and the resultant stereotype of the "submissive and silent non-Western woman" (Mohanty 2003, p. 127), it is important to dwell briefly on state, Islam and gender politics. Moroccan philosopher Mohammed Abed al-Jabiri (1980), in his book *Nahnu wa al-tharwa* (We and Our Heritage), provides evidence of how, in Islam, the politicians realized that they could only authoritatively manage the present by using the sacred past as a standard. Following al-Jabiri, Mernissi (1992, p. 16) talks about how the sacred text has been used as a political weapon since the eighth century AD when "the Muslim savants began to make a catalogue of *Hadith* (the deeds and saying of the Prophet), the *fiqh* (religious knowledge) and *tafsir* (the explication of the Koran)". Since then, empires and nation states have been using this catalogue to suit their political purposes and needs. Hence, the 'natural truths' about Islam and gender (modesty, sex-segregation, roles) should be understood in the political and social context.

In Turkey, the more than decade-long dominance of the religiously conservative Justice and Development Party (AKP), has 'normalized' religion in political discourse (Evans and Kaynak 2015, p. 145). The influence of religion in politics can be observed in President Erdoğan's discourse on gender:

> Some ladies talk about gender equality on TV. If this means equal rights we are fine with that. But the other goes against creation.
>
> (Denizaltı, 17 October 2010)

What Erdoğan means is that by challenging the 'natural' differences between men and women, this would go against God's creation. The religiously framed differences between women and men are creational, of divine origin and, as such, normal and unchangeable. In a speech he made in 2014 Erdoğan clarifies this point:

> You cannot bring women and men into an equal position; this is against nature [...]. You cannot make women do everything men do like the communist regimes did [...]. This is against her delicate nature.
>
> (*ISR Weekly*, 24 November 2014)

In another speech where he uses religious laws of truth to justify gendered division of labour, he accuses feminists of not appreciating the importance of the archetypal value of motherhood:

> Our religion [Islam] has defined a position for women [in society]: Motherhood. Some people can understand this, while others can't. You cannot explain this to feminists because they don't accept the concept of motherhood.
>
> (*Hürriyet Daily News*, 24 November 2014)

In this speech the woman is constructed as an element of the family, not as an individual (Belge 2011). By referring to Islam as the body which issued women their role, it is also implied that questioning this role would also mean questioning religion. On a similar note, Ali Bulaç, a columnist for *Zaman Daily*, states that men could marry up to four women "for it was in their nature", however women cannot "because they are monogamous by nature. That is how God created them" (*Milliyet* 24 June 2014). Such statements, by using religion as their source, aim at strengthening and naturalizing the discourse on the holiness of the heterosexual family (Güvenli and Tanrıöver 2009, p. 109; Coşar and Yeğenoğlu 2011). They are also used to justify gender division of labour that positions women differentially to men in the workplace and political arena which sets a perfect example for Mernissi's (1992) theory on using the sacred texts as a political weapon.

Natural differences discourse in Turkish football culture

The natural differences discourse is also highly dominant in football culture in Turkey. In this section, two phenomena, which, I believe, are the two manifestations of this discourse in football, will be discussed. The first one is the widespread stereotype of the woman that does not get the offside rule. In this analysis, this stereotype will be discussed as it manifests in/through the Turkish media. The second is the crowd restrictions that were in effect for three seasons (2011–2012, 2012–2013 and 2013–2014) during which 58 football matches were played in front of women and children spectators only.

Turkish women and the offside rule

'The woman who does not get the offside rule' is a stereotype widely used by Turkish advertisers and endorsed by brands and consumers alike. On a recent nationwide campaign the car manufacturing company Renault announced reductions on prices with the tagline 'You wouldn't be this happy unless you were able to explain the offside rule to your girlfriend'. The target customer is male and the company obviously finds the number of potential buyers who will be offended by this sexist statement negligible. Mobile service provider Vodafone, which is one of the market leaders in Turkey, also made use of the same stereotype while announcing its new discount plan a few years ago. A young man struggles to explain the offside rule to his girlfriend on the phone. Although it is likely to take forever, he is not concerned about his next phone bill since his charges will be reduced.

This stereotype, which is peddled by the advertising industry, is also proliferated, almost on a daily basis, through social media. The satirical, hypertext, online dictionary *Ekşi Sözlük* (which literally translates as 'The Sour Dictionary'), which is also a very popular social networking site, is one of the effective mediums where it is reproduced. *Ekşi Sözlük* attracts around 50,000 contributors who create dictionary-like entries on any topic imaginable: historical or current events, people – including but not limited to politicians, celebrities, professors, doctors – groups, political issues, places, quotations, etc. The entries are not moderated for factual correctness yet the website receives over 14 million visitors a month. According to Zeynep Tüfekçi, it is "Wikipedia, a social network, and Reddit rolled into one" (Kantrowiz 2013). It can also be considered a dynamic public space where contributors often respond to each other's entries and debate socio-political issues on the pages of this unconventional dictionary. Under the entry 'Explaining the offside rule to women' there are over 200 contributions by anonymous writers, most of which recreate the idea that, no matter how hard you try, women just do not get it:

> Take 4 olives and a salt container and when all the efforts fail tell her that you will try to explain it in drawings one day and get the hell out of this madness.
> It is harder than teaching quantum physics.
> I think it is impossible. Once my dad and I attempted at explaining it to my mom and sister.... And, not surprisingly, we failed....
> It can drive men crazy.
> It is harder than getting a camel (to) jump over a trench.

Some contributors also try to account for this impossibility by appealing to the natural differences discourse: all the efforts are futile because it is not in women's nature to get the offside rule; their brains are wired differently:

> It's impossible. Because she is a girl. Their brains are different. Girls do not have an offside centre in their brains. They have a shoe centre. I think we should talk to them about shoes.

Some take the above stated preconception that women have a shoe/fashion centre in their brains a step further and try to translate the rule into the language of fashion:

> You entered Mango to buy the perfect bag during sales. There is only one left, and it is behind the cashier's (till, the goal). You are not the only one after that bag. Another potential customer, (your opponent), also her eyes on the bag. You both attempt at the cashier's (till, the goal) [...]

Some contributors bring in men to the discussion and simultaneously recreate the stereotypes about men and masculinity:

> It is like explaining men the fashionable colours of the season. They are both futile.

While others, in order to strengthen their argument, add transphobic remarks to their entries:

> If she gets it immediately run away. She is probably not a woman.

These preconceptions and stereotypes, which are reproduced in social media every day, also get support from the football community in Turkey. For instance, at the time translator for foreign players, Samet Güzel, writes, "I'm wondering about the reactions to possible offside situations today when only ladies will be occupying the stands. I just sent out a tweet about ladies and the offside rule before the game" (*Takvim* 21 September 2011). In the following section, the crowd restrictions Güzel is referring to, and how they stemmed from and also recreated the stereotypes about women, football and female football fans, will be explored.

The crowd restrictions

The crowd restrictions in Turkey which attracted a lot of attention from the international football community and sports media were actually the indirect result of crowd violence during a pre-season game between the Istanbul team Fenerbahçe and Shakhtar Donetsk of Ukraine on 21 July 2011. During this game, which Fenerbahçe hosted in its Rüştü Saraçoğlu stadium, several supporters invaded the pitch. This disruptive fan behaviour, which can frequently be observed in Turkey, prompted the

Turkish Football Federation (TFF) to take radical action. The initial order was to have Fenerbahçe play two of their home matches behind closed doors. However they later amended the rules so that women and children would be allowed to watch these 'no spectator' events with free tickets. In other words, only males over the age of 12 would be barred from attending the games in question. The representatives of both the federation and Fenerbahçe announced this as an historic decision. Turkish association deputy chairman Göksel Gümüşdağ declared that this was what Turkish football needed to address crowd violence in the stadium.

Their first assumption was that since it was the male fans who terrorized the passers-by before or after the games, vandalized the stadia, lit up torches and invaded the pitch, if these natural troublemakers were barred from attending games violence could be reduced. The second assumption was that since women and girls and boys under 12 were 'naturally' well behaved, allowing only these uncontaminated fans would help transform the football culture in Turkey. Before the first match in front of women and children only, which was played on 20 September 2011, strict ID checks were done by an all-women police squad ensuring that the male fans above 12 were not allowed in the stadium. The next day, Turkish mainstream media reported that, despite all these measures, one man, disguised under a headscarf and women's clothing, made it into the stadium. International sports media also shared the story (*Der Spiegel* 21 September 2011). Simultaneously, it was reported that, defying expectations, swearing and 'ugly chants' were heard during this women and children-only game. The immediate reaction was to bring these two 'facts' together and jump to a quick conclusion: other male intruders were probably responsible for this masculine behaviour. Political authorities also endorsed this theory. After the match, Suat Kılıç, then Minister of Youth and Sports, announced that he was very proud to see women and children inside the stadium. When asked about the swearing he responded:

> I heard it through social media sites. Looks like some men infiltrated the stands. I have seen some pictures in the newspapers today. This must be their doing. It can't be women's doing. Turkish women do not sing ugly chants.
>
> (*Habertürk* 21 September 2011)

A couple of days later, the Fenerbahçe fan who both the media and the minister referred to as 'the male intruder' turned out to be a woman wearing the hijab. Kılıç's and the media's non-hesitant explanation for the glitch – 'ugly chants' coming from a stadium filled with women and children only – exhibits belief in natural, dimorphic gender differences. The same glitch was detected during the other women and children-only matches as well. On 8 January 2012 during the women and children-only game Galatasaray played against Bursapor. The Bursapor fans chanted the homophobic slur: "Cimbom (Galatasaray) what the hell is going on, your ass and head keep moving" which was even audible on live coverage (*HaberVesaire* 18 May 2012). A similar incident occurred on 2 February, the same year, during a match between Beşiktaş and Mersin İdman Yurdu in Istanbul. The chant targeted Beşiktaş' biggest rival, Fenerbahçe: "Here I'm up on the stone, my legs spread out, come Fener, go down on me and suck my balls" (*HaberVesaire* 18 May 2012). During the Fenerbahçe vs. Beşiktaş derby on 3 May the homophobic chant, "Fener fags, you can't be champions" was so loud it could not be blamed on the imaginary 'male intruders' or go undocumented (*HaberVesaire* 18 May 2012). As a result, Beşiktaş was fined 60,000 TL (about $20,000) for female fan trouble. About two years later, on 19 April 2014, a female Galatasaray fan was detected on Lig TV, the channel that airs Turkish premier league football, giving the finger to a Kasımpaşa player. This time, having learned from experience, the media refrained from repeating the 'male intruder' story. Instead this unexpected sound that defied traditional gender expectations in Turkey was reported as 'shocking'. As argued, the crowd restrictions that were in effect for three seasons both stemmed from and helped recreate the natural differences discourse in football. Even the glitches did not destabilize the dominant gender re/presentation. In what follows, the stereotypical representations of female fans will be discussed in the light of the arguments above.

Female fans

The natural differences discourse is dominant in the stereotypical representations of female football fans in Turkey. Since the stadia where the game is played are still seen as public spaces where the so-called masculine qualities of aggression, toughness, competitiveness, control, anger, and violence are praised (Erhart 2013) women are often represented as the 'Other' to men. This 'Other' could be a fragile, high-pitched, perfumed lady fan who is disturbed by foul language or the bickering aunt. They both are depicted as strangers who are tangential to the game. The only type of female fan who belongs in the stadia is the 'crazy-blooded' fans who have internalized hegemonic masculinity. In what follows, I will try to show that, despite their differences, all these three stereotypes are inspired by the natural differences discourse. I will focus mostly on the matches during which only women and children were allowed inside the stadia since it was during and after these matches that they got the most attention from media and contributors to social networking sites.

The high-pitched, perfumed lady

The female fans who were allocated free tickets for the 'women and children only' matches were often referred to as 'ladies' by the football community as well as in the traditional and social media. 'Lady' (*bayan*) is often used a euphemism for 'woman'. It aims to strip sexuality off the word 'woman', and as Kocaman (2012) suggests, sometimes, also serves as a 'public virginity test'. For instance, Fenerbahçe defender Joseph Yobo thanked the 'ladies' for their support after the first game played in front of women and children only on 20 September 2011, between Fernerbahçe and Manisaspor. These stereotypically well-behaved lady-guests had temporarily filled the stadium with unusual sounds, sights and smells. Rahşan Gülşan wrote in her column for *Habertürk* that during that unique evening the whole neighbourhood of Kadıköy, where the stadium is located, "was filled with the smell of perfume". Many contributors on *Ekşi Sözlük* added "instead of the usual B.O." to her observation. The smell of the roses the players threw at the female fans was also mentioned on *Ekşi Sözlük*. As Caudwell suggests (2011, pp. 125–126), sound is also a significant dimension of spatiality. Sonic spatiality of the stadia during the women and children only games attracted a lot of attention and the descriptions of the sound space contributed to the subordination of female fans. Turkish sports media often described the 'unusual' soundtrack from the stands, as 'high decibel' and 'high-pitched'. Andrew Das (2011), a writer for the *New York Times* soccer blog, likened the roar after Fenerbahçe's goal to that of the moment the lights go down at a Justin Bieber concert. One fan on Twitter likened it to the sound of a vuvuzela and asked his fellow Fenerbahçe supporters what they preferred: "Vuvuzela or stadium filled with women?" Another fan commenting on *Ekşi Sözlük* asked the Turkish Football Federation to reconsider its decision since even absolute silence would be better than the sounds women produced. Yet another suggested that the federation should open a course on whistling for women.

In the eyes of many writers and male fans these high-pitched, perfumed ladies were not there for the football but for a 'tea party' or a 'night out' with other women. In fact, 'Ladies' Night' was the most frequently used headline to describe the evening on *Ekşi Sözlük*. To devalue their fandom, they mentioned other activities these women would be willing to engage in while at the stadium. One commentator wrote, "If they sold high-heeled shoes and bags at Fenerium [the official Fenerbahçe store] the club can become the richest in Europe in a couple of hours. This chance should not be missed." Another mentioned the nail polish bottles the women were likely to throw to the pitch:

> Soon we will see them throwing lipsticks, perfume bottles and bras (instead of booze bottles).

They were also devalued for not 'getting the offside rule' and taking offside for a goal:

> They cheered for the opposing team for 30 seconds. One should have seen the joy in women who were so happy they won 2–1 – when the game was actually tied at 1–1.
>
> (*Mynet* 2011)

> 'In the end, we won' are the first four words of an emotional speech delivered by a pretty lady fan who took offside for a goal. For this kind to get the rule at least 40 games should be played in front of women only.
>
> (*Ekşi Sözlük* 2011)

The bickering aunt

Another stereotype, which was prevalent in sports media and social networking sites, especially through the seasons when the gendered crowd restrictions were in effect, was that of the bickering aunt. Just like the perfumed lady, she is also an outcast. She bickers, cannot follow the game, and does not get the chants. She brings her motherly habits and concerns to the stadia. She is there to check on the players' health and well-being and punish them in motherly ways – bicker all day, throw slippers at the players and referees – if they are defeated. The following *Ekşi Sözlük* entries exemplify how this stereotype is reproduced:

> You can hear women yelling 'Alex, son, please do not run that much, you'll get sick'.
> 'Alex, son, come over here. Have a couple of these *dolmas.*'
> The referees are expected to be targeted by flying slippers.

These entries bring gender roles in Turkish society to the foreground; the implication is that male fans are the real owners of the stadia who are disturbed by these old women who keep asking questions during an almost sacred activity. With their odd (and old) ways and habits and decaying mental capacities they are represented as misfits. Their presence has a disrupting effect on the genuine (male) fans.

The crazy-blooded tomboy

Dunkerly (2007, p. 14) argues that historically women were excluded from societal institutions because they were believed to be "weaker, less moral, and possessing less capacity for reason, control and logic". Within these institutions, the hegemonic masculine ideal was supported and the gendered norms were naturalized. To challenge the relations of power, women had to show that they were actually not so different from men. In a way, to prove themselves equal, they felt the need to comply with the hegemonic masculinity (Price and Shildrick 1999). Since the key features of hegemonic masculinity are the subordination of women and the celebration of toughness, aggressiveness and rationality (Connell 2000), women felt pressured to act accordingly. The following extract illustrates how a female fan uses this strategy to fit in Turkish football culture:

> I watch the game like a man. I'm not disturbed by foul language. In fact, I join in. I do not mind the rain or the cold. Other women are in need of protection. They come with their husband or boyfriends. They fear they'll be raped otherwise. I do not.
>
> (Şentürk, 2001)

According to Şentürk, who seems to have internalized the masculine standard, only the women who swear, who are not afraid of being targets of violence, are the real fans. These women are also referred to as 'women who get the offside rule' on *Ekşi Sözlük*. As such, they are also expected to enjoy *işkembe* soup and *kokoreç* which are dishes usually associated with toughness. On the blog titled *Beşiktaş Ruhu* (The Soul of Beşiktaş) these types of fans are described as:

> They are crazy-blooded. They enjoy going to places men go before the games.
> They dress casually; they do not put on make-up.
> They are as creative as men on the terraces.

These descriptions clearly show that hegemonic masculinity determines the standards of football fandom in Turkey. Women can be considered real fans only if they meet these standards; otherwise they are positioned among other women misfits.

Conclusions and discussion

One of the entries on *Ekşi Sözlük* on female football fans reads:

> Women, actually do not like football yet they pretend to like it to appear cute to their boyfriends.

This chapter was an attempt at challenging this idea and showing that Turkish female fans do exist. Examining the fandom practices of Turkish women also significantly enables us to broaden an understanding of their relationships with sport, revealing aspects of their identities beyond physical participation in sport to include wider sport consumption practices and behaviours (Toffoletti and Palmer, 2015). For Turkish female fans, they exist yet are trapped and confined to stereotypes about gender roles and expectations of behaviour. These stereotypes arise in conjunction with debates about femininity, masculinity, football and spectatorship, and are often underpinned by the natural differences discourse prevalent in Turkey. Political discourse and media discourse also contribute to the creation and sustainability of these stereotypes. As a result, negative, hegemonic images of female fans as perfumed ladies, bickering aunts and crazy-blooded tomboys are constructed and are circulated.

However, it is not only in Turkish culture that women are seen as 'others' invading the male football domain and are ridiculed, mocked, and questioned about their 'inauthentic' fandom. The myth about women misunderstanding the offside rule perpetuates and dominates all cultures (Western and Eastern) because of the androcentric and masculinist nature of footballing subcultures. Sometimes even women referees are questioned. In 2011 football presenters for Sky Sports, Richard Keys and Andy Gray, were recorded during transmission of a Premier League match between Wolverhampton Wanderers and Liverpool "complaining that the assistant referee, Sian Massey, probably did not know the offside rule and that someone 'fucked up big' by appointing a female match official" (Booth 2011). The sad reality is that the offside myth itself has been the subject of comical debates and sexist banter in news articles, stand-up comedies, movies, and TV and radio shows, in and beyond English and European football.

In the 2006 Iranian movie *Offside* director Jafir Panahi challenges the status allocated to female fans in Iran:

> Like the footballer who is offside, women supporters are too far forward in their contestation of the structural and cultural barriers to women's sports participation in Iran religious values of modesty and purity for Muslim women and culturally gendered notions of fan behaviour.
>
> (Toffoletti 2014, p. 80)

Pope's research, on the other hand, challenges the binary opposition, "genuine, traditional, good fans/lads" against "new, consumers, bad fans/women" and illustrates that not all female fans want to sit and/or are obsessed with stadium safety (Pope 2010, p. 474). On the contrary, some of them found the new "family/female friendly" Leicester stadium in England to be "placeless", "too peaceful" and "too regimented" (p. 482). I would argue that such research and works of art which focus on and display a nuanced and diverse range of female fandom will eventually counterpoint stereotypical images. Social media campaigns by female fans themselves who want to free themselves will also help challenge the preconceptions. While gathering data for this chapter I have observed some reactions from fans themselves, like starting a *change.org* campaign against the Renault slogan 'You wouldn't be this happy unless you were able to explain the offside rule to your girlfriend'. The fans objected to the media campaign on the grounds that it peddled the stereotypes and recreated the patriarchal conception that sports and technology are masculine areas. Renault responded to the campaign which included 1542 signees and took down the posters. Such reactions and activism could be ideas for further research in and beyond the spectator spaces of football in Turkey and elsewhere.

References

Ayata, A. and Tütüncü, F. (2008) 'Party politics of the AKP (2002–2007) and the predicaments of women at the intersection of the Westernist, Islamist and Feminist discourses in Turkey', *British Journal of Middle Eastern Studies*, 35(3): pp. 363–384.

Belge, B. (2011) 'Kadın Bakanlığı Kaldırıldı, Kadın Örgütleri Öfkeli', *Bianet*. Available from: www.bianet.org/bianet/kadin/130585-kadin-bakanligi-kaldirildi-kadin- orgutleri-ofkeli [20 January 2016].

Booth, R. (2011) 'Sky presenters in the firing line over sexist jibes at female match official', *Guardian*. Available from: www.theguardian.com/global/2011/jan/23/sky-presenters-sexist-remarks-female-official [17 May 2017].

Bourdieu, P. (1977) *Outline of a Theory of Practice*, London: Cambridge University Press.

Butler, J. (1989) 'The body politics of Julia Kristeva', *Hypatia*, 3: pp. 104–118.

Caudwell, J.C. (2011) 'Does your boyfriend know you're here? The spatiality of homophobia in men's football culture in the UK', *Leisure Studies*, 30(2): pp. 123–138.

Connell, R.W. (2000) *The Men and the Boys*, Sydney: Allen & Unwin.

Coşar, S. and Yeğenoğlu, M. (2011) 'New grounds for patriarchy in Turkey? Gender policy in the age of AKP', *South European Society and Politics*, 16: pp. 555–573.

Das, A. (2011) 'In Turkey, game day becomes ladies' night', *Goal Blog*. Available from: http://goal.blogs.nytimes.com/2011/09/21/in-turkey-gameday-becomes-ladies-night/?src=tp [17 January 2016].

Denizaltı, S. (2010) 'Yaratılışımız Farklı Bayan', *Simurg*. Available from: https://simurg.info/2010/10/17/yaratilisimiz-farkli-bayan/#more-5514 [17 May 2017].

Der Spiegel (2011) 'Ladies' night at Fenerbahce: male fans banned from Turkish soccer match', *Der Spiegel*, 21 September 2011. Available from: www.spiegel.de/international/europe/ladies-night-at-fenerbahce-male-fans-banned-from-turkish-soccer-match-a-787627.html [17 May 2017].

Dick, P. and Nadin, S. (2006) 'Reproducing gender inequalities? A critique of realist assumptions underpinning personnel selection research and practice', *Journal of Occupational and Organizational Psychology*, 79: pp. 481–498.

Direk, Z. (2013) 'Queer Kuram ve Cinsiyet Farklılığı', *Zeynep Direk Blog*. Available from: https://zeynepdirek.wordpress.com/2013/01/04/queer-kuram-ve-cinsiyet-farkliligi/ [17 January 2016].

Dunkerly, R.M. (2007) *Women of the Revolution: Bravery and Sacrifice on the Southern Battlefields*, Charleston, South Carolina: The History Press.

Ekşi Sözlük (2011) '20 Eylül 2011 Fenerbahçe-Manisaspor Maçı'. Available from: https://eksisozluk.com/20-eylul-2011-fenerbahce-manisaspor-maci--3050310 [17 May 2017].

Erhart, I. (2013) 'Ladies of Besiktas: a dismantling of male hegemony at Inönü Stadium', *International Review for the Sociology of Sport*, 48(1): pp. 83–98.

Erman, T. (2001) 'Rural migrants and patriarchy in Turkish cities', *International Journal of Urban and Regional Research*, 25: pp. 118–133.

Evans, M. and Kaynak, M.S. (2015) 'Media framing in religious–secular conflict in Turkey and Israel', *International Political Science Review*, 36 (2): pp. 139–152.

Foucault, M. (1991) *Discipline and Punish: The Birth of the Prison*, London: Penguin.

Güvenli, G. and Tanrıöver, H.U. (2009) 'Ders kitaplarında toplumsal cinsiyet', in G. Tüzün (ed.) *Ders kitaplarında İnsan hakları II tarama sonuçları*, İstanbul: ed. Tarih Vakfı: pp. 97–114.

Habertürk (2011) 'Bakanlıktan Yeni Adım', *Habertürk*, 21 September 2011. Available from: www.haberturk.com/spor/futbol/haber/671656-bakanliktan-yeni-adim [17 May 2017].

HaberVesaire (2012) 'Küfür, kadının tribüne kabul söylemi', *HaberVesaire*, 18 May 2012. Available from: http://habervesaire.com/kufur-kadinin-tribune-kabul-soylemi/ [17 May 2017].

Hürriyet Daily News (2014) 'Turkish President Erdoğan says gender equality "against nature"', *Hürriyet Daily News*, 24 November 2014. Available from: www.hurriyetdailynews.com/turkish-president-erdogan-says-womens-equality-with-men-against-nature.aspx?pageID=238&nID=74726&NewsCatID=338 [17 May 2017].

ISR Weekly (2014) 'Erdoğan: You cannot bring women and men into an equal position; this is against nature', *ISR Weekly*, 24 November 2014. Available from: http://rcweekly.reasonedcomments.org/2014/11/erdogan-you-cannot-bring-women-and-men.html [17 May 2017].

Jabiri, M.A. Al. (1980) *Nahnu wa al-tharwa*, Beirut: Marqez Derasat a-Wehdeh Al-Arabia.

Kantrowitz, A. (2013) 'How the founder of Turkey's original social network explained it to his Microsoft co-workers', *Forbes*, 7 July 2013. Available from: www.forbes.com/sites/alexkantrowitz/2013/07/10/how-the-founder-of-turkeys-original-social-network-explained-it-to-his-microsoft-coworkers/ [20 January 2016].

Kocaman, C. (2012) 'Dili Cinsiyetsizleştirmek mi?' Available from: www.sendika.org/2012/02/dili-cinsiyetsizlestirmek-mi-ceren-kocaman-bianet [20 January 2016].

Linville, S. (1998) *Feminism, Film, Fascism: Women's Auto/biographical Film in Postwar Germany*, Austin: University of Texas Press.

Lorber, J. (1993) 'Believing is Seeing: biology as ideology', *Gender & Society*, 7(4): pp. 568–581.

Marshall, G.A. (2008) 'A question of compatibility: feminism and Islam in Turkey', *Middle East Critique*, 17(3): pp. 223–238.

Matthews, C.R. (2014) 'Biology ideology and pastiche hegemony', *Men and Masculinities*, 17(2): pp. 99–119.

Mernissi, F. (1992) *The Veil And The Male Elite: A Feminist Interpretation of Women's Rights in Islam*, London: Basic Books.

Milliyet (2014) 'Ali Bulaç: Erkek dört eş alabilir, kadın alamaz,' *Milliyet*, 24 June 2014. Available from: www.milliyet.com.tr/ali-bulac-erkek-dort-es-alabilir--gundem-1901821/ [17 May 2017].

Mohanty, C.T. (2003) *Feminism without Borders: Decolonizing Theory, Practicing Solidarity*, London: Duke University Press.

Mulvey, L. (1993) 'Marie/Eve. Continuity and discontinuity in J.L. Godard's iconography of Women' in M. Locke and C. Warrenean (eds) *Luc Godard's Hail Mary: Women and the Sacred in Film*, Carbondale: Southern Illinois University Press: pp. 39–53.

Mynet (2011) 'Kadın taraftarın yorumları koparttı'. Available from: http://spor.mynet.com/fenerbahce/18656-kadin-taraftarin-yorumlari-koparttı.html [17 May 2017].

Offside [Motion picture] (2006) Jafir Panahi (Director), Artificial Eye: World Cinema Ltd, Iran.

Öztamur, P. (2004) 'Defining a population: women and children in early republican Turkey, 1923–1950'. MA thesis, Boğaziçi Üniversitesi, Istanbul.

Pope, S. (2010) '"Like pulling down Durham Cathedral and building a brothel": women as "new consumer" fans?', *International Review for the Sociology of Sport*, 46(4): pp. 471–487.

Price, J. and Shildrick, M. (1999) 'Openings on the body' in J. Price and M. Shildrick (eds) *Feminist Theory and the Body: A Reader*, New York: Routledge: pp. 190–202.

Smith, J. (1979) 'Women in Islam: equity, equality, and the search for the natural order', *Journal of the American Academy of Religion*, XLVII(4): pp. 517–537.

Şentürk, D. (2001) 'Tribünde Kadın Olmak', *Tribün*, 3: pp. 12–13.

Takvim (2011) 'İşte Fenerbahçe Geyikleri', *Takvim*, 21 September 2011. Available from: www.takvim.com.tr/fenerbahce/2011/09/21/iste-fenerbahce-geyikleri [17 May 2017].

Tekeli, Ş. (1979) 'Türkiye'de Kadının Siyasal Hayattaki Yeri' in N. Abadan, A, Eğitim, E.Yayınları (eds), *Türk Toplumunda Kadın*, İstanbul: Ekin Yayınları.

Toffoletti, K. (2014) 'Iranian women's sports fandom: gender, resistance, and identity in the football movie *Offside*', *Journal of Sport and Social Issues*, 38(1): pp. 75–92.

Toffoletti, K. and Palmer, C. (2015) 'New approaches for studies of Muslim women and sport', *International Review for the Sociology of Sport*, doi: 10.1177/1012690215589326.

Chapter 10

Sport coaching and the inclusion of Black women in the United Kingdom

Alexandra J. Rankin-Wright and Leanne Norman

Introduction

Equality and diversity issues feature strongly in the strategies and activities of the United Kingdom (UK) (England, Wales, Scotland and Northern Ireland) sport and coaching agencies in response to wider societal drives and legislative pushes to address social inequalities. Through the recent UK Equality Act (2010), sports organisations need to demonstrate their commitment to improving diversity within their workforce and the services that they offer. For instance, the UK Coaching Framework advocates "a more diverse [coaching] workforce" as one of its central strategic objectives (Sports Coach UK, 2012). In terms of addressing either gender and/or 'race' more directly, this usually includes increasing the number of women as participants and coaches on the one hand, and the drive amongst coaches to recruit and include BME[1] groups in their professional practice on the other. Notably, the representation of BME men or women as leaders and coaches is largely missing from such policy agendas. Despite broad calls for equity amongst UK sport organisations and national governing bodies (NGBs), existing statistics and research continue to suggest that diversity within sport, especially in positions of leadership, remains low. This is evidenced by the under-representation of minoritised ethnic groups in all leadership positions.[2]

The underrepresentation of Black (see below for use of this term) coaches, and particularly Black women coaches, in the UK sport coaching context has been prominently highlighted by quantitative studies documenting the number of qualified coaches (North, 2009; Sports Coach UK, 2011). In comparison to the UK's adult population (92% White and 8% 'BME'), these studies reported that 99% of qualified head coaches and assistant coaches self-defined as White and 1% self-reported as 'BME' (North, 2009, Sports Coach UK, 2011). The reports also stated that 82% of qualified coaches were men and 18% were women, in comparison to the UK's population of men (49%) and women (51%). The limitation of these data sets is that 'race' and gender continue to be addressed as separate stand-alone categories and thus, there is no gender breakdown of the 99% of White qualified coaches, or the ethnic breakdown of the 18% identified women coaches. These one dimensional approaches fail to account for intersecting identity constructs (Bruening, 2005; Collins, 1986, 2000; hooks 1984; Brah, 1996; Mirza, 2009). As a result, Black women occupy a blind spot in these mainstream monitoring procedures, which categorise coaches according to either gender *or* ethnicity and not a combination of both positionings. Qualitative research has further demonstrated that women coaches regardless of 'race' and ethnicity often experience fewer opportunities to practise, learn or develop their skills. They also often experience unequal gendered relations with their male colleagues and superiors, are assumed to be less competent as effective coaches or leaders, and as a result of problematic working environments, cite lower self-confidence (Shaw and Slack, 2002; Allen and Shaw, 2013; Kilty, 2006; Fielding-Lloyd and Mean, 2011; LaVoi and Dutove, 2012; Norman, 2010a, 2010b, 2012). What remains particularly absent within this literature is a more in-depth, focused understanding of the lived experiences of Black women coaches and their negotiations of and challenges within the racialised and gendered structural practices and power relations embedded within sport coaching (c.f. Sporting Equals, 2011; Norman *et al.*, 2014; Carter-Francique and Olushola, 2016). It can be claimed that this writing has largely failed to acknowledge the whiteness of sport coaching as an institutional field, and the connected White privileges of representing a racial majority in this arena. This chapter is therefore a much-needed departure from much of the existing sports coaching literature. Rooted in a Critical Race Theory and Black feminist theoretical framework, the approach adopted both supplements and challenges previous established epistemologies, methodologies, and theoretical perspectives in sport coaching by offering an alternative way of knowing, a counter narrative to the dominant ideologies espoused from within 'the coaching system'. This approach also facilitates an understanding of the identities and experiences of Black women as coaches whose contributions and voices have long been systematically marginalised or ignored.

Notwithstanding critiques in the literature of the term 'Black', and recognising the multiplicity of identities and experiences within and across the group of coaches interviewed for this research, we have employed the term 'Black' as a unifying, political and theoretical term (Hylton, 2009; Mirza, 2009). In relation to Black feminist thought, Collins (1986: 16) writes that whilst "all individuals possess a unique standpoint on, and perspective of their experiences ... there will be certain commonalities of perception [and experience] shared by Black women as a group". Hence, Black feminism, as a political project, is a meaningful act of identification for individuals with different experiences and patterns of knowledge that marks a collective presence against common challenges (Mirza, 2009). However, where appropriate we have used the coaches' self-identified terminology as selected by them so as not to divorce this terminology from the wider context in which their particular coaching experiences are situated.

Theorising 'race', gender and their interconnections in sport coaching: a CRT and Black feminist approach

Critical Race Theory (CRT) guided the epistemological framing of the research. CRT is a theoretical approach that fundamentally reveals and challenges racial stratification and unequal power processes in society, which marginalise racially oppressed individuals and groups (Hylton, 2012). Whilst accepting the constructed falsehood, and contested and problematic nature of 'race', and based on the understanding that 'race' and racism are the product of power relations, CRT begins from the premise that 'race' and racism are commonplace, endemic and enduring within society (Ladson-Billings, 1998; Solórzano and Yosso, 2002). Based on the five precepts depicted by Solorzano and Yosso (2001), Hylton (2005) outlined five key elements of a CRT framework relevant for sport/coaching scholars and practitioners. These included: (1) The centring of 'race' and racism as core factors in the study of the social relations in sport, and recognising their connection with other forms of subordination and oppression. This centring of 'race' and interconnecting oppressions is key due to the persisting unequal patterns of recruitment and retention in sport coaching based on gendered and racialised structures that privilege certain coaches and disadvantage others. (2) Resisting and challenging dominant ideologies around meritocracy, equal opportunity, 'race-neutrality' and colourblindness. Because sporting success is widely perceived to be based on merit and talent, CRT challenges those ideologies, which are controlled from a position of power that ignores racialised processes and disparities that function merely as a way to maintain the interests and privilege of dominant groups in sport coaching, for instance. (3) A commitment to social justice that incorporates elements of an agenda for liberation and transformation. Applying this critical element of social transformation engages political ideas in order to influence 'race' and positively change mainstream sport coaching agendas where 'race' and gender issues have not been centred and contested. (4) Centring the lived experiences and stories of marginalised groups, and empowering them to speak their lived truths as a counter narrative to representations and terms of oppression in sport. This includes the voices of Black women coaches who are rarely heard and often marginalised in sport coaching research and practice. (5) A transdisciplinarity element that encourages researchers to continually broaden their theoretical and methodological frames to ensure that social justice agendas highlight the multidimensionality of oppression.

The transdisciplinary nature of CRT is powerfully explicated through Crenshaw *et al.*'s (1995) work. Crenshaw was appropriating the critiques of Black feminist intellectuals when she sought to combine feminist legal work with CRT to expose and to challenge inequalities regarding both 'race' and gender in the field of law. Thus, thinking in and between 'race' and gender links CRT and Black feminist thinking. For this research, more specifically, CRT was used as a guiding framework in addition to Black feminist concepts and language, which further supported the interpretation of the coaches' everyday experiences. Thus, the combined CRT and Black feminist approach builds upon the complementary alignment of these two theoretical perspectives. The critical paradigm adopted by Black feminists moves beyond merely describing gender and 'race' as distinctive systems of oppression to naming and critiquing interconnecting systems of institutional, structural and cultural oppression as being part of one overarching structure of domination (Crenshaw, 1989; hooks, 1989; Collins, 2000; Mowatt *et al.*, 2013). Research framed by a combined CRT and Black feminism agenda has rarely been centred in sport and even less so in sport coaching. A major premise of this approach is that within sport coaching, as in society, whiteness and masculinity have been positioned as the desirable 'norm' status (Singer, 2005a). Thus, the power relations within sport coaching systematically advantage whiteness whilst disadvantaging Blackness (Hylton, 2012), and advantage certain forms of masculinity whilst disadvantaging femininity (Norman, 2010a, 2010b, 2012).

Both CRT and Black feminism seek to centralise the lived experiences and identities of those who have been traditionally excluded and inadequately represented in sport policy and practice. Black women coaches, who are often excluded from the privileged centre, are argued to occupy a position of "perspective advantage" (Rollock, 2012: 65), or 'outsider within status', providing a distinctive standpoint on existing social paradigms and 'sociological spaces' (hooks, 1984; Collins, 1986, 2000). hooks (1984: ix) captures the unique perspective that 'outsiders within' can generate in the following quote:

> Living as we did – on the edge – we developed a particular way of seeing reality. We looked both from the outside in and from the inside out. We focused our attention on the center as well as the margin. We understood both.

In many cases, the distinct personal, social and cultural lives of Black women are not synonymous with either the experiences of Black men or White women. Thus, Black feminist thought is grounded in a political standpoint that emancipates and empowers Black women through validating and privileging their testimonies. Furthermore, in line with the social justice and emancipatory politics and praxis element of both CRT and Black feminism, this chapter attempts to reveal and challenge the subtle practices and policies that perpetuate racial and gender stereotypes, ideologies and inequalities within sport coaching. As part of this framework and through the process of privileging those voices that have been traditionally marginalised, we recognise our own privileged position as White, middle-class scholars and the responsibility to disrupt rather than perpetuate power structures within the research process and within coaching literature (see below for further debate). This approach provides Black women coaches with a platform to voice their lived experiences and perspectives, rather than be marginalised or understood through the agendas of the dominant sport coaching writers, policy makers and practitioners. This knowledge can then be used to transform sport coaching for the benefit of Black women coaches.

Methodology

The data (re)presented in this chapter was collected across two qualitative research studies. The first study, commissioned by sports coach UK, the UK's central agency for the recruitment and progression of coaches, aimed to explore the 'Sporting experiences and coaching aspirations among Black and Minority Ethnic (BME) groups'. Interviews were completed with six coaches over the telephone by Author A. The second study was part of Author A's doctoral research, in which she completed face-to-face interviews with four coaches (two of the coaches, Carol and Amelia, were interviewed for both studies) to explore their coaching experiences within their particular sport and NGB. The coaches were purposively selected primarily on their self-identification of being a 'BME' woman with coaching experience and a UK Coaching Certificate (UKCC[3]) between level one to level four, in one of four sports (two team and two individual sports). Table 10.1 profiles the eight coaches that were interviewed along with their self-selected pseudonyms. Due to the potential high profile of the participants and the low representation of Black women coaches in the UK, anonymity in relation to the coaches' names and the specific sports they coached was necessary in order to create the freedom for the coaches to be honest and open about their experiences of the coaching system.

Prior to the interview, each coach was briefed over the phone about the research and the interview discussion themes. A pre-planned interview guide, devised for the purpose of the studies, was used to direct interaction with the coaches. Interview guide themes for the first study included: personal background, getting into the sport, playing and coaching context, enablers and barriers to participating, getting into coaching, enablers and barriers to coaching, and improving the recruitment and representation of

Table 10.1 Profile of the coaches interviewed

Coach	*Self-identification of ethnicity*	*Age range*	*UKCC coaching qualification level achieved*	*Coaching status at the time of the interview*
Seema	Asian British Pakistani	20–30	Level 1	Previously coached in primary schools but no longer coaching.
Olive	Pakistani	20–30	Level 2	Previously coached in secondary schools but no longer coaching.
Amelia	Black British	40–50	Level 4	Actively coaching at high performance level as a full-time head coach.
Carol	Black Caribbean	40–50	Level 2	Actively coaching at high performance level as a part-time coach.
Barbara	Black British Caribbean	40–50	Level 2	Actively coaching at county level.
Faith	Half Caribbean	20–30	Level 2	Actively coaching at national junior level.
Tina	Indian	40–50	Level 2	Actively coaching at county level.
Sabia	British Muslim	20–30	Level 2	Actively coaching at club level.

'BME' groups. Interview guide themes for the second study included: personal background, getting into coaching, progressing in coaching, other coaching ambitions, and connected insights and reflections. The aim of these interviews was to give the coaches the opportunity to explore and recall detailed accounts of their own views, feelings and experiences (Sparkes and Smith, 2014). The telephone interviews lasted between 30 and 60 minutes. The face-to-face interviews lasted between 30 and 80 minutes. All of the interviews were digitally recorded and transcribed verbatim. Thematic analysis was used to aid the identification, analysis and reporting of themes across the data set.

Three fundamental principles underpinning feminist and 'race'-based methodologies were specifically applied during this research. This included (1) adopting the view that we, as the researchers were "part of the research" (Bhopal, 2010: 2), allowing participants to address their lives and express themselves and their situation in their own terms; and researching with and for the coaches, not just about them (Bhopal, 2010; Few *et al.*, 2003; Pillow, 2003; Norman, 2010a); (2) In relation to this, we endeavoured to acknowledge and highlight through the research analysis the relevancy of our own identities, experiences and practices and how these may have influenced and informed the production and (re)presentation of knowledge (Frankenberg, 2004; Rollock, 2012; Ladson-Billings, 2000; Ladson-Billings and Donnor, 2005), and (3) it is important to note that the journeys and experiences of all the coaches were individualised and multidimensional, and therefore cannot be essentialised nor generalised. Yet, the coaches' narratives provide a critique of sport coaching organisations in order to help unpack the cultural norms and taken-for-granted assumptions operating within this space. Therefore each counter-story, within a racially and gendered structured organisation, makes a particularly insightful contribution to the research, and the broader sport coaching landscape. Such a perspective lends researchers a clearer understanding of the major structures, power processes, and inequalities within sport organisations that have consistently been ignored by both practitioners and mainstream theorists (Hylton, 2009). The findings are (re)presented under three themes: feeling hyper visible, overcoming the burden of doubt, and everyday experiences of sexism.

Feeling hyper visible

The coaches across the group voiced concern that their 'different' bodies were used to symbolise racial and gender diversity for their organisations, to evidence commitment, good practice and institutional progress (see also Ahmed, 2009). Amelia, who represented one of the few Black women who had broken into a powerful, culturally visible role within high performance coaching, expressed concern that she did not want to be seen as merely ticking a box for the organisation. She explained:

> I know I'm being silly aren't I because I'm trying to be undercover and I can't can I, you know, so like when I go to somewhere and it's like 'Let's introduce [Amelia] from [sport] ...' and I'm like really, must I? I'm Black, yes I'm Black, I can't help it, and I'm female ... but that's what I kind of worry about sometimes, I don't want people thinking 'oh we'll tick [a box], she's Black and she's female'.
>
> (Amelia)

Carol, who self-identified as Black Caribbean, and had coached within the high performance environment for a number of years, expressed similar doubts over her initial appointment as an apprentice coach:

> When I got the job with [NGB] I think there's a tick box that everybody has to tick isn't it? ... so I think that was just a tick box, 'Oh we got a Black girl, Black female'.

This fear of evidencing an organisational commitment to diversity and the continual physical and emotional toll of 'standing out' within an occupation traditionally dominated by whiteness and masculinity was further illustrated by Olive's experiences, when she attended coach meetings for her team sport:

> Nobody sort of comes up to your face and says it but you almost get that unsaid feeling sometimes around a room where probably there is one third of the room sat there thinking 'Well we know why you're here and we know why you've been picked', ... I went to a meeting a while ago and there was about 35/40 people in this room and number one I was the only ethnic face in the room and number two I was the only female in the room, so it does sometimes make you think is everybody else sat around this room thinking 'Well you are just here to tick a box', and that would frustrate me if they did think that.
>
> (Olive)

Olive, a Pakistani coach, felt like an outsider and an anomaly within this space. She was surrounded by "everybody else sat around" and frustrated by the questioning gaze of those who have possibly determined her body to be 'out of place'. This process of racialisation not only marks Olive's Pakistani female body as different, but interrogates her presence within the spaces of sport coaching. Olive's encounter resonates with Ahmed's (2012: 157) work in which she states that "because of the culture of equal opportunities, arriving as an ethnic minority person can risk being seen as advantaged *because* of your minority status". Consequently, Olive feels the need to legitimise her existence, to justify her visibility as the only female and only South Asian coach and refute the suspicions that she is there as a 'tick in the box' for the organisation (Ahmed, 2012). These narratives also illustrate the interrelatedness of multiple oppressions that shape Black women's experiences within sport coaching experiences that are unique from those of Black men and White women, and are unique to each of the coaches within this group (Bruening, 2005).

The coaches included in both studies carried what Puwar (2004: 62) terms the "burden of representation". This burden related to being seen as fitting in, being seen to be overtly accepted by other coaches, athletes and organisational personnel, even if motives were continually questioned and actions continually challenged. The burden also related to the responsibility to succeed as coaches not only to represent the capabilities of Black women within coaching, but also to act as an inspiration to other women. Carol testified to this responsibility, "I have to [do well] for the females, at least for the next generation – they need to see that women can do it and do a good job". This responsibility to act as a role model had been embraced by some coaches, as Sabia, a British Muslim level two coach, explained:

> I've always looked at it as a positive way to say, look, if I'm an Asian girl, I stand out as well, so you know, if I've made it through, it's a new thing … and you've got to keep going … because there's a lot of girls out there that will turn away from it, they are talented and they've got the potential but they won't have anyone to look up to, so being an Asian girl, it will help a lot of the younger generation to come forward and actually take it up as a sport.
>
> (Sabia)

However, being seen to be a role model was not welcomed by Amelia, as illustrated in the following testimony:

> Everybody says 'You are a role model', which I hate, I don't want to be a role model I just want to be [Amelia], but then I thought to myself well if somebody sees me, another female and Black, doing a role and it inspires somebody else then that is a positive.
>
> (Amelia)

Faith, who self-identified as half Caribbean, and coached at national level for an individual sport, further indicated the challenges of being a role model in relation to balancing her time to pursue her own training as a national player. She explained:

> I sometimes get asked to do too much coaching and I have to turn things down because I have to kind of think about my own training and my own time.
>
> (Faith)

Overcoming the burden of doubt

The challenges and subsequent negotiations attached to being 'different' often resulted in questions surrounding their coaching capabilities – something Puwar (2004: 59) labels "a burden of doubt". The coaches were seen as lacking something, which if they otherwise possessed would make them 'fit in'. For example, Carol explained that she had been "lumped as thick, illiterate and inarticulate" because she was Black, and had also been stereotyped as being unable and inexpert because she was a woman:

> They [coach recruiters in her NGB] think I'm not capable of doing it, I'm not good enough, I haven't had the experience even though I have and I've had it so much but I think I've had it because I'm everything that they don't want to be in the sport. I'm not a part of the old boys' [network] that was there.
>
> (Carol)

Carol had a proven track record of coaching successful Olympic athletes, yet was not overtly accepted, not embraced as 'one of us' within her coaching organisation and networks due to doubt about her capabilities and expertise. Seema also discussed the multiple and interconnecting burdens confronted by Black women, including racial and cultural issues.

> There are so many barriers and I think they are more so faced by women but more so faced by BME women where they are fighting a different battle than White Caucasian women would be.... And cultural hindrances as well.
>
> (Seema)

Sabia, a British Muslim coach, highlighted the different battles she fought to become a player and a coach. When asked about any challenges experienced, Sabia responded:

> Just being Asian, it's not something that, you know, is encouraged in the family ... I think being a Muslim girl as well, sometimes when fasting for Ramadan, there's been some restrictions where I couldn't really get out to go and play a game.
>
> (Sabia)

Discussions of cultural and religious difference to dominant sport discourses were only mentioned by Sabia and Seema, illustrating the experiences of these two coaches. Seema further explained that she had struggled to engage women from her South Asian community in coaching sessions for her sport (a traditionally White male-dominated sport), in part due to the expectations that they had regarding appropriate activities for South Asian women as well as the feeling that they did not conform to the 'norms' of mainstream sport settings:

> People would rather come here [community based gym rather than the sport facility] because they can fit in because they can wear traditional clothing but then just stick a pair of trainers on underneath and not have funny looks or people stare at them weirdly.
>
> (Seema)

The fear of prejudice against cultural and religious difference to the dominant discourse of sports sheds further light on the different persisting challenges that South Asian women have to negotiate in terms of cultural identity to feel accepted as sport coaches within their own communities and within dominant sport settings (Ahmad, 2011a; Ratna, 2011). According to Sabia's and Seema's viewpoint and experience, some women of South Asian background have to negotiate various cultural barriers but this is not to say that this is the norm for all South Asian girls and women.

Author A, as a researcher and a coach, was conscious of her racial and cultural identity, racial privilege and in this context, her own outsiderness in terms of ethnicity during the interviews. For example, Author A struggled to relate to Carol's everyday reality of being racially stereotyped or Seema's fear of prejudice against cultural difference due to her *inexperience* of racism and her own privileged position as a White coach. Indeed, Author A may have been positioned as an outsider by some of the coaches during the interviews because she did not, and could not, share a view of the world stimulated by the experiences of living as a Black woman (Collins, 2000). Yet at other points during the interviews, Seema for example explained that sharing the same gendered identity as Author A encouraged her to disclose experiences of sexism that she would not have openly discussed with a male researcher irrespective of their racial similarities and/or differences. For example, Seema talked about feeling singled out and belittled by the (White) male tutors:

> I think they were quite pessimistic as well because they were like, when I was the only female they'd say certain things like, treat you kind-of different and it was almost like patronising at times, you know, in terms of like 'Oh well are you sure you are going to be able to cope when you go out on the [sports ground]?'
>
> (Seema)

Different identity characteristics became more or less relevant and pertinent at different times within each interview and in our positions as researcher and participants. Conversations often departed beyond the topic of sport coaching to discussions around, for example, age, motherhood, families, relationships and religion. Arguably, the dynamics of power and lines of enquiry were constantly negotiated and re-negotiated (Bhopal, 2010) during the interview process by both Author A and the research participants. This led to the active production and reproduction of social identities, and the recognition of commonalities of experience, as well as differences, between the interviewer and participants during the research process (Phoenix, 2001; Carrington, 2008; Fletcher, 2014; Song and Parker, 1995; Flintoff and Webb, 2012).

Like Seema, Carol foregrounded her gendered identity as she reflected on having to prove her competences as a female coach in response to the constant challenges of feeling undervalued:

> You know you have to be that much better than all the coaches in the building because you are a female and because you know you are going to get the barriers, … It's like they talk to you and say 'Oh this is my assistant coach' – I'm not assisting you in anything, I'm coaching [athlete] on my own, don't be telling people that I'm your assistant …

> he's [male coach] very patronising and he likes to lord it over you ... just to belittle me and they [other male coaches] say that I'm paranoid ... I should get the recognition for what I've done, not somebody else getting my recognition, or not even being valued for what you put in.
>
> (Carol)

These experiences of feeling undervalued and trivialised resonate with the feelings expressed by the female coaches interviewed by Norman (2010b) who also felt that they operated in the shadows of male coaches. These narratives also illustrate how the coaches' embodied differences are viewed through a sexist lens by the masculine governance of sport coaching that serves to 'Other' them through the use of gendered stereotyping. Barbara, who had completed her level two coaching qualification, shared her story of being initially prevented from completing a higher coaching qualification due to the assumption that she was an assistant coach:

> I think the only barrier that I had was being held off from doing the [coaching qualification] and I think there was some misunderstanding in that not realising that I wasn't reporting to another coach, I was the coach and I probably didn't get that across firmly enough because, as I said, I wished I'd done the [qualification] sooner because that would have really helped me a lot to help the athletes a lot more.
>
> (Barbara)

These coaches suggested a form of embedded prejudice, which left them feeling unsupported in their coaching and unable to progress. As Puwar (2004: 145) argues, "marked" bodies are under "super-surveillance" in that their presence within a space (in this case, sport coaching) is viewed suspiciously and therefore trivialised; 'they' are not automatically expected to embody the relevant competences. This burden may also account for Amelia's reluctance to take on the mantle of 'role model'; that in part, Amelia also accepted this evaluation of her competency and thus did not deem herself worthy of such a title. These examples illustrate how, within the sporting culture, it is automatically assumed that Black women coaches are lower ranking than (White and Black) male coaches; they are incapable of occupying senior positions. Whereas the image and performance of (White) men as coaches had become institutionalised as 'normal', unproblematic and unchallenged in terms of being part of the dominant group (McIntosh, 1997; King, 2004). In contrast, the Black female body was immediately gendered, and assumed to be unable to perform the competencies required to be a coach. This reflects and reproduces the gendered discourses underpinning sport coaching and women's position within this male dominated space (Scraton *et al.*, 2005; Flintoff, 2014) and also, negates the racialised contours of these coaching encounters. Amelia's narrative reveals that she doubted that she would ever be able to progress further to the head coaching position, above her current coaching role:

> I really can't ... although I would love to say it, but I can't see myself getting the [top] job, ... I don't think they're ready for a female, never mind Black female, to do the job.
>
> (Amelia)

Here, Amelia's pronounced visibility as a 'different body' within a space that has traditionally employed and promoted White men, and to a lesser degree White women, has lead to a degree of reservation and uncertainty towards progression that is not likely to be experienced by her (White) counterparts. Amelia also illustrated a reluctant acceptance of these regimes; "that's just 'cos it is", thus these inequalities were normalised and accepted as part of the culture (Claringbould and Knoppers, 2012).

Everyday experiences of sexism

Although we approached the interpretation of the coaches' experiences through an intersectional lens, within specific contexts, the coaches' identity as women was often expressed as more salient by the participants than their racialised identity. Previous research has similarly found that some Black female athletes (Massao and Fasting, 2014) and British Asian female football (soccer) players (Ratna, 2008, 2013) chose to forefront sexist discrimination in the production of their testimonies, rather than racism. Ratna (2008, 2013) suggested that this was a coping strategy in an attempt to facilitate a sense of belonging in a predominantly White space, which in/advertently denied racism. In the unpacking of these British Asian players' narratives, it became clear that racism was interconnected to sexism and also contributed to their negative experiences of the game. In our study, although a number of the coaches noted their gender connection with Author A – and sexism was further probed and developed – she did not similarly probe if more insidious forms of racism lurked beneath and connected to the manifestation of everyday sexisms. In reviewing the interview transcripts, the authors acknowledge that Amelia, for instance, did provide cues about her experiences of everyday racism: that is, the implications of walking her son to an all-White school and having difficult conversations with a head teacher who did not recognise the impacts of whiteness on her or her son's daily experiences of 'the education system'. Arguably, as stated above, moving beyond the sports coaching literature and thinking about mechanisms to facilitate a more equitable sports coaching system (see above) demanded the Authors better engage with some of the wider critical 'race', gender and sport scholarship, and use that knowledge to more effectively unpack whiteness and White privileges operating both within the institution of sport and the research production process. In future studies, the process of reflective learning has indeed sharpened our sensitivity to our own White privileges as well as the necessity to use our positional power as researchers and interviewers, to further probe the possible inter-relationships between racism and sexism, and thus to critically unpack what the participants say and/or do not say during the interview process (see Ratna, 2008).

However, by making this point, experiences of everyday sexism should not be erased as unimportant and thus insignificant. Indeed, despite the racial and ethnic differences between the participants, they all in various ways questioned the sexist inequalities operating within this White yet still male-dominated space. In particular, the coaches reflected on incidents of everyday sexism which they and the female athletes they coached had been subjected to by male colleagues. In the first example, Carol described how she and her athlete had to move from their warming up area due to the dominance of certain male coaches:

> The first time I went in there [the warm up area] I was scared.... The men don't make you feel welcome at all and I would say they even feel threatened by you.... It's not that I'm not confident it's just that it is a horrible cauldron and they might – like three men, when we were warming up (athlete and I), they came and stepped right in our way. They could see the cones were out, they could see us there because we'd been warming up for ages and they came and they stood right in front of us and stopped [my athlete] from warming up ... they're very undermining.
>
> (Carol)

The presence of these men, deliberately choosing to occupy the space which Carol and her athlete were using, reinforces the masculine dominance within sport coaching and the symbolic statement that certain bodies are naturally entitled to this space while others are not (Puwar, 2004). Seema, who had completed her level one coaching award in a traditionally White male-dominated team sport, provided a further example of feeling like an intruder into a territory in which she was not welcome:

> I don't think the provision was there for females to be actually like welcomed. [Females] have that dreaded feeling like 'What am I doing here?' [The coach education courses were] quite sexist in terms of [feeling like the tutors were saying] 'it's a man's world, you're out of your depth' so that did come across heavily in there.
>
> (Seema)

This territory of sport coaching was reserved for the privileged positions of masculinity (and whiteness) in that these identities were unproblematised; they embodied an "unmarked normative position" (Puwar, 2004: 58,

Singer, 2005b). The arrival of a female body disturbs the masculine culture; it evokes a reaction from the men. Carol provided a further example that illustrated the physical manifestation of discrimination when male coaches approached her athletes after events:

> Some coaches, they go up to my athletes and tell them what they've done wrong in the [event] ... and it really bugs me because they would not do that to another male coach so why do they feel they have the right to do that to me? I mean it really irritates me, it really winds me up ... I want to tell them what they did right, that's my role, I'm their coach! I don't want anyone else to tell them what they did right or wrong, that's not their role, they're not their coach and a lot of the male coaches do that. It's quite rude actually, disrespectful.
>
> (Carol)

These subtle discriminatory actions were not only enacted by male colleagues, but were also enacted by male parents of athletes. Tina, who self-identified as Indian, and had achieved her level two coaching qualification within a typically male-dominated team sport, reflected:

> I think that the main problem was some of the parents, for instance, they thought that I could be a bit of a pushover.... So they would approach me, and in fact one of the [White male] coaches [who was also a parent] came up to me and challenged me in front of the players and other coaches, which was a bit daunting. So it did create, it created a lot of upset for me ... personally I find people take male coaches a lot [more] seriously and women have to really struggle and stand their ground unless you come in at a really high level.
>
> (Tina)

Tina's example illustrates how the Indian/female body is read as a 'passive' body, a body that can be challenged by those in dominant and privileged positions. In relation to her involvement as a coach, Olive explained her frustration at having to battle against some South Asian men within her community who held traditional ideals and around South Asian femininity and cultural norms, derived from religious beliefs from her South Asian heritage. She was continuously challenged regarding her participation as a coach and her involvement in sport. Yet Ahmad (2011b) notes that contrary to assumptions that Islamic requirements restrict Muslim women from participating in sport, the Qur'an and Hadith actively encourage participation. Challenges related to religious heritage were absent from the other coaches' narratives, indicative of the different experiences of, and challenges, facing different groups of women within groups. The normalisation of these practices, such as challenging women coaches in front of athletes, illustrates the power of masculine superiority to shape and control the gender relations within sport coaching (Massao and Fasting, 2010). These everyday social practices, such as the examples above, caused other athletes and coaches to mark out and behave in disparate ways towards those coaches who are not afforded the same unearned privileges due to their gender (McIntosh, 1997). These practices support Norman's (2010a, 2010b) argument that it is not necessarily the structural processes that prevent women, and in this case, Black women coaches, entering and developing as sport coaches, nor is it overt discrimination. Rather oppression is "subtle, [and] insidious ideologically based", embedded within an organised system of beliefs and practices that are evident in the everyday interactions and experiences of the coaches (Norman, 2010b: 100).

Concluding thoughts and implications for sport coaching

The focus of this chapter was on exploring the everyday lived realities of eight Black women sport coaches across a range of sports in the UK context. The research, on which this writing is based, provides a unique, empirical contribution to sport coaching sociology through a critical exploration of how gendered and racialised discourses operate within sport coaching organisational practices. The contribution of this research is also in foregrounding these coaches' lived experiences, providing counter, even uncomfortable, stories, in stark contrast to the commonly documented coaching issues and debates within the wider subject area. The empirical material was (re)presented under three themes: feeling hyper visible, overcoming the burden of doubt, and everyday experiences of sexism. Through this, a further impact of the research is in presenting some of the complexities inherent in the coaching context and coaching identities. In particular, the research demonstrates the complex influences of 'race' and gender on different women's involvement in sport coaching and the unique challenges they face in negotiating multiple layers of oppressions. Although negotiating the gendered culture of sport coaching was centralised in all of the coaches' narratives, these experiences were interconnected with negotiating whiteness and issues of 'race' and ethnicity. The sport coaching context provided different challenges for the women based on these interconnecting factors, for example whereas Carol, as a Black Caribbean coach, discussed racialised stereotypes related to intelligence, Olive, Seema and Sabia discussed challenges in relation to the attitudes within, and of, their South Asian communities regarding the appropriateness of sport and a sport coaching role for South Asian women. Thus, some South Asian women may have to negotiate parental and cultural resistances to varying degrees, some more so than others. Specific factors, barriers and experiences were unique to all of the coaches and different aspects of racialised and ethnic identities were more or less pertinent for coaches at different times and in different situations. We are conscious that our analysis of these coaches' accounts is limited in terms of providing a detailed exploration of these differences to further entangle the complexity of gender, 'race' and ethnicity and the ways in which these factors impact on the identities and experiences of different groups of women coaches. However, by critically exploring the stories and experiences of the coaches included in this chapter, including women of different ethnicities and religious biographies, we provide evidence of some of the nuances between groups of women within sport. This is one area that previous research into the area of women in coaching is yet to properly and systematically address. We, in hindsight, advocate that researchers should follow Watson and Scraton's (2001: 274; see also Watson and Scraton, this volume) principles and engage in greater reflexivity with responsibility, acknowledge whiteness within research, and crucially translate this 'acknowledgement of privilege into action' in terms of thinking more carefully about the questions asked/not asked and the deeper interrogation of experiences being re-told and recounted. The findings in this respect indicate that there is still a clear need for continued analysis of sport coaching to further examine the complexities of inclusion and exclusion for Black women coaches and the operation of sexism with racism as interlocking systems of oppression. There is a further need for research that elucidates the differences within groups of groups to bring alternative realities from the margin to the centre of feminist theorising.

Arguably, thinking critically about the experiential knowledge derived from Black women coaches' real life experiences can still help sport organisations and NGB to recognise, challenge and overturn the routine practices and situations of everyday coaching that are viewed and experienced as 'normal' by the dominant coaching group (Essed, 1991). For example, foregrounding the Black women coaches' counter-narratives will inform analyses of unequal social relations, unequal ideologies and stereotypes related to 'race', ethnicity and gender, constructions of sport and coaching 'spaces', and structural discrimination as processes of exclusion. Sport organisations will then be able to name, problematise, understand and begin to challenge the taken-for-granted dominance of whiteness, masculinity and the everyday sexisms that operate within sport coaching. In line with the CRT and Black feminist commitment to emancipatory work and social justice, a number of policy and practitioner implications have already been drawn from the research and fed back to sport coaching organisations. For example, NGBs should seek out new ways to diversify the coaching workforce with transparent systems for recruitment and development, rather than using social networks to appoint positions, and organisational workshops on inclusive cultures should be mandatory for all staff including coaches, coach educators and those working at an organisational leadership level. Crucially, NGBs need to focus greater attention on reforming the sport coaching culture within their institutions, and on the problematic and exclusionary nature of normative gendered and racialised power relations and not on the individuals who are forced to negotiate them.

Notes

1 BME (Black and Minoritised Ethnic) is a popular acronym used in policy circles in the UK, used to denote the diverse positions and identities of all those individuals classed as 'in the minority'. In this chapter, we use the term 'Black' as an inclusive and political term.

2 There is a scarcity of statistical research pertaining to the presence of BME men and women in sport coaching positions. The existing reports (North, 2009; Sports Coach UK, 2011) that do evidence the underrepresentation of BME men and women coaches do not provide sport specific or cross-sectional statistics to determine the percentage of BME male and females across different sports.

3 The UKCC established a training and education pathway for coaches, offering five levels of achievement (now revised to four levels of achievement).

References

Ahmad, A. (2011a) 'British muslim female experiences in football: Islam, identity and the hijab' in D. Burdsey (ed.) *Race, Ethnicity and Football.* Oxon: Routledge: pp. 101–116.

Ahmad, A. (2011b) 'British football: where are the Muslim female footballers? Exploring the connections between gender, ethnicity and Islam', *Soccer & Society*, 12: pp. 443–456.

Ahmed, S. (2009) 'Embodying diversity: problems and paradoxes for Black feminists', *Race Ethnicity and Education*, 12: pp. 41–52.

Ahmed, S. (2012) *On Being Included: Racism and Diversity in Institutional Life*, Durham, North Carolina: Duke University Press.

Allen, J. and Shaw, S. (2013) 'An interdisciplinary approach to examining the working conditions of women coaches', *International Journal of Sports Science and Coaching*, 8: pp. 1–18.

Bhopal, K. (2010) 'Gender, identity and experience: researching marginalised groups', *Women's Studies International Forum*, 33: pp. 188–195.

Brah, A. (1996) *Cartographies of diaspora.* London: Routledge.

Bruening, J.E. (2005) 'Gender and racial analysis in sport: are all the women white and all the blacks men?' *Quest*, 57(3): pp. 330–349.

Carrington, B. (2008) '"What's the footballer doing here?" Racialized performativity, reflexivity, and identity', *Cultural Studies↔Critical Methodologies*, 8(4): pp. 423–452.

Carter-Francique, A.R. and Olushola, J. (2016) 'Women coaches of color: examining the effects of intersectionality' in N. Lavoi (ed.) *Women in Sports Coaching.* Oxon: Routledge: pp. 81–94.

Claringbould, I. and Knoppers, A. (2012) 'Paradoxical practices of gender in sport-related organisations', *Journal of Sport Management*, 26(5): pp. 404–416.

Collins, P. (1986) 'Learning from the outsider within: the sociological significance of Black feminist thought', *Social Problems*, 33(6): pp. 14–32.

Collins, P. (2000) *Black Feminist Thought: Knowledge, Consciousness and the Politics of Empowerment*, London: Routledge.

Crenshaw, K. (1989) 'Demarginalizing the intersection of race and sex: a Black feminist critique of antidiscrimination doctrine, feminist theory and antiracist politics', *University of Chicago Legal Forum*, pp. 139–168.

Crenshaw, K., Gotanda, N., Peller, G. and Kendall, T. (eds) (1995) *Critical Race Theory: The Key Writings That Informed the Movement*, New York: New Press.

Essed, P. (1991) *Understanding Everyday Racism: An Interdisciplinary Theory*, California: Sage Publications, Inc.

Few, A.L., Stephens, D.P. and Rouse-Arnett, M. (2003) 'Sister-to-sister talk: transcending boundaries and challenges in qualitative research with black women', *Family Relations*, 52(3): pp. 205–215.

Fielding-Lloyd, B. and Mean, L. (2011) '"I don't think I can catch it": women, confidence and responsibility in football coach education', *Soccer & Society*, 12(3): pp. 345–364.

Fletcher, T. (2014) '"Does he look like a Paki?" An exploration of "whiteness", positionality and reflexivity in inter-racial sports research', *Qualitative Research in Sport, Exercise and Health*, 6(2): pp. 244–260.

Flintoff, A. (2014) 'Tales from the playing field: black and minority ethnic students' experiences of physical education teacher education', *Race Ethnicity and Education*, 17(3): pp. 346–366.

Flintoff, A. and Webb, L. (2012) '"Just open your eyes a bit more": the methodological challenges of researching black and minority ethnic students' experiences of physical education teacher education', *Sport, Education and Society*, 17(5): pp. 571–589.

Frankenberg, R. (2004) 'On unsteady ground: crafting and engaging in the critical study of whiteness' in M. Bulmer and J. Solomos (eds) *Researching Race and Racism*. London: Routledge.

hooks, b. (1984) *Feminist Theory: From Margin to Center*, Boston, Massachusetts: South End Press.

hooks, b. (1989) *Talking Back: Thinking Feminist. Thinking Black*, Boston, Massachusetts: South End Press.

Hylton, K. (2005) '"Race", sport and leisure: lessons from critical race theory', *Leisure Studies*, 24(1): pp. 81–98.

Hylton, K. (2009) *'Race' and Sport: Critical Race Theory*, Oxon: Taylor & Francis.

Hylton, K. (2012) 'Talk the talk, walk the walk: defining Critical Race Theory in research', *Race Ethnicity and Education*, 15(1): pp. 23–41.

Kilty, K. (2006) 'Women in coaching', *The Sport Psychologist*, 20(2): pp. 222–234.

King, C. (2004) *Offside Racism: Playing the White Man*, Oxford: Berg.

Ladson-Billings, G. (1998) 'Just what is critical race theory and what's it doing in a nice field like education?' *International Journal of Qualitative Studies in Education*, 11(1): pp. 7–24.

Ladson-Billings, G. (2000) 'Racialized discourses and ethnic epistemologies' in N.K. Denzin and Y.S. Lincoln (eds) *Handbook of Qualitative Research*. Second ed. Thousand Oaks, California: Sage.

Ladson-Billings, G. and Donnor, J. (2005) 'The moral activist role' in N.K. Denzin and Lincoln Y.S. (eds) *The SAGE Handbook of Qualitative Research*. Third ed. Thousand Oaks, California: Sage.

Lavoi, N.M. and Dutove, J.K. (2012) 'Barriers and supports for female coaches: an ecological model', *Sports Coaching Review*, 1(1): pp. 17–37.

Massao, P.B. and Fasting, K. (2010) 'Race and racism: experiences of black Norwegian athletes', *International Review for the Sociology of Sport*, 45(2): pp. 147–162.

Massao, P.B. and Fasting, K. (2014) 'Mapping race, class and gender: experiences from black Norwegian athletes', *European Journal for Sport and Society*, 11(4): pp. 331–352.

McIntosh, P. (1997) 'White privilege and male privilege: a personal account of coming to see correspondences through work in women's studies', in R. Delgado and J. Stefancic (eds) *Critical White Studies: Looking Behind the Mirror*. Philadelphia: Temple University Press: pp. i–vi.

Mirza, H. S. (2009) *Race, Gender and Educational Desire: Why Black Women Succeed and Fail*, Oxon: Routledge.

Mowatt, R.A., French, B.H. and Malebranche, D.A. (2013) 'Black/female/body hypervisibility and invisibility: a black feminist augmentation of feminist leisure research', *Journal of Leisure Research*, 45(5): pp. 644–660.

Norman, L. (2010a) 'Bearing the burden of doubt: female coaches' experiences of gender relations', *Research Quarterly for Exercise and Sport*, 81(6): pp. 506–517.

Norman, L. (2010b) 'Feeling second best: elite women coaches' experiences', *Society of Sport Journal*, 27(1): pp. 89–104.

Norman, L. (2012) 'A crises' of confidence: women coaches' responses to their engagement in resistance', *Sport, Education and Society*, 19(5): pp. 1–20.

Norman, L., North, J., Hylton, K., Flintoff, A. and Rankin, A. (2014) *Sporting Experiences and Coaching Aspirations among Black and Minority Ethnic (BME) groups*, Leeds: Sports Coach UK.

North, J. (2009) *The Coaching Workforce 2009–2015*, Leeds: Sports Coach UK.

Phoenix, A. (2001) 'Practising feminist research: the intersection of gender and "race" in the research process' in K. Bhavnani (ed.) *Feminism and 'Race'*. Oxford: Oxford University Press.

Pillows, W. (2003) 'Race-based methodologies: multicultural methods or epistemological shifts?' in G.R. Lopez and L. Parker (eds) *Interrogating Racism in Qualitative Research Methodology*. New York: Peter Lang Publishing.

Puwar, N. (2004) *Space Invaders: Race, Gender and Bodies out of Place*, Oxford: Berg.

Ratna, A. (2008) 'A "fair game": British Asian females' experiences of racism in women's football' in J. Magee, J. Caudwell, K. Liston and S. Scraton (eds) *Women, Football and Europe: Histories, Equity and Experience*. Eastbourne: Meyer and Meyer Sport: pp. 69–88.

Ratna, A. (2011) 'Flying the flag for England? National identities and British Asian female footballers' in D. Burdsey (ed.) *Race, Ethnicity and Football*. Oxon: Routledge Ltd: pp. 117–130.

Ratna, A. (2013) 'Intersectional plays of identity: the experiences of British Asian female footballers', *Sociological Research Online*, 18(1): p. 13.

Rollock, N. (2012) 'The invisibility of race: intersectional reflections on the liminal space of alterity', *Race Ethnicity and Education*, 15(1): pp. 65–84.

Scraton, S., Caudwell, J. and Holland, S. (2005) 'Bend it like Patel: centring race, ethnicity and gender in feminist analysis of women's football in England', *International Review for the Sociology of Sport*, 40(1): pp. 71–88.

Shaw, S. and Slack, T. (2002) ' "It's been like that for Donkey's Years": the construction of gender relations and the cultures of sports organizations', *Sport in Society*, 5(1): pp. 86–106.

Singer, J.N. (2005a) 'Addressing epistemological racism in sport management research', *Journal of Sport Management*, 19(4): pp. 464–479.

Singer, J.N. (2005b) 'Understanding racism through the eyes of African American male student-athletes', *Race Ethnicity and Education*, 8(4): pp. 365–386.

Solorzano, D. and Yosso, T. (2001) 'Critical race and latcrit theory and method: counter-storytelling', *Qualitative Studies in Education*, 14(4): pp. 471–495.

Solórzano, D.G. and Yosso, T.J. (2002) 'Critical race methodology: counter-storytelling as an analytical framework for education research', *Qualitative Inquiry*, 8(1): pp. 23–44.

Song, M. and Parker, D. (1995) 'Commonality, difference and the dynamics of disclosure in in-depth interviewing', *Sociology*, 29(2): pp. 241–256.

Sparkes, A.C. and Smith, B. (2014) *Qualitative Research Methods in Sport, Exercise and Health: From Process to Product*, Oxon: Routledge.

Sporting Equals (2011) *Insight: BME Coaching in Sport*, Birmingham.

Sports Coach UK (2011) *Sports Coaching in the UK III: A Statistical Analysis of Coaches and Coaching in the UK*, Leeds: Coachwise Business Solutions.

Sports Coach UK (2012) *The UK Coaching Framework: Embedding Excellent Coaching Practice*, Leeds.

Watson, B. and Scraton, S. (2001) 'Confronting Whiteness? Researching the leisure lives of South Asian mothers', *Journal of Gender Studies*, 10(3): pp. 265–277.

Index

Page numbers in *italics* denote tables.

Abney, R. 63
academic institutions, Black scholars in 109–22
African American men: misogyny of 75; representations of in research 12; *see also* Black sportspeople; BME (Black and Minoritised Ethnic) people
African American women 78–9; agency of 72; Black feminism 65, 66, 67–8, 70–3, 78; Critical Race Feminism (CRF) 73–4, 78; Hip-Hop feminism 74–8, 79; and intersectionality 68; negative historical images 71–2; representations of in research 14, 17–19; scholars 64–5; standpoint of 64–7; womanist theory 68–70, 78, 112; *see also* Black scholars; Black sportspeople; Black women; BME (Black and Minoritised Ethnic) people; ethnic 'Other' girls and women; non-white women; women of colour
African American women in sport 63–4, 140; Black feminism 72; Critical Race feminism 73; elite athletes 17; Hip-Hop feminism 76, 77; and intersectionality 68; organisational barriers 63; and womanism 70
African Caribbean women cricketers 143–4
African Games 39
Africana feminist theology 70
Africana womanism 70
agency, and 'sporting Muslim women' 49–53
agitative brownness 172, 173
Ahmad, A. 218
Ahmed, S. 39, 86, 89, 94, 95, 96, 99, 122, 211
AKP (Justice and Development Party), Turkey 191–2
al-Gassra, Ruqaya 46
al-Jabiri, Mohammed Abed 191
Alcoff, L. 111
Aldridge, D.P. 77
Alexander-Floyd, N.G. 21, 22
Amara, M. 39
anger 109, 121–2; as empowerment 110; as resistance 113, 114
anti-racist campaigns 96
Anzaldúa, G. E. 1, 174
Arai, S. 97–8
area studies 20
Armstrong, K.L. 72
Asian American women 20
Asian feminism 12
Asian Mediterranean Games 39
assimilation, refusal of 116
Atlanta Plus 42
Australia 136; 'White Australia' immigration policy 134–5; ethnic 'Other' women and girls 7
Azzarito, L. 74

Baartman, Saartjie 18
Baker, Ella 67
Bambara, Toni Cade 67
Basquiat, Jean-Michel 185n1
Begum, Ruqsana 152–3
Bell, D. 66
Benn, T. 35, 39
Best, A. 100–1
Beyoncé 101

Birrell, S. 11, 13–14, 23, 88
Black, terminological issues 3, 205–6
Black feminisms 1, 5, 6, 12, 17, 22, 65, 66, 67–8, 70–3, 78, 87, 88, 118, 205–6; and 'talking back' 11; Black women in sports coaching 205, 206–8, 220; and critical research 20; and intersectionality 20
Black Lives Matter movement 174–5
Black scholars 2; 'writing back' to experiences in academic institutions 109–22; becoming 'raced' 114–17; and language 118–21
Black sportspeople: female 101, 117–18, 130; male 12; racialised stereotypes 96; re/presentation of as 'Others' 117–18; *see also* BME (Black and Minoritised Ethnic) people
Black women: and intersectionality 21; representations of in research 14, 17–19; *see also* African American women; BME (Black and Minoritised Ethnic) people; British Asian girls and women; ethnic 'Other' girls and women; non-white women; South Asian women; women of colour
Black women in sports coaching 6, 204–6; burden of doubt 212–16, 219; conclusions and implications 219–21; CRT and Black feminist approach 205, 206–8, 220; everyday sexism 216–19; hypervisibility 210–12, 219; study methodology 208–10, *209*; underrepresentation of 204–5
BME (Black and Minoritised Ethnic) people: identities 88–9; sport and leisure experiences 85, 97; stereotypical representations of 114–15; terminological issues 221n1; and UK sports coaching 204; *see also* African American men; African American women; Black women; British Asian girls and women; ethnic 'Other' girls and women; non-white women; South Asian men; South Asian women; women of colour
Border Studies 174, 182
Boulmerka, Hassiba 42
Bourdieu, P. 190
Brah, Avtar 19–20, 87, 92, 95, 99
Breedveld, K. 148
Bremen, Cindy van den 45
British Asian girls and women: and football 112, 119, 120–1; *see also* Black women; ethnic 'Other' girls and women; non-white women; South Asian women; women of colour
brown commons 171, 172, 174–5, 180, 181, 183, 184–5
Bruening, J.E. 72
Buckland, Mollie 134
Buford May, R.A. 91–2, 93
Bulaç, Ali 192

Captain, G. 2–3, 129, 130, 137
Carby, H. 17, 98
Caribbean women's cricket 136–7
Carrington, B. 130
Carter-Francique, Akilah R. 5, 63–84
Caudwell, J.C. 197
Chand, Dutee 175
Channon, A. 157
Chicana Cultural Studies 20, 174, 182
Chicana feminisms 6, 20, 22, 174, 176
Choi, Yeomi 171–88
Civil Rights Movement, US 71
coaching, Black women in sports coaching study 204–21
Coachman, Alice 63
Collins, Patricia Hill 64, 70–1, 71–2, 77, 90, 99, 111, 205
colonialism, in cricket 131–2
colonisation 37, 38
combat sport *see* ladies-only kickboxing, the Netherlands
communal sense of brown 177, 181–2
Conesa, Andrés 173
Cook, Nicole 48
Cooper, Anna Julia 67
Corbett, D.R. 47
Corona, Fabiola 172
counterpublicities 179–80
Crenshaw, K. 18, 20, 68, 73, 99, 207
creolisation theories 98
CRF (Critical Race Feminism) 73–4, 78
cricket: institutional racism 130; racial mythologies/stereotypes of non-white cricketers 140–1; racism and imperialism in 126, 131–2; *see also* men's cricket; women's cricket
CRT (Critical Race Theory) 6, 73, 74, 86, 93, 97–8, 102; Black women in sports coaching 205, 206–8, 220
cultural geographies 20
cycling, sexism in 48

Dart, J. 119–20
Das, Andrew 197
David, K. 54
Davis, Angela 67
decolonisation 38–9, 55; and 'sporting Muslim women' 36, 37, 40–53
deconstruction 38; *see also* decolonisation
diaries, as historical sources 128; *see also* women's cricket
Dick, P. 190
disidentification 173, 174, 175–6, 177, 179–80, 181, 182
Douglas, Gabrielle 63, 73
dual heritage women 7
Dunkerly, R.M. 197
Durham, A. 75, 77

ECB (England and Wales Cricket Board) 141
Egyptian Muslim women, and sport 35
Ekşi Sőzlük 189, 193–4, 197–8, 199
el-Mountawakel, Nawal 42
empowerment, and Moroccan-Dutch girls and women in kickboxing 148, 152–5, 162
England and Wales Cricket Board (ECB) 141
English language, and Black scholars 118–21
Equality Act 2010, UK 204
Erdoğan, Recep Tayyip 191–2
Erhart, Itir 6, 189–203
ethnic 'Other' girls and women: and intersectionality 19–23; representations of in research 14–19, 20–3; scholarship on 1–3; in sport and physical activity 6–7, 20–4; terminological issues 3–4; *see also* African American women; Black women; BME (Black and Minoritised Ethnic) people; British Asian girls and women; non-white women; South Asian women; women of colour
ethnic 'Other' scholars 2
Evans, L. 77
everyday sexism, in sport coaching 216–19

Fasting, K. 35
Felix, Allyson 46
feminism: Turkey 190–1; *see also* Africana feminist theology; Asian feminism; Chicana feminisms; CRF (Critical Race Feminism); Hip-Hop feminism; Islamic feminism; Marxist feminism; post-structural feminism; postcolonial feminisms; postmodern feminism; queer of colour feminism; transnational feminisms; white feminism
FIFA, and veiling 44, 45; *see also* football
First Nation people 20
football: and British Asian girls and women 112, 119, 120–1; offside rule 189, 190, 193–4, 198, 200, 201; representations of South Asian men in research 15; women referees 200; *see also* FIFA; Turkish female football fans; women's football
Fortyn, Pim 149
Frankenberg, Ruth 85, 87, 88, 96, 97
Freeman, Cathy 46
Frelier, M. 148

gender segregation 155; in Muslim culture 37–8; and 'sporting Muslim women' 46–9; *see also* ladies-only kickboxing, the Netherlands
Gibson, Althea 63
Giddings, Paula 67
Gillman, L. 118
global girl subject 171, 172–7, 182–5
Gray, Andy 200
Green, T.S. 63
Griffith, Florence 46
Guevara, Ana 172
Guha, Isa 129
Guiner, Lani 73
Gülşan, Rahşan 197

Habertürk 189, 195, 197
Hague, The 149; *see also* ladies-only kickboxing, the Netherlands
'halal sports' 161, 162
Hannon, J. 74
Harding, S. 90
Hargreaves, Jennifer 14, 19, 117–19, 158
Hargreaves, R. 137
Harris, J.C. 109
Harrison, L. 77
Heyhoe-Flint, Rachael 137, 141
hijabs *see* sports hijabs; veiling
Hill, Anita 73
Hip-Hop feminism 71, 74–8, 79
hooks, bell 64–5, 67, 87, 94, 95, 99, 113, 114, 116, 118, 119, 120, 121, 207

Howard-Baptiste, S.D. 109
Hudson-Weems, Clenora 69–70
Hürriyet 189, 192
Hylton, K. 93, 99, 102, 206

identities 5; hyphenated 54; Muslim women 54
Ifekwunigwe, J.O. 76, 101
India: intersex athletes 7; women's cricket 136, 139–40, 142
institutional racism 86, 89, 94, 95–100, 130
International Women's Cricket Council (IWCC) 127–8, 136–7
intersectionality 1, 5, 19–23, 39, 68, 98, 99
Iran: female football fans 200; veiling 45; women's football 47
Islam: and colonisation 37–8; and gender politics 191–2; and 'sporting Muslim women' 35, 41–4, 218; women's status in 54n6
Islamic feminism 35, 50, 191
Islamic Solidarity Games 39
Islamic Women's Games 39, 47
Islamophobia, the Netherlands 149–50; UK 46
IWCC (International Women's Cricket Council) 127–8, 136–7

Jamaica, women's cricket 137
James, S.M. 67
Jamieson, Katherine M. 1–2, 6, 171–88
Japan 7
Johnstone, Brian 141
Jonsson, T. 100, 102
journal editors 119–20
Justice and Development Party (AKP), Turkey 191–2

Kaepernick, Colin 174
Keys, Richard 200
Kick it Out 96
kickboxing *see* ladies-only kickboxing, the Netherlands
Kim, B.C. 184
Kim, Christina 182
King, Mae 143
Kivel, B.D. 97–8
Kılıç, Suat 195
Kocaman, C. 197
Kwon, S.Y. 184

ladies-only kickboxing, the Netherlands 148–9, 151–6, 162–4; 'empowerment' discourses 148, 152–5, 162; comfort in gender-segregates environment 156–8; geographical factors 158–60; religious factors 160–1; social context 149–50
language, and Black scholars 118–21
Latinas: Critical Race Feminism (CRF) 73, 78; critical research on 20
leotards 46, 55n4
Levine-Rasky, C. 99
Liberti, R. 65
Lopez, Nancy 178
Lorde, Audre 67, 113, 119, 121–2
Lorena Ochoa Invitational 181–2
Lugones, M. 174
Lutz, H. 54

Macpherson Report (1999) 96
Mahmood, S. 52, 155
Mansour, Asmahan 45
Manyonganise, M. 70
Marqusee, Like 143
Marshall, Annecka 116
Marxist feminism 19
Massey, Sian 200
Mathewson, A.D. 68
Matsuda, Mari 73
Matthews, C.R. 190
McDonald, I. 130
McDonald, M. 85–6, 97, 98, 102
men's cricket: institutional racism 130; Pakistani team, 1987 and 1992 132; racism and imperialism in 126, 131–2, 143; West Indian pace bowlers 132; *see also* cricket; women's cricket
Messner, M. 158
mestiza consciousness 1–2
Mexicanas, critical research on 20
Mexico *see* Ochoa, Lorena 'La Reina'
Mirza, H.S. 90
misogyny, of African American men 75
modesty 47, 49, 161–2
Mohanty, C.T. 53
Moore, L.W. 77
Moraga, C. 174
Morgan, Joan 75
Moroccan-Dutch girls and women *see* ladies-only kickboxing, the Netherlands
Muay Thai *see* ladies-only kickboxing, the Netherlands
multi-heritage women 7
Muñoz, José Esteban 171, 174–6, 177, 179, 180, 181, 182, 183

Muslim communities, representations of in research 16; *see also* Islam; 'sporting Muslim women'
Muslim men: criminalisation of in the Netherlands 150; exclusion from women-only sporting arenas 47; representations of as violators of gender equality 49–50
Muslim women: agency 49–53; and colonisation 37–8; empowerment discourses 148, 152–5, 162; identities of 54; representations of as subordinate/oppressed 36, 37–8, 47, 148–9, 150, 152–5, 163 *see* ladies-only kickboxing, the Netherlands; 'sporting Muslim women'

Nadin, S. 190
narrative analysis 101–2
national governing bodies *see* NGBs (national governing bodies), UK
Native American women, Critical Race Feminism (CRF) 73, 78
natural differences discourse 189–90; Turkish female football fans 189, 192–6; Turkish gender politics 190–1
neoliberalism 153, 154
Netherlands, the 149–50; *see also* ladies-only kickboxing, the Netherlands
New Zealand 7
NGBs (national governing bodies), UK: and diversity issues 204, 220–1; *see also* Black women in sports coaching
Nicholson, Rafaelle 5–6, 126–47
nicknames 73
non-white women: cricketers 6, 126, 127, 129, 130, 131, 138–9, 141–2; representations of in research 13–14; *see also* African American women; Black women; BME (Black and Minoritised Ethnic) people; British Asian girls and women; ethnic 'Other' girls and women; South Asian women; women of colour
Norman, Leanne 6, 204–24, 215, 219

Ochoa, Lorena 'La Reina' 6, 171–2, 184–5; as/and the global girl subject 171, 172–7; career successes and awards 172–3; disidentification practices 176, 177–82, 183
Odreda, Sonia 129
offside rule 189, 190, 193–4, 198, 200, 201
Ogunyemi, Chikwenye Okonjo 70
Olson, P. 118
Olympic Games: Barcelona, 1992 42; London, 2012 44, 153; Los Angeles, 1984 42
oral testimonies, as historical sources 128, 129; women's cricket 137, 138, 139, 142–3
Orientalising 135
Osborne, C. 144
'outsider within' 110, 111, 112, 122, 207

Pakistani cricketers 132
Palmer, C. 17, 35, 43, 52, 53
Pan-Arab Games 39
Panahi, Jafir 200
Parks, Rosa 67
participation: alternative forms of 43, 44; as a concept 43, 55
Pastore, D.L. 72
patriarchy 13, 18, 21, 35, 47, 50, 155
Peoples, W. 77
Phillips, L.D. 72
photographers, exclusion from women-only events 47–8
politics of location 112–13
Pope, S. 200
post-structural feminism 38–9
post-title 9/11 frameworks 177
postcolonial feminisms 5, 22, 36, 40, 54; and women's cricket 130–1, 135, 144
postcolonial research 127
postmodern blackness 98
postmodern feminism 21–2
Pough, Gwendoline 75
Puwar, N. 211, 212, 215

queer of colour feminism 20

'race matching' 91–2
Race Relations Theories in Sport (Birrell) 11
race, social constructions of 13–14
racelessness 87, 88
racial mythologies in sport 12–13; in women's cricket 127, 130, 133, 135, 140–4
Raimist, Rachel 75
Rainsford-Brent, Ebony 129
Rana, Jasmijn 6, 148–67
Rankin-Wright, Alexandra J. 6, 204–24
Ratna, Aarti 1–9, 5, 10–32, 100, 109–25, 153, 216

reflexivity with responsibility 87, 89–91, 93, 101, 220
Renault 193, 201
'representational intersectionality' 18
research methodologies: feminist debates on 89–90; narrative analysis 101–2; and whiteness 86, 87–8, 90–1, 98, 101–2
research overview 4–5, 10–11, 23–4; categorical research 11–14; difference, intersectionality and voice 19–23; dominant discourses in 14–19
resistance 16–17
Rheinberg, Netta 133, 134–5, 141
Rich, Adrienne 120
Richey, D. 63
Roberts, L. 114
role models 211–12, 215
Rollock, N. 112
Royal and Ancient Golf Club of St. Andrews 172
Rudolph, Wilma 63, 65
Rugby League 15

Sadiq, Ambreen 152
Said, E. 136
Samie, Samaya Farooq 1–9, 5, 10–32, 35–62, 153
Sandoval, Chela 174
Saudia Arabia 45
Schipper, Edith 150
Schomberg Center for Research on Black Culture 64
Scraton, Sheila 5, 19, 23, 85–106, 131, 220
Sehlikoglu, S. 40–1, 43, 44, 153
sense of brown 171, 175, 176, 178, 182, 184; communal 177, 181–2
Şentürk, D. 199
sexism: in cycling 48; in sport coaching 216–19; and Hip-Hop feminism 76–7
Sholock, A. 90
silence, as resistance 16, 17
Skillen, F. 144
Slowe, Lucy Diggs 63
Smith, Barbara 67
Smith, J. 191
Smith, M.M. 65
Smith, Y.R. 2, 65
social media 73; *Ekşi Sőzlük* 189, 193–4, 197–8, 199
sociocultural analysis of sport 118; Black scholars' experiences in academic institutions 110, 111, 112, 113–22
Solomon, M.A. 74
Solorzano, D.G. 206
South Africa 7
South America 7
South Asian men, representations of in research 15
South Asian women: cricketers 143; representations of in research 14, 15–16, 17; sport and leisure experiences research 85, 90–1, 92–3, 94; in sports coaching 211–12, 213, 216, 218, 219; *see also* Black women; BME (Black and Minoritised Ethnic) people; British Asian girls and women; ethnic 'Other' girls and women; non-white women; women of colour
sport: as a 'social service' 12; as a concept 43; and development 23; institutional racism 86, 96–100; and integration 150; race relations 12; and racial myths 12–13, 127, 130, 133, 135, 140–4; research overview 10–24; whiteness, and research 82–102
'sporting Muslim women' 35–7, 53–5; and agency 49–53; decolonisatation 39, 40–53; factors influencing participation 35; and gender segregation 46–9; Islamic/cultural barriers and challenges 41–4, 48; and Muslim men 49–53; and veiling 39, 44–6; *see also* Muslim women
sports coaching, Black women in sports coaching study 204–21
sports hijabs 45; *see also* veiling
sports history: maleness of 126–7; women's 144; *see also* women's cricket
Srinivasan, Amia 109, 121
Stephens, D.P. 72
Stewart, J.B. 77

'talking back' 111, 113, 114
Tate, Shirley Anne 120
terminological issues 3–4
Terrell, Mary Church 67
Thai boxing *see* ladies-only kickboxing, the Netherlands
third wave feminism 71
Title IX of the Education Amendments of 1972 63–4
Toffoletti, K. 17, 35, 43, 52, 53, 200
transactional friendships 118, 121
transnational feminisms 22, 52
Truth, Sojourner 67
Tubman, Harriett 67

Tüfekçi, Zeynep 193
Turkey: gender politics 190–1; veiling 45
Turkish female football fans 6, 189–90, 192, 199–201; 'bickering aunt' stereotype 189, 198, 200; 'crazy-blooded tomboy' stereotype 189, 198–9, 200; 'perfumed lady' stereotype 189, 197–8, 200; crowd restrictions 194–6; natural differences discourse 189, 192–6; and the offside rule 189, 190, 193–4, 198, 200, 201

UK: Black women in sports coaching study 204–21; Islamophobia 46
UK Coaching Framework 204
UKCC (UK Coaching Certificate) 208
US-LPGA (US-Ladies Professional Golf Association) 171, 172, 173, 175, 178, 179, 180, 181

van Gogh, Theo 149
van Ingen, C. 126
Varnish, Jess 48
veiling 37, 44–6, 161
Vertinsky, P. 2–3, 129, 130, 137
Vodafone 193

Walker, Alice 68–9
Walseth, K. 35
Washington, M. H. 7
Watson, Beccy 5, 85–106, 220
WCA (Women's Cricket Association) 130, 137, 138, 141, 142–3; archive sources 127–8; and class 138; and Indian cricketers 139–40; as a white, middle-class organisation 132
Wells, Ida B. 67
West Indies: men's cricket 132, 140–1; women's cricket 142
white feminism 68, 70, 71
white minoritised groups 7
whiteness: 'declarations' of 86, 89, 94, 95; heterogeneity of 95
whiteness, in sport and leisure research 5, 85–6; insider-outsider issues 91–5; institutionalisation of whiteness 95–100; re-confronting of 100–2; reflexivity with responsibility 87, 89–91, 93, 101, 220; situatedness of white researchers 86, 87–9
Wiggins, D.K. 12
Wilkes, K. 99–100
Williams, Jack 126
Williams, Patricia 73
Williams, Serena 63, 76, 101, 175
Williams, Venus 63, 76, 175
Wimbledon 76
Wing, Adrien 74
womanist theory 68–70, 78, 112
women of colour: heterogeneity of 67; representations of in research 13–14; scholars 2; terminological issues 3; violence against in US 20; *see also* African American women; Black women; BME (Black and Minoritised Ethnic) people; British Asian girls and women; ethnic 'Other' girls and women; South Asian women
women's boxing 126
women's cricket 5–6; absence of in cricket history 126–7; dress codes 141–2; etiquette and behaviours 138; non-white women cricketers 6, 126, 127, 129, 130, 131, 138–9, 141–2; oral testimonies 137, 138, 139, 142–3; racial mythologies/stereotypes in 127, 130, 133, 135, 140–4; tour diaries evidence 127–8, 133–7; white, middle-class nature of 127, 129–30, 133, 134, 136–7; *see also* cricket; men's cricket
Women's Cricket Advisory Group 141
Women's Cricket Association *see* WCA (Women's Cricket Association)
Women's Cricket Association of India 139–40
women's football 47, 116; British Asian girls and women 112, 119, 120–1
Wright, C. 116
'writing back': Black scholars' experiences in academic institutions 110–22; and language 118–21

Yosso, T.J. 73, 206

Zinbabwe 70